LIGHTING THE NIGHT

LIGHTING THE NIGHT

Revolution in Eastern Europe

William Echikson

William Morrow and Company, Inc.
New York

Recognizing the importance of preserving what has been written, it is the policy of William Morrow and Company, Inc., and its imprints and affiliates to have the books it publishes printed on acid-free paper, and we exert our best efforts to that end.

Library of Congress Cataloging-in-Publication Data

Echikson, William.
    Lighting the night : revolution in Eastern Europe / William Echikson.
        p. cm.
    ISBN 0-688-09200-4
    1. Europe, Eastern—Politics and government—1945–1989.
I. Title.
DJK50.E24 1990
947.084—dc20

                                                            90-38756
                                                            CIP

Printed in the United States of America

First Edition

1 2 3 4 5 6 7 8 9 10

Contents

Acknowledgments

In the following pages I have included the names of many people for whose trust and friendship I am grateful. I have been careful about identifying them. When I was at Yale a decade ago, I was fortunate to have John Hersey as a teacher. Professor Hersey impressed me not only with his creative and important contributions to American non-fiction, but also with the deep sense of duty he felt towards the subject of his writing. He would repeat that the journalist has an equal responsibility to his reader and to his subject. In our rush to inform, we too often privilege the reader and abuse the subject. This lesson was crucial in Eastern Europe, where to print the names of many of the people I met threatened them with harassment, even arrest. Those who have been identified here accepted the risks of helping a Western journalist. They deserve great credit for their courage.

I am particularly grateful to my translator–researchers: Grazyna Gorska, Dorota Kowalska, Malgarzata Dutkiewicz and Krystyna Wróblewska in Poland; Michál Donath and Eva Turková in Czechoslovakia; Agnes Major and Magda Seleanu in Hungary; and Aleksandar Zigic in Yugoslavia. They were much more than simple wordsmiths; they served as guides to their countries, accompanying me through the rich but dense forests of their respective lands.

This is a truly international book. I am grateful to Hilary Davies, my British editor at Sidgwick & Jackson, for speeding up publication. Margaret Talcott, my American editor at William Morrow, deserves thanks for her sharp eye and persistence about the title. My agent Barbara Lowenstein deserves credit for originally conceiving this project. Chrystia Freeland provided invaluable help with the research.

At the *Christian Science Monitor* former managing editor David Anable and my two foreign editors Paul Van Slambrouck and Jane Lampmann offered me the invaluable opportunity of covering Eastern Europe. Whenever I was frazzled, I could always count on soothing words from European regional editor Gail Russell Chaddock. Daniel Franklin at *The Economist* provided invaluable insights. John Panitza graciously permitted me to use portions of articles first commissioned for *Reader's Digest*.

At Harvard, Professor Marshall Goldman provided me with the invaluable resources of the Russian Research Center. Thanks also to my new editor at the *Wall Street Journal*, Europe, Robert Keatley, who generously pushed back my arrival so that I could finish this book, and to David Thomas, who gave up his spare time to help with proof reading.

Most of all I want to thank my parents for giving in me the curiosity to become a roving journalist; and Anu, who put up with my long absences away in Eastern Europe.

William Echikson
April 1990

EASTERN
EUROPE

NORWAY

Oslo

FINLAND

Helsinki

Stockholm

SWEDEN

Baltic Sea

DENMARK

Copenhagen

EAST
GERMANY

WEST

Berlin

Bonn

Leipzig

Gdansk

Warsaw

POLAND

Krakow

UNION OF SOVIET
SOCIALIST REPUBLICS

Prague

CZECHOSLOVAKIA

Vienna

AUSTRIA

Bratislava

Budapest

SWITZERLAND

HUNGARY

ITALY

Ljubljana

Zagreb

Belgrade

YUGOSLAVIA

ROMANIA

Timisoara

Bucharest

Black Sea

BULGARIA

Sofia

Plovdiv

Tiriana

ALBANIA

GREECE

TURKEY

LIGHTING ᴛʜᴇ NIGHT

Introduction

The Bearable Lightness of Being
Dienstbier

What happens but once might as well not have happened at all. The history of the Czechs will not be repeated, nor will the history of Europe.
Milan Kundera, The Unbearable Lightness of Being

During my five years of reporting from Eastern Europe, I witnessed the world turn upside down. Communists who received me in their palatial offices in 1985 had fled from the scene by the beginning of 1990. Dissidents whom I first met in small, cramped apartments had suddenly become national leaders. For me this remarkable revolution is personified in one man, Czechoslovakia's new Foreign Minister Jiří Dienstbier. When I first met Jiří, we went to a smoke-filled pub and ordered two beers. Over a long evening he told how he had been a Communist Party member and star foreign correspondent for the National Radio. He covered the Vietnam War and was appointed to the plum post of senior correspondent in Washington.

After Soviet tanks squashed the Prague Spring in 1968, Jiří was recalled home. He refused to sign a declaration saying that the invasion was necessary to crush a "counterrevolution." For his defiance, he and half a million others were expelled from the Party. The heart was cut out of his career. He floated from job to job. In 1977 he signed the Charter 77 human rights declaration. For that "crime," he was arrested and imprisoned between 1979 and 1982. Upon his release, only his old dissident friends dared stay in touch. He ended up working as a stoker, shoveling coal into a furnace, for the Prague subway system.

Over the next few years I became a regular visitor to the Dienstbier flat on Nekazanka Street near Wenceslas Square. In the spacious study and dining room I spent many evenings with Jiří, eating hearty Czech dumplings and discussing the world. He never lost his courage – nor his wry sense of self-deprecating humor. Police tailed him, often placing guards outside his apartment building and conducting regular searches for samizdat material. The point wasn't to hide the surveillance, he once explained. It was to make it so blatant as to frighten him. The tactics gave his wife Věra serious migraines. He ignored the police. He, the caged dissident, was freer than any other Czechoslovak because he lived as if he were free. "You know, I sort of like my job," he once admitted. "I don't work too hard and I get four days a week off for my real work." His "real" work remained journalism – spiced with opposition politics.

After Prague erupted with street protests in November 1989, Jiří Dienstbier became the spokesman for the opposition group Civic Forum. He was brilliant in the job, charming the assembled mob of foreign correspondents in nightly press conferences at the Magic Lantern Theater. "Will there be a Green Party?" he was once asked. "This country needs all parties to be Green," he responded. When journalists pestered him for his opinion on the divisions within the Communist Party and the relationship between the Czech and Soviet Parties, questions which we had no way of answering, he responded with another ironic jibe about the "fraternal assistance" invoked by the Warsaw Pact as its reason for invading Czechoslovakia in 1968. "We won't ask for international assistance any more," he remarked.

Exhausted, he told me that he wasn't sleeping more than three hours a night. Events left him dazed. At one point, someone proposed him as head of the National Radio. "Can you believe it – me as the chief of radio?" he asked. He himself couldn't believe it. When the new Czechoslovak government was finally announced on December 10, 1989 (International Human Rights Day), Jiří Dienstbier wasn't appointed head of the National Radio. Instead, he became Czechoslovakia's Foreign Minister. Along with Jiří, eleven of the twenty-one ministers in the new Czechoslovak government were noncommunists – with seven from the opposition Civic Forum, including Finance Minister Václav Klaus, Social Affairs Minister Petr Miller and Interior Minister Jan Čarnogurský, who had been in prison only weeks before.

Dienstbier was amazed. He, the longtime enemy of socialism, would be sitting in the beautiful baroque chambers of the Czernin Palace directing the Czechoslovak Socialist Republic's foreign policy. It wasn't only he who had trouble keeping up with Czechoslovakia's dizzying transformation. So did the police. Just before the protests exploded, they cut his home telephone line. "Don't try to call me," a smiling Jiří warned the assembled press corps. It was restored only the day before he took office. Ever the master of witty repartee, he announced that before taking over as Foreign Minister he would first have to find a replacement for his job as stoker.

For forty years, occupiers had ruled Czechoslovakia. Soviet troops had crushed the Prague Spring and put unqualified louts into power, their only recommendation being their loyalty to Moscow. External force had fed the country a sleeping pill. Now Czechoslovakia was awakening and the best were rising normally, naturally, to the top. Jiří Dienstbier has made a superb Foreign Minister. How many of his communist predecessors in the post spoke four foreign languages? How many could converse on world affairs as fluently as he did?

Freedom did not come to Eastern Europe as a gift from Moscow or Washington. It came from more than forty years of struggle – a daily, grinding struggle against a corrupt and evil system. This book is about people who exposed communism's fraud and brought about its collapse. It is about the people whom I have known, written about and socialized with for years, men such as Jiří Dienstbier in Czechoslovakia, Solidarity's parliamentary chief Bronisław Geremek in Poland, the Free Democrats' leader Miklós Haraszti in Hungary. It is also about the ordinary people who danced on the breached Berlin Wall and stared down tanks in Bucharest's Palace Square; the people who shook their keys in Prague's Wenceslas Square and lit candles in front of Budapest's neo-Gothic Parliament. Traveling through Eastern Europe for the past five years, I came across countless examples of moral courage and intellectual integrity, which forced me to drop my air of American superiority. In Eastern Europe, the abstract notion of struggling for fundamental human rights and self-determination came alive. The issues are not about power and money. They are about right and wrong, truth and lies.

In Part I, I introduce these themes by recounting the climactic events of 1989. This section should be read as an impressionist outline, not a comprehensive narrative. It draws on my own personal experiences and travels. The technique, I hope, will permit readers who were not in Eastern Europe at the time to experience the heady atmosphere of the revolution. In Part II, I move on to the more solid, sober ground of hindsight. The chapters profile the revolution's major players: not just its protagonists but also its adversaries; not just its principal actors but also its supporting cast – deposed communists, threatened apparatchiks, rebellious workers, courageous intellectuals and radical students. In Part III, I look at the various passions that ate away at the old communist order, the faltering centrally planned economic and political systems, the burgeoning democratic opposition, the mounting anger over a polluted environment, the growing attraction of religion and the renewed pull of nationalism.

Structuring the book by themes, not by individual countries, raises inevitable difficulties. Eastern Europe, after all, is a misnomer. It never was a monolithic bloc. It is a region full of deep differences – different nationalities, different traditions, different histories. The imposition of Soviet-style communism not only failed to wipe out these differences: one of the exhilarating and dangerous aspects of the present revolution is the rediscovery of unique national identities. My contention remains, however, that the former Soviet Empire can be dealt with as a whole. Eastern Europeans face common problems. All are small countries, fearful for their very existence. All have broken the Communist Party's monopoly of power. All now must pick up the pieces of their bankrupt centrally planned economies. Everywhere in these societies which long preached egalitarian ideals, inequality has mounted. Religious belief has become more powerful. A defiant young generation has emerged.

Communism was imposed on Eastern Europe after World War II only with the backing of Moscow. In some places – Czechoslovakia and Bulgaria – the communists enjoyed a fair amount of support. But nowhere did they have a majority. Stalin envisioned building the same system for all these countries, by brute force if necessary. He never succeeded. Soviet-installed regimes failed to win full legitimacy. The people of Eastern Europe always considered communism alien, associating it with the Russians, whom, with their oriental heritage, they perceived as culturally second rate compared with Western cultural, religious and intellectual heritage. "The Russians are peasants," my friends in Prague snickered.

These prejudices persist, despite Mikhail Gorbachev and *glasnost*. After Solidarity took power in August 1989, the Polish historian Marcin Król, who has taught at Yale, still refused to visit the Soviet Union. "I am afraid the KGB would make me vanish," he confided. "It happened to a friend of mine." After I had been to Moscow, friends in Warsaw subjected me to a rude grilling. "Wasn't it backward?" I told them that both Poland and the Soviet Union reeked of the same sad socialist "realist" façades on their modern buildings, the same sparsely stocked shops and the same unappetizing restaurants. They were shocked. "But Russians smell," they insisted. To avoid a fight, I described being pushed and shoved while shopping at the GUM department store. My friends smiled. At least in Poland, they said, our queues are civilized.

In contrast, the prosperous, democratic West is considered a reference point. While Western Europeans often ridicule Ronald Reagan as an ignorant cowboy and George Bush as a cautious do-nothing, both men are heroes in Eastern Europe. They stood up to the Soviet Union. As Vice President, Bush visited Warsaw and became the first Western leader after martial law to meet with Solidarity leader Lech Wałęsa in public. When he returned as President, he offered little concrete aid, but Poles didn't seem to care. They waved American flags and sang "The Star-Spangled Banner."

Until recently, we in the West did not return the loving attention. We forgot about Eastern Europe as soon as one of its periodic eruptions cooled down. Proud Hungarian patriots lobbing Molotov cocktails at Soviet tanks in 1956, joyous Czechs screaming for "socialism with a human face" in 1968, and throngs of striking Polish workers in 1980 once captured the world's attention. But without such volatile confrontations, the press assumed there was no news. When I first met Jiří Dienstbier, few correspondents bothered to come to stagnating, repressive Czechoslovakia. "We don't have a story here," he said. "We have a situation – the same situation for the last sixteen years."

Change was taking place outside the glow of television lights, in a more subtle, elusive fashion, in church basements where independent lectures were given and in private apartments where independent magazines were edited. None of these slow, incremental actions made headlines. The inevitable explosion caught most of the media off guard. American television networks had closed their Warsaw offices after the declaration of martial law in 1981; when new strikes broke out in 1988, they could not be on the scene. The quiet in Eastern Europe was deceptive. Even before Mikhail Gorbachev, discontent was always bubbling beneath the surface.

Anyone who takes Mr. Gorbachev as a point of departure for analyzing the bewildering Eastern European vista is mistaken. Not every new development in his farflung empire can be treated as a result of Soviet *glasnost* and *perestroika*. If Gorbachev has been important, even crucial, it has been more for what the Soviet leader didn't do than for what he did. Before he came to power, Eastern Europe seemed set in a deep freeze. Although reform looked necessary, the examples of the 1968 Soviet invasion of Czechoslovakia and the 1981 suppression of Solidarity in Poland showed that it was dangerous for satellite countries to question the status quo. Gorbachev removed this fear. As part of his "New Thinking," he said that each communist country should have the right to find its own path to socialism. His stress on non-interference, his denial of the universal application of Soviet experience, his decision to thin out Soviet forces – all these things undermined the Soviet position in Eastern Europe and left its communist regimes exposed. "Our leaders can no longer claim that Soviet tanks are waiting on the border," explained Jacek Kuroń, the Polish dissident turned Minister of Labor. "Everybody knows that the decision to bring Solidarity back depended on our own government – and not on the tanks over the border."

Communism counted on fear. It depended on the knowledge that if one stood up and spoke out, one could lose job, car, home, and in some cases face prison or death. That choice silenced everyone except a few courageous dissidents like Dienstbier. Most didn't like the system but were too frightened to do anything about it. With the Soviet leader conceding the failure of the Soviet model, Eastern Europeans found more courage to press their individual claims. "I see a definite increase in civic courage," noted Jiří Hájek, Czechoslovak Foreign Minister during the 1968 Prague Spring, who became one of the original spokesmen for the Charter 77 human-rights group. "People are no longer so afraid." Hundreds of thousands of once-timid Czechs took to the streets in November 1989, demanding democracy. The revolution's spiritual spark, the decisive moment, came when the masses of individual Eastern Europeans stood up and said, "I am no longer afraid."

The collapse of fear first happened in Poland in 1980, with Solidarity's birth. The Solidarity revolution turned the dissident minority into a majority. It changed the way people thought. And for the first time people said aloud what they thought. They ended their internal isolation and became involved in public life. Even after martial law was declared the following year, people lived as if in a free country. In 1989, the rest of Eastern Europe discovered the same sensation. The moment the lid of repression was lifted, the communist system collapsed.

People realized that they all felt the same, and that together they could be strong.

Everybody in Eastern Europe seems to remember that one special moment when fear stopped. For baby-faced Czech drama student Pavel Chaloupa, it took the beating of some fellow students in November 1989 to transform him into a revolutionary leader: "I said, we can't continue to live in a country where people don't say what they think." He thought the police would take over their campuses and expel him and other strikers from the university. But the police never came. Journalist Jana Smidová of the Czech newspaper *Svobodné Slovo* thought her article about the student demonstrations would be censored. It was not. So she went ahead and wrote an honest story.

Even if it sometimes seemed insincere and opportunistic, the transformation was remarkable, turning the most unexpected people into revolutionaries. For two long decades newscaster George Marinescu mouthed lies on Romanian television about the greatness of despot Nicolae Ceausescu. As soon as demonstrators took over the television studios in Bucharest in December 1989, he went on the air and offered a *mea culpa*: "I lied. I was commanded to lie." He put on the revolution's blue, yellow and red armband as a badge of honor and became the chief anchorman for Free Romanian Television. "I was not a hero," he said afterwards. "I had to feed my family and there was no other television station for which I could work." If his apology revealed little courage, at least it rang with truth.

The Rubicon of fear crossed, it will be almost impossible to restore the former status quo. Before, the old communist order came under attack only in isolated bursts. There were two tragic weeks of Hungarian freedom in 1956. The ill-fated Prague Spring in 1968 lasted only eight months. Solidarity's first legal existence in 1980 was sustained for just thirteen months. In 1989, however, change took place all over Eastern Europe. The only historical analogy that seems to capture the scope of these dramatic events is 1848, "the Springtime of Nations," when a wave of revolution swept continental Europe. Eastern Europe's revolutionaries no longer want to "reform" stagnant communism: they aim to install a new democratic, capitalist system. In a few years, today's events could be described as another Springtime of Nations.

The analogy, to be sure, offers few solid assurances for the future. Europe's first Springtime ended in disaster, with the old repressive emperors crushing the national liberation movements. It was to take decades of struggle before the captured nations could free themselves. But the omens look better this time. Outside threats of intervention are fading. The main threat facing the countries of Eastern Europe comes from within. In long-closed societies, a little hope can be a dangerous thing. The nineteenth-century French historian Alexis de Tocqueville noted that the most dangerous period for a repressive society comes with the first stirrings of change. Long-oppressed people see the possibility of freedom and suddenly make new demands, which inspire either more reforms or a return to repression. Perceptive Eastern Europeans recognize the danger. "Either we will manage a calm evolution," Lech Wałeşa has often told me, "or we will face an uncontrollable revolution."

As I wonder whether the accelerating process of change can be kept from spinning out of control, my thoughts keep returning to that dramatic day in June 1989 when the Poles voted the communists out of office. I witnessed the historic events in a small village, Rejszew, and as voters emerged from the booths I asked for whom they had voted.

"Solidarity, of course."

"Why?"

"Because it gave me hope."

The answer was the same – thirty-five times in a row.

That evening I returned to Warsaw to learn about the massacre in Beijing's Tiananmen Square. A demonstration was taking place outside Warsaw's Chinese Embassy. While a few policemen looked on sympathetically, the protesters lit candles. They prayed. They hung posters reading "Freedom, Peace for China." Most of all, they asked if Solidarity's electoral victory could become tomorrow's Tiananmen Square.

"We must move slowly," one student cautioned. "Each change needs time to be digested."

"You're a lousy gradualist," another young student shot back. "Poland doesn't have any more time."

"Calm down, calm down," an older onlooker implored. "We have to find a common language. If we're going to get anywhere, we're going to have to learn to cooperate."

Revolution

Chapter One

The Revolution:

Ten Years to Ten Hours

Poland, Ten Years.
Hungary, Ten Months.
East Germany, Ten Weeks.
Czechoslovakia, Ten Days.

Prague graffiti, December 1989

Winter winds whipped through Gdańsk. As 1989 approached, the days were short and dark, and so was the mood of the people in this Baltic seaport, the birthplace of Eastern Europe's revolution. The Lenin Shipyard was to be closed down, bankrupt. Everyone knew that the yard was losing money. Every other shipyard in Poland was also losing money. The real issue wasn't economic. It was political. The communist regime was taking on Solidarity in its stronghold, the place where workers had revolted in 1970, 1976, 1980, and twice again in 1988. Here, for the first time since World War II, an Eastern European nation had forced the communist monolith to shudder, for more than just a few days or weeks.

I expected to see flowers and banners announcing "Occupation Strike," grim-faced strikers in overalls flashing their "V-for-Victory" signs and shouting "Solidarity." But there was little passionate outpouring of pent-up emotion. Few work stoppages were reported. People seemed skeptical, embittered by martial law and eight long, wasted years. They just didn't believe the shipyard would be closed. "The authorities are trying to provoke us," said Brunon Baranowski, a welder in the yard since 1974. "They just can't close the shipyard and kick us out on the streets."

Lech Wałęsa, with a bigger belly and grayer hair than in former days, no longer beamed the same old defiant enthusiasm. I waited for him in the rectory of St. Brygida's Church. When he entered, he threw off his sheepskin jacket, slumped

11

into a chair and announced, "I feel lousy." His bad back bothered him. His room for maneuver was narrow. Because of the shipyard dispute, he had been forced to call off plans for a scheduled "round table" with the communist authorities. But with winter approaching, an occupation strike would have been suicidal. Freezing buildings can't be occupied. Wałeşa opted for caution, and impatient young union members were criticizing him for his moderation. They wanted action. "There is still a chance of avoiding things," he told me. "We need dialogue – dialogue is best for Poland."

Although on this blustery day the deal still seemed far away, Wałeşa perked up as our interview proceeded. He believed time was on his side. The economy was going from bad to worse. The Communist Party was bleeding members. In the two strike waves of 1988, a new generation of Poles had shown itself ready to take up the struggle. Wałeşa used one of his idiosyncratic metaphors to describe the situation. "It's like bananas," he insisted. "I like bananas. But if I try to plant them here, it won't work. I have calulated now that strikes won't work. My decision could change tomorrow." He explained, "If there is no solution, the people will become fed up and throw themselves against the power."

After our talk, I went down to the church basement to meet some young union activists. Mirosław Żak and Grzegorz Frydrych were in high school when Solidarity was born. While many of the movement's veterans had drifted away, Grzegorz and Mirosław had become fervent supporters. "We don't have apartments, we don't have benefits, we have nothing to lose," Mirosław said. "Older workers worry about losing their job, their seniority ranking, their retirement benefits, their apartment."

On their meager salaries, Grzegorz and Mirosław lived in grim workers' hostels, with peeling façades, broken windows and bare lightbulbs. A guard at the door made sure all visitors signed the guest register and left before 10 p.m. They had little hope of ever obtaining their own apartments. "When I went to see the housing cooperative, they laughed," Grzegorz recalled. "They said, 'Possibly, you'll get an apartment in thirty-eight years.' Thirty-eight years!"

I realized Lech Wałeşa was right. Poland's fuse was lit.

Unlike in Poland, where the impetus for change stemmed from below, from frustrated youngsters like Mirosław and Grzegorz, Hungary's Communist Party led the way towards democracy. Budapest buzzed with a new spirit at the beginning of 1989.

The pale-red "goulash" communism of past years had outlived its usefulness. "Our old model of socialism was based on an unhappy mixture of Tsarist traditional and Hapsburg enlightened absolutism," said János Barabás, a leading Communist Party official. "In the fast-developing world of computers and high-tech, this mixture no longer works." He and the other new Party chiefs ordered their economists to prepare a new reform plan. At the Hungarian National Bank, housed in a baroque palace next to the American Embassy, officials could not control their enthusiasm. "All of a sudden the word came: 'The sky's the limit; do what is necessary,' " said István Ipper of the National Bank. "The taboos vanished."

The new laws took effect on January 1, 1989. A stock exchange was established. Western capitalists were invited to own 100 per cent of Hungarian firms. Soon Hungarian officials would be touring Western Europe trying to sell off many of the country's leading industries. Private entrepreneurs were encouraged to make larger profits. Instead of being limited to thirty workers, they were allowed to hire almost as many as they needed. At the Rollitron Computer Company, president László Steiner outlined bold plans for issuing stock and starting a joint venture with a West German partner. "We used to be blocked by so many artificial limits," he said. "Now we could become just like a Western company."

The political landscape was shifting. When the Jurta Theater opened on the outskirts of Budapest in 1987, it became the first privately owned theater in Eastern Europe. Architects avoided erecting a soulless glass-and-steel socialist structure, choosing instead to draw from national traditions and erect a building which evokes a cowboy tent out on the Hungarian *Puszta*. Without any state control, independent groups can rent the attractive premises. That freedom didn't make much difference at first – the few dissidents who existed in 1987 found it hard to fill a private coffee house. But now in January 1989, almost every evening I found myself squeezed into a packed house at the Jurta. One night I heard speakers from the populist Democratic Forum lament the plight of Hungarians under Romanian rule. Another evening there was a passionate meeting of the Network of Free Initiatives, a group bringing together various opposition factions. A new students' union, FIDESZ, used the Jurta for its inaugural congress. "The political process has speeded up," said László Romhányi, the Jurta's long-haired, jeans-clad director. "We've started to come out of a thirty-year coma."

A few months before, only the most daring dissidents had imagined true democracy in Hungary. I considered them incurable optimists. "Micky," I asked Miklós Haraszti, "don't you think you should be realistic?" As publisher of an underground journal and a blacklisted writer, Haraszti had endured countless hours of police interrogations. He clenched his fist and answered defiantly, "Why not dream the impossible?"

When I returned to Budapest in January 1989, the impossible had happened: top-ranking communists were endorsing the idea of a Western-style democracy. "I think a multi-party system is unavoidable," said Imre Pozsgay, a Politburo member, sitting in his spacious office in Budapest's wedding-cake Parliament building. "It should be realized within two years."

Pozsgay was the Communist Party's best advertisement for change. Born in 1933 to a peasant family in a small village on the Hungarian Plain, his peasant origins and looks helped his popularity. He joined the Party at the height of the Stalinist era. In 1957, the year after the Hungarian Uprising, he received his teaching degree in Marxist-Leninism. After a career in the provincial apparatus in Kecskemét, he was made Minister of Culture. Demoted in 1982 to head of the Patriotic People's Front, a meaningless communist-controlled umbrella organization, he used the opportunity to build strong ties with emerging interest groups. He wore a well-tailored gray suit like a Western politician, and seemed bright and articulate. Unlike other communist politicians, he didn't fidget and weasel around questions with wooden language.

"Mr. Pozsgay, Poland also has several political parties in addition to the communists," I said. "Are you thinking of creating a Polish-type situation, or something closer to Austria?"

"Much more like Austria," Pozsgay answered without hesitation. "When I think of a multi-party system, it's not like Poland."

Next to this clear statement, the voice of Gorbachev sounded like communist orthodoxy. Pozsgay himself criticized the Soviet leader for moving too slowly. "Gorbachev personally is a strong figure," he said, "but I am concerned about the pace of his progress."

As our conversation neared an end, I wondered why Pozsgay had embarked on such a risky course. "There is no other way," he answered. "The old communist system has reached a dead end." He mentioned the economic crisis. He talked about a spiritual crisis. The old system kept people silent, their emotions and energies bottled up. "We must create an outlet for citizens' emotions," he explained. For him the choice was simple. Either Hungary liberalized quickly, or the combination of slow anger about falling living standards and disappointed expectations over *perestroika* and *glasnost* would combine into "a swelling of protest. The conservatives say that we must not move too fast in order to maintain stability," he said. "I say our greatest enemy is the unchanged situation."

In neighboring Prague, as 1989 opened, Communist Party leader Miloš Jakeš was fighting a rearguard action to preserve the crumbling status quo. A stocky hunk of a man with a cold, chiseled face, he represented the quintessential opportunist. Born in 1922, he worked as an electrician before World War II. He joined the Party in 1945, rising through the bureaucracy without distinguishing himself. His higher education was limited to the Soviet Party school from 1955 to 1958. During the Prague Spring, he kept in close contact with the Soviet leadership, approving the invasion and, as chairman of the Central Control and Auditing Commission, supervising the ensuing purge of reformers, in which almost 500,000 Party members were expelled. University professors became window-cleaners, engineers turned into garbage collectors, lawyers into bus drivers. Jakeš refused their rehabilitation. He insisted that no one would return to the Party until he offered a public confession.

When he was named First Secretary, Czechs mocked him bitterly.

"Somebody kidnapped Jakeš and they're asking for a ransom of $50 million," my friend Michál Donath told me.

"What will happen?" I asked.

"If we don't pay it, we get him back," Michál responded. "If we pay it, they keep him."

Since Soviet tanks crushed the 1968 Prague Spring, Czechs had struck a cynical bargain which they themselves called "salamis for submission": as long as you kept your head down, you could enjoy relatively high living standards. If you spoke up, your career would be ruined. By the late 1980s, however, sporadic shortages had appeared in the shops, and a growing number of people were prepared to risk something in order to speak their minds. A spiritual revival was visible. In 1988 a religious petition collected hundreds of thousands of signatures. New dissident groups proliferated. There were the John Lennon Peace Club, the Czech Children, even a pranksterish

Society for a Merrier Present, which armed itself with truncheons made of cucumber and salami.

On January 16, 1989, a small group of youngsters made their way, slowly, peacefully, towards the top of Prague's Wenceslas Square, towards St. Wenceslas's statue, where exactly twenty years earlier a student named Jan Palach had set himself on fire to protest against the Soviet invasion. Before they could commemorate his sacrifice, police began using water cannon and tear gas. Within moments, the calm square was transformed into a smoke-filled battle zone. Off to the side, a short, solid man with fair hair and a moustache watched in horror. When he tried to leave, a plainclothes policeman grabbed him and threw him into the back of a police van. The target was no potential rioter – it was Václav Havel, the country's pre-eminent playwright and human-rights champion. The prosecutor claimed Havel had incited the demonstrations by giving interviews to foreign radio stations. In fact, Havel had warned his countrymen against using violence to press their grievances. "I consider the way I am treated as an act of vengeance for my ideas," he told the court. "Rather than using laws, it would be more honest to say, 'Havel, you annoy the authorities, so you will be convicted.' "

The judge sentenced him to nine months in prison.

Imprisoning Havel proved a terrible mistake, provoking protests from the East as well as the West. Hungarian Prime Minister Miklós Németh disapproved in public; Polish opposition leaders went on hunger strike; and more than 100 Bulgarian intellectuals signed a petition calling for his release. Within Czechoslovakia itself, over 4,000 people, including many of the country's leading actors, academics, writers, film directors and artists, signed two petitions calling for Havel's release. "I didn't want to take any risks before," admitted screenwriter Jiří Křižán, one of the petition's organizers. "Now some type of morality is re-emerging; people are showing courage."

In mid-May, Havel was released on parole. I attended his hearing at the Pankrac Prison. The playwright's small figure looked emaciated. His distinctive moustache was clipped off. As the judge announced clemency, Havel smiled and threw his fist into the air. He rushed out of the room, his normal Chaplinesque walk transformed into a kind of racing shuffle. In the afternoon, the deposed hero of the 1968 Prague Spring, Alexander Dubček, who in the past had kept his distance from the hard-core opposition activists, visited the Havel apartment. This was the first time they had met. That evening, Havel

16

threw a wonderful victory party in his home. Other than Jiří Dienstbier, who had to work his shift as a stoker, the entire Czech opposition was there. Jiří Křižán and his fellow artists who had signed the influential petition attended. The singing, dancing and drinking went on well into the small hours.

When I met Havel two days later, he was a bundle of nervous energy. "A lot has changed since I went into prison," he said. "Budapest Radio now calls me and interviews me for an hour. Dubček comes to see me. All this was impossible a few weeks ago." In prison, he told me, he had received 500 letters a month. "This surprised me. These were unknown people – students, workers, peasants, different groups from different parts of the country." He was optimistic. "For twenty years, this society has been demoralized," he said. "Everybody now knows that our leadership is isolated from its foreign partners and its own society."

Amidst Eastern Europe's mounting discontent, East Germany appeared an island of relative tranquility. But when I went to Berlin in February 1989, discontent was breeding beneath the placid German surface. Although East Germans lived much better than their communist cousins, they compared themselves not to poor Poles but to the rich West Germans.

At the Zentrum Department Store on Alexanderplatz, Jörg Schaffer was searching for ice-hockey skates. A tall, gangly eighteen-year-old with size twelve feet, no pair would fit him. "The skates are good," he said, "but there's little choice."

Down on the first floor, saleswoman Karin Fluke arranged a pile of textiles. Her shelves were overflowing with purples and pinks, reds and roses. But she wasn't smiling. "It's all polyester," she complained. "We're always running short of good cotton."

The biggest complaint concerned travel. Although the communist regime permitted more and more of its citizens to visit the West, passports were still controled. Husbands and wives could not leave together. Police refused privileges without explanation. "My brother was able to visit our cousins in Stuttgart," my friend Volker Ebermann complained. "But I never received permission."

Later in the week, I was lost in Weimar, East Germany. A beautiful city, home to Goethe and Schiller, Weimar lies close to the West German border. Marko, a young train conductor, helped me find my hotel. We began talking. He told me that, despite the new travel privileges, he was refused his passport to visit West Berlin. He asked me where I lived. I told him Paris. At most, Paris is only an eight-hour drive away.

"Paris, France," he said, sipping his beer. "I'll never see the Champs-Elysées."

After finding frustration in East Germany, I headed off for a weekend in Transylvania. In the spring of 1989 tensions were mounting between the forward-looking Hungarian communists and their backward-looking Romanian comrades. For the past three years I had been unable to obtain a journalist's permit to visit Romania, so I traveled on a tourist visa. At the border the Romanian guard demanded that all luggage be taken from the car and placed on a bench. He ripped through the bags, skimmed through the books and flipped through the papers. Another guard passed a mirror under the car body and pulled up the seats to see if anything was hidden.

"Any firearms?" he asked.

"No."

"Any Bibles?"

"No."

He took my passport. Three-and-a-half hours passed. The guard finally returned and signaled that I could cross the border.

In the morning the hotel restaurant had no coffee. Outside, beggars pleaded with me for coffee, gas and, most of all, Kent cigarettes. For some mysterious reason, Kents had replaced the leu as the national currency.

I went on to the Transylvanian city of Cluj. When I arrived, I tried to visit a Hungarian poet, Lajos Kántor. A small, blond man stopped me. He was well-dressed and polite. In perfect English, he invited me to the police station. He pulled out a badge. It read "Captain Gheorghiu."

"I have some information for you," he explained.

At the police station I was locked inside a small room while Captain Gheorghiu conferred with his superiors. When he returned, he took the film from my camera.

"In Oradea you took pictures which were not those of a normal tourist," he said. "You will have to leave the country tonight."

It was 10:30 p.m. The border with Hungary was a three-hour drive away.

"Tonight?" I asked. "Not even tomorrow morning?"

"Tonight," he repeated.

A police car trailed me. At the border the guards took an

eternity to inspect my car. They pulled me into a bare room for a body search. By the time the border gate went up, it was 4 a.m. I had spent a total of thirty hours in the beleaguered Stalinist outpost.

My next stop was Moscow. During his five years in power, Mikhail Gorbachev had been passive towards Eastern Europe. When he visited Prague in 1987, he deflected all questions on the 1968 invasion, calling it an affair "for our Czechoslovak comrades." For that matter, the reform-minded Soviet leader had refrained from criticizing any of his hidebound hardline allies, the so-called "Gang of Four" (Czechoslovakia, East Germany, Bulgaria, or even hideous Romania). Now in February 1989, everybody seemed preoccupied by domestic events in Moscow. Preparations were under way for the freest parliamentary elections in Soviet history. Discussions centered on the remarkable developments in the Baltic nations, the unrest in Armenia and Azerbaijan, and, most of all, on the deteriorating economy. No one seemed interested in Eastern Europe.

When I probed, Russians said all they wanted in their European empire was stability, nothing less, nothing more. They didn't want to worry about Poland and Hungary. If pressed, they explained that bullying allies was bad politics for Moscow. It cut into the goodwill generated in the rest of the world by the new pragmatic, peaceful Soviet foreign policy. "Everybody knows that we need good neighbors, not satellites," said Yuri Mitiunov, a leader of Moscow's Democratic Union. "This is the only way of avoiding a tragedy." By tragedy, Mitiunov meant another convulsive upheaval which would represent a serious threat to Gorbachev's own reforms, even to his hold on power.

Unfortunately for the Soviet leader, his most perceptive advisers realized that stability would be difficult to achieve. I met Oleg Bogomolev, who survived long Brezhnev years by establishing a think-tank, the Institute of Socialist Economies, out in the Moscow suburbs. Under Gorbachev, he was given a more direct policymaking role. In our talk, he stressed Moscow's worry about "instability" in Eastern Europe and called for talks with the West to prevent a disaster. The Kremlin had no intention of intervening. He insisted that all the Eastern Europeans would soon be forced to reform, whether they wanted to or not, whether they were pushed by Moscow or not. "The quiet we are seeing now is superficial, on the surface, even in places like East Germany," he explained. "History's clock cannot be turned back, changes are impossible to avoid."

The first taboos fell in Poland. At the outset of negotiations with the government in February 1989, Solidarity leaders hoped to win back their union in return for endorsing painful economic reforms. Instead, the discussions plunged far beyond their original brief. The Solidarity negotiators realized that their government had a free hand. "Moscow's message was, 'Don't be so careful. Do whatever is necessary to get your house in order,' " explained Andrzej Stelmachowski, one of the talks' key mediators. On April 18, the historic social contract was initialed. It called for a series of breakthroughs unparalleled in the communist world, everything from restoring private schools to giving Solidarity its own newspaper. The outlawed independent trade union – both its workers' and farmers' divisions – was restored. Most important, free elections were scheduled for a new upper house of Parliament, the Senate, and for 35 per cent of the seats in the existing lower house, the Sejm. The vote was set for June 4, giving the opposition little time to organize a campaign.

After the agreement was announced, I called on a key Solidarity adviser, Tadeusz Mazowiecki. We sat in his cramped office at the Warsaw Catholic Intellectuals' Club. He looked tired, worn out. He said he would refuse to run for Parliament. He believed Solidarity should stay out of politics and concentrate on the safer area of trade-union activities. Lech Wałeşa and other Solidarity leaders overruled him. Mazowiecki's pessimism was haunting. "I don't see the possibility of a Christian ruler in Poland," he said. "A lot is being said and discussed, but I think it is very, very far away."

Within days Solidarity's first campaign posters were printed. They soon covered Warsaw's Constitution Square. Thousands of young volunteers crisscrossed the country. They needed 3,000 signatures to register Solidarity candidates in the ballot. They gathered hundreds of thousands. Solidarity's rallies were full of blaring loudspeakers, rousing music and stands selling posters and buttons. Even in the remotest, most isolated rural districts, Solidarity candidates were visible, thanks to support from local priests. While posters for Solidarity all proclaimed their allegiance with the familiar red logo, posters for the communist campaign played down any connection with the Party, or even with the existing regime. Communist candidates spoke of the need for "harmony," "good sense" and "moderation."

They hinted at chaos ahead if Solidarity should win. "With us," one poster preached, "you can be sure of things."

When the results came pouring in on June 5, 1989, the trade union showed itself to be a formidable political machine. It swept up between 70 and 80 per cent of the vote. Most humiliating for the communists was the rejection of all but one of its special "protected list" of thirty-five candidates, including Prime Minister Mieczysław Rakowski. To pass, all the voters had to do was leave the ballot unmarked. I remember scenes of voters taking their ballot papers and with a sense of immense physical pleasure crossing out each of the thirty-five names. The landslide was so complete that the communists, who were supposed to be guaranteed a working majority, could not put together a credible government.

In August 1989, Tadeusz Mazowiecki, the reluctant politician, became Prime Minister.

Even before Solidarity took power, Hungary's communists realized that their only hope of survival was to drop all pretenses of Party ideology. At the beginning of 1989 they began preparing to delete all references to Marxist-Leninism from their platform and to change their name from the Hungarian Socialist Workers' Party to the Hungarian Socialist Party. Roundtable talks were opened with the opposition to set a date for an election.

The most important concession, however, concerned 1956. For years, the bloody and daring uprising crushed by Soviet troops was referred to as a "counterrevolution." In 1956 a friend of mine, Imre Mecs, coordinated student resistance by distributing pamphlets and passing messages. Arrested as a "traitor" and sentenced to death by a "people's court," he was spared at the last moment because he had not used a weapon. Between 130 and 500 rebels, including Prime Minister Imre Nagy, were hanged and their bodies dumped into an unmarked mass grave.

On the uprising's thirtieth anniversary in 1986, I joined Mecs to bring flowers and a candle to the Rakoskeresztur Cemetery. We headed towards Section 301, overgrown by wild poppies and weeds. Here, Mecs believed, Nagy and his executed comrades were buried. A gray Lada was parked nearby. Beside it, three mustached men in leather jackets puffed cigarettes. One flashed a police badge. They took Imre's identity card and my notebook. "Some liberalism," Imre muttered. "You can't even put flowers on your friends' graves."

In the spring of 1989 the Communist Party dropped the term "counterrevolution" for the more acceptable "popular uprising," and Imre Mecs helped organize a massive public funeral for his fellow Hungarian patriots. On June 15, before more than 200,000 people in Budapest's Heroes' Square, he stood up and said, "We will never forget. We will have a democracy like we dreamed of in 1956." Plot 301, only months before a swampy wasteland, was transformed into a garden for a decent burial. Funeral music sounded. A guard of honor stood erect. Everything was shown live on national television.

The next evening, Imre and I met for dinner. A bottle of wine was uncorked. A gypsy band struck up some swirling strains. Imre dug into a huge plate of chicken paprika, and tried to explain the astounding events. "You know that policeman who searched us three years ago?" he said. "Well, the other day he came to see me at my home. He wanted to apologize. He said, 'Please excuse me. What I did was so stupid.'"

Along with rehabilitating their martyrs, the Hungarians began tearing down the barbed-wire fences and watchtowers on the Austrian border. To the Hungarians the particular significance was minimal: the border had already been open to their own citizens since the beginning of 1988. To the East Germans, however, the event portended momentous change. Word went around that it might be possible to walk across the border from Hungary into Austria. From there it was even easier to reach West Germany, where they received automatic citizenship.

The numbers, small at first, kept growing. By midsummer thousands of East Germans had gathered in refugee camps in Budapest. At the stroke of midnight on September 13, Hungary suspended its bilateral consular agreement with East Germany and officially opened its western border. The "Great Escape" began. A stream of freedom-seekers turned into a flood – 15,000 in three days.

At home in East Germany, Church-protected opposition was gathering strength. Every Monday in Leipzig the faithful met for a "peace service" in the St. Nikolai Church. Afterwards they spilled out on to the Karl-Marx Platz to march for freedom. They included such unlikely demonstrators as Marlis Flüssen, a middle-aged matron who wore a prim, proper dress and spoke in the soft, sure tones of a middle-class Fräu. Happily married for three decades, she was the proud mother of two strapping children, twenty-one-year-old Stefan and fifteen-year-old Sandra. "I've never protested before," Mrs. Flüssen said. "None of us used to have the courage." With elderly parents living nearby, she herself couldn't leave, but her children didn't face the same constraints. "My son Stefan was considering going, he was so frustrated with his prospects here," she said. "As a mother I felt a responsibility to do something." On October 9, the fear of losing her family overcame the fear of speaking out. For the first time she went to St. Nikolai and joined the demonstrators.

If one can identify a turning-point, it was this day. Riot police, state security forces and members of the factory's paramilitary "combat groups" stood ready with live ammunition. Thousands like Mrs. Flüssen demonstrated regardless. The police, called off at the last moment, did not shoot. The Monday evening demonstrations continued to swell. The protesters demanded a new travel law. It was granted. By now virtually all of East Germany seemed to have taken to the streets. They demanded an end to the Berlin Wall – and, climactically, it came down, on November 9, 1989.

Dancing on the Wall was a marvelous street-party, perhaps the most marvelous street-party the world has ever seen. The next day came the hangover. In East Berlin, my friend Volker Ebermann told me that he had been to West Berlin for the first time in his life. He enjoyed the book stores, the food; but on his return home he was depressed. Every night on television he had seen that the West was better off economically. Now for the first time, he could smell it, feel it, absorb it – and the sensation was sickening. "After the first night in the West, I was ill almost all the time," he said. "I had known we were behind. I just didn't know we were so far behind."

In late November and early December, with freezing weather settling in, the tone of Leipzig's peaceful, determined Monday evening demonstrations began to turn angry. One week, protesters stormed the seven-storey stone Stasi secret-police headquarters. Another week, strident banners called for a united Germany, complete with a map of the old 1937 borders. On the Monday I attended, the pastor of St. Nikolai warned against too much emotion. If we were not careful, he said, violence could result. "People have lost valuable things in the last few months: hope, ideas, belief, peace, convictions, influence, status, power. Let us all feel responsible for one another."

People streamed out on to Karl-Marx Platz and headed down the main boulevard towards the huge baroque train station. They started off good-humored. Many chanted, "Bravo, bravo." Others shouted, "We are the People."

Then shouts were heard.

"Germany, Germany – a single Fatherland."

The demonstrators started breaking up into groups. Anti-unification youngsters waved banners proclaiming, "We don't want a Fourth Reich."

"If Germany unites," one explained, "then we will become aggressive."

Pro-unification people heckled them.

"We've been cheated for forty years," an older man shouted. "I won't be cheated any more."

"We're definitely in the minority," the young anti-unification protester admitted.

Back in West Berlin, I visited a "relocation center" in a high school on Onkel Tom Strasse in the American sector. Cots covered the entire gym space. Since the Wall had come down, the flow of East Germans to the West had stayed steady at around 2,000 people a day. In the whole of 1989 some 300,000 East Germans left the country permanently. The Schultzes – father Jürgen, mother Uta and their two boys, nine-year-old Florian and six-year-old Tobias – were typical. Even though their home country was democratizing, they did not plan to go back. "Our life is here," the stocky, muscular thirty-eight-year-old Mr. Schultz said. "To be honest, I really don't care what happens there."

Nowhere else in Eastern Europe did a similar problem exist. Hundreds of thousands of Poles were leaving for the West; their departure did not throw into question the future existence of Poland. Czechoslovakia's new leaders threw open their country's borders in November 1989 without much real effect. There was no rich West Czechoslovakia where Czechs could go and receive immediate citizenship. In East Germany, however, emigration was a crucial, *the* crucial, issue. As the flight of skilled workers and professionals continued, the country's economy crumbled. Before the Wall came down, few dared criticize those who wanted to leave. Afterwards, many of the opposition intelligentsia denounced the departees. They should stay and help rebuild a new democratic East Germany. "Those who left before the Wall came down had ideals – they were leaving for freedom," said Klaus Wiczynski, a diplomatic correspondent at the *Berliner Zeitung*. "Those who are leaving now leave for crass material reasons, to live in a big apartment and drive around in a big car."

Men such as Wiczynski opposed unification. They believed that West Germany was not the best of all possible worlds, that there was less inequality and more human caring in East Germany. They wanted to make a different East Germany, neither communist nor capitalist, but genuinely socialist. As Wiczynski put it, "We want a free society – but a free society without elbows."

The problem with this dream was that the majority of East Germans didn't believe in it. Certainly emigrants such as the Schultzes didn't see any "Third Way." They saw West Germany – and they saw that it worked. They were willing to accept a tougher life in the West with "elbows" in return for the possibility of prosperity. Although neither Jürgen nor Uta Schultz had found a job, they weren't even considering returning to the safety of East Germany's welfare state. "I contributed thirty-eight years to East Germany – for nothing," Schultz told me. "There is no way I will be a laboratory rabbit for any new experiment."

With East German freedom trains passing through Prague, the Czech national spirit was roused. "When we saw all those East Germans leaving, it told us anything could happen," recalled Michál Čech, another drama student. "I myself helped more than forty East German students escape." Everybody realized freedom was within reach. On November 17, 1989, police used truncheons to disperse peaceful student demonstrators. Many were taken to hospital; a rumor circulated that one person had died. That provided the needed spark. The students went on strike. Actors joined them. Each day, for ten days in a row, the demonstrators gathered in Wenceslas Square. They waved banners: "Down With Communism." They jingled keys and shouted, "The bells are ringing."

Václav Havel brought all the existing opposition groups together to form "Civic Forum." It set up headquarters in the Magic Lantern Theater. The Forum demanded the resignation of Party leader Jakeš and President Gustáv Husák. The puppet Socialist Party defected. The Socialist Party newspaper *Svobodné Slovo* had offices on Wenceslas Square, from the balcony of which Havel began addressing the crowds below. Later in the week, Alexander Dubček appeared and the crowd roared with joy. "DUBČEK! DUBČEK!" Afterwards, the two leaders gave a joint press conference. On November 24 they were just starting to field questions when someone brought the news that Jakeš and the entire Politburo had resigned. Havel leapt to his feet, gave a V-for-Victory sign and embraced Dubček.

Much more drama remained to be played out. One government was named by the communists and rejected by Civic Forum before a second, including Jiří Dienstbier as Foreign Minister, was accepted. Husák resigned as President; his replacement was none other than Havel.

Prague seemed hypnotized, caught in a magical trance. It had never ceased to be one of Europe's most beautiful cities, but for two long decades a cloud of repressive sadness had enveloped the Gothic and baroque towers. Now it vanished. The crowds were calm, confident and civilized. Each day, people assembled after work at 4 p.m., filing politely, patiently and purposefully into Wenceslas Square. When the protest was over, they filed out just as politely, patiently and purposefully. Everyone seemed to have the Czech tricolor pinned to his breast. Flags flew from the rooftops. The city burst with color: posters were plastered on walls, on shop windows, on any inch of free space. An entire country was awakening. After each mass rally, the crowd sang the National Anthem, a lullaby-like tune:

> Where is my home, where is my home?
> Streams are rushing through the meadows.
> Orchards decked in spring's array.
> Scenes of paradise portray.

As they intoned the haunting melody, the dour faces disappeared. Everyone smiled.

At my hotel, the receptionist whom I had once nicknamed "Witch Woman" on account of her demeanor, greeted me with a "Hello." There were no rooms, she said, but let's see what we can do. She found me a room. At the border the guards no longer rummaged through my belongings. One wished me a good trip. I mentioned Civic Forum, and he gave out a joyful squeal: "Victory."

The revolution spilled over into Bulgaria, long the most docile, subdued Soviet satellite. On the day the Wall came down in Berlin, a new, young, reform-minded team led by Foreign Minister Petar Mladenov replaced the rigid, repressive rule of Todor Zhivkov. Roundtable talks were held. A free vote was promised. When I had last visited Sofia, the American Embassy had still been unable to find enough dissidents to have a good cocktail party. Now fear had vanished. Walking down streets in Sofia, I encountered groups of pedestrians engaging in spirited conversation.

The new-found freedom of expression, however, often resulted in more demands than compromises. People shouted.
They didn't listen to the opinions of others. "We still have to
learn democracy," said opposition leader Deyen Kiuranov.
"People have to calm down and talk out problems."

In Sofia's Lenin Square, the proud socialist realist statue of
Lenin still stood erect, while a huge red star remained perched
on top of the Communist Party's Central Committee building.
At night it was lit up. In Poland, statues of Lenin had already
been ripped down, and in Budapest the same red stars were
gone. Although reformers controlled the top of the Bulgarian
Communist Party, they had no time to weed out the old Party
bosses, who formed and financed protests against the country's
Turkish minority. Opposition figures continued to complain
about difficulties with the police. "My telephone is bugged and
my conversations often cut," complained Stanimir Dossev of
the Democratic Youth Union. "The leaders at the top of the
Communist Party promise reform, but under them, the repressive apparatus remains intact."

The incredible year ended in Romania. When the explosion
came in the most repressed outpost of the Soviet Empire,
it came with a bang. In mid-December, secret police in the
Transylvanian city of Timisoara staged a raid on the Inner City
Reform Church. They wanted to arrest the pastor, a fiery ethnic
Hungarian named László Tökés. A human chain formed outside
the church. The police dragged Tökés away. By the following
evening, crowds of students and workers joined the pastor's
followers in the streets, breaking windows and building bon-
fires. The army occupied Timisoara. Tanks rolled into Opera
Square. The troops opened fire.

Protests spread around the country, toppling dictator Nicolae
Ceausescu. A new National Salvation Front took power. When
the army joined the uprising, the security police – the notorious
Securitate – resisted and heavy fighting took place. It subsided
only after Ceausescu and his despised wife Elena had been
executed by firing squad on Christmas Day.

When I arrived, signs of another "People Power" victory were
everywhere. Passers-by grinned. Boys flashed V-for-Victory
signs. The national blue, yellow and red tricolor hung from
factories and houses – with its central symbol, the communist
hammer and sickle, cut out. But this victory was different. It
was soaked in blood. Mourners stood twenty-four-hour vigils
at memorials to the dead, which can be found in the square of

every major city. They held candles, mementos and photographs.

Most of the victims were young. The rage and commitment of their children came as a shock to many parents. I visited Lajos and Erzsébet Hegyi, who had lost their twenty-six-year old son, also named Lajos. Eyewitnesses to the shooting told them how it had happened. Security forces had confronted a crowd of schoolchildren shouting "Down with Ceausescu." Young Lajos stepped forward and pleaded, "Don't shoot." They shot anyway. It was not until the next morning that his parents learned about the gunfire in the square. "I learned about it from the lady next door, that he had been outraged even before the events of Timisoara," his father told me. "She said to us, 'You still did not know what your son was really like.' " Later that morning, Mr. Hegyi went to the hospital. There he found his son's body riddled with bullets. "The only consolation is the knowledge that although they died, at least they triumphed so far," Mr. Hegyi told me. "The country has ceased to be a prison."

Five days after Ceausescu's execution, soldiers and tanks still occupied the streets. Army checkpoints were set up along the roads for fear of rogue Securitate agents. The soldiers were dressed in olive-drab wool and carried machine guns of World War II vintage. Only after car and body searches did they let me pass. Off on the side of the road between Oradea and Cluj, I spotted a truck with its windshield shattered. "I was coming under the underpass and there was a shot," the unharmed driver said. "Be careful."

Many ruling Salvation Front members worried that their ranks were being infiltrated by their old oppressors. "We still haven't got rid of the telephone bugging," complained János Vincze, the Front's vice president in Cluj. "When I raised the issue at our meeting, only one person backed me. They are scared." Few were confident about a democratic future for Romania. "This country is not ready for elections," the courageous dissident Doina Cornea told me. "We need the army to step in and restore order."

In the coming months each of Eastern Europe's new democratic experiments would encounter similar difficulties. Politicians became locked in squabbles, presenting vague, sketchy programs and blurry ideologies, while the economies stagnated and living standards declined. On the campaign trails, anger mounted. In Hungary I visited my old dissident friend Miklós Haraszti, who was running for Parliament. Together we went to Paszto, an agricultural town of about 20,000 people about fifty miles north of Budapest, to attend a meeting at the local Cultural Center, a nondescript modern building on the town's outskirts.

After Haraszti had explained his political program, a man in work clothes rose to speak. "There's a communist in this room," he said in an accusing tone, pointing at a man in the audience. He pulled a small Christian cross from his pocket. "See, I'm no lousy communist."

"Shut up," yelled the accused man, who wore a dark-brown suit. "I have as much right to be here as you."

Another spectator rose. "No, you haven't," he said. "We should kick all the communists out. They still control all the power here in Paszto."

Haraszti was horrified. He had spent all his adult life fighting communism. Within sight of victory, he feared that the public's long-suppressed anger could destroy his cherished dream. "I'm shocked by the people's reaction," he said. "They really hate the communists. They almost want to lynch them."

For me the year of revolution ended on an appropriate bitter-sweet note, one that summed up both the exhilaration and exasperation of the tumultuous events in Eastern Europe. I was in Romania, in the Transylvanian town of Cluj. The baroque dining hall at the Hotel Continental was empty on New Year's Eve. There was going to be no celebration of the new decade. "It's too soon for people to dance," the hotel clerk explained. "We're still mourning." I drove on to the nearby city of Tirgu Mureș, to the home of Pastor Filöp Dénes. A few weeks before, police had detained his children and interrogated them about meeting with foreigners. Guests from The Netherlands, Hungary and the United States now filled the room. As midnight approached, the group assembled for a moment of silence. The pastor then picked up the Bible. Champagne bottles were uncorked. Everybody raised glasses. The mood was of hope and joy mixed with grief and sorrow. There was the thrill of freedom. There was the bitter memory of those who had lost their lives. The New Year's toast was bittersweet too. "We know that life can be destroyed as easily as a flower," Pastor Dénes said. "Let us then pray that we will break down walls. Let us pray that goodness will triumph. Let us pray, above all, that God will bring us peace."

Chapter Two

The Landscape:

Squeezed Between East and West

From Stettin in the Baltic to Trieste in the Adriatic, an
iron curtain has descended across the Continent . . .

Winston Churchill, Fulton, Missouri, 1946

Winston Churchill's Iron Curtain always was an unnatural
concept, an accidental by-product of World War II when Soviet
and Western armies met in conquered Germany. It enjoyed no
deep historical or geographic roots. In ancient times, Europe
was split between Rome and Byzantium. Romanians, Bulgarians, Greeks and Serbs looked eastwards to Constantinople.
Poles, Czechs, Slovaks and Hungarians looked westwards to
Rome. Turkish occupation from the tenth to the nineteenth
centuries deepened the divide between their backward Balkan
lands and the more advanced territories ruled by the Austrian
Hapsburgs. Poles, Czechoslovaks and Hungarians always refused the label "Eastern Europe." If asked where they came
from, they replied "Central Europe." When Mozart went from
Vienna to Prague, after all, he didn't feel he was traveling to
the "East." Why should he have? Physically, he was moving
west. Emotionally, spiritually and ideologically, he stayed in
Europe's cultural heart.

Even before the Iron Curtain was dismantled, it was difficult
to locate today's East–West divide. Greece, at the south-eastern
end of the Balkans, gave off an Eastern flavor while remaining
politically and economically in the Western camp. Yugoslavia
was communist but non-aligned. Austria was democratic and
capitalistic. Within the vanishing Soviet Bloc itself, the profound
"north–south" divide persisted, between the Roman Catholic
"Europeanized" countries, Poland, Czechoslovakia and Hungary, and the Orthodox Christian "Balkanized" nations of
Romania and Bulgaria. How can you compare a Czech steel-
worker from the industrial city of Plzeň, puttering about in his

Škoda automobile, with a Romanian peasant from the Wallachian countryside, plodding along in his horse and cart? Both reside in the same post-communist universe. But they live in two different centuries, in two different worlds.

Amidst these different traditions and histories, one strong common factor unites the Eastern European countries – their smallness, their fragility, their preoccupation with obtaining real independence. Powerful, successful countries like America or Britain enjoy the nationalism of victors. The vulnerable Eastern European nations have fallen back on a different, difficult sort of nationalism, the nationalism of victims. Over the centuries, three great empires, Ottoman, German and Russian, have kicked them around like a football. They have been traded, abused, mocked. Sporadically they have managed to break free of outside domination. These moments of independence, cherished as they are, never lasted. For Westerners, especially Americans, growing up in a stable, settled environment, it is hard to imagine how each Eastern European nation has lived through a roller-coaster of a history, full of sharp ups and downs, where just existing represented a sort of success.

No nation illustrates this checkered past better than Poland. Poles often refer to themselves as "the Jesus Christ of nations", suffering oppression for the promise of general salvation, and at the end of most Catholic Masses, parishioners join together to sing the National Anthem, which begins: "Poland has not yet perished . . ."

Exaggerated though this victim's sense of self-importance may sound, it isn't. Poles defended Roman Catholicism against the threat of the infidel Turk in the seventeenth century, then against the Orthodox Cossack in 1920, and in 1939 against the atheist Nazi. Within the Soviet Empire, Poland was the key link. It was the largest, most populous, most strategically located satellite, and the most volatile, combining a virulent anti-Russian sentiment with a romantic self-consciousness. When Soviet-imposed communism began to teeter, the Poles were the first to the barricades and the first to succeed in toppling it.

The defiant Polish character is rooted in the bad fortune of the country's geography, squeezed between Germany and Russia. These two powerful nations conspired to wipe Poland off the map at the end of the eighteenth century. After World War I, the modern Polish state emerged, impoverished and divided. A generation later, the Germans and Russians tried again to wipe out Poland. They almost succeeded. On September 1, 1939, the Nazis launched their Blitzkrieg from the west and two weeks later, on September 17, under the secret provisions of the Molotov–Ribbentrop Pact of August 23, 1939, the Russians invaded from the east. No country suffered more from the war. In German-occupied Poland, the infamous death camps were built. In Soviet-occupied Poland, army prisoners and suspect "bourgeois" Poles were sent eastwards to the labor camps. The bodies of thousands of officers, the cream of the Polish army, were later discovered buried in the Katyn Forest, each with his skull shattered by a bullet.

In 1944, when the advancing Red Army approached Praga, on the far side of the Vistula river from Warsaw, the Polish Home Army rose up to liberate their capital. As the Soviet forces stood by, refusing to help, the Nazis proceeded to crush the insurrection, march the few survivors off to the countryside and raze the entire city. By the time the country was freed, a total of 6 million Poles had lost their lives, half of them Jews. The sheer devastation is hard to grasp. On my first trip to Poland I visited Warsaw's City Museum in the Old Town Square. The museum's film opened with images of the capital in 1945 – pictures of mountains of rubble. Warsaw is still a city of scars. Except for the restored Old Town, the overriding impression is of grime and dirt, and crumbling gray concrete blocks.

Almost all of Poland spreads out like a flat pancake. Since time immemorial, this open plain has provided a perfect stage for wave after wave of nomads and settlers, raiders and invaders, from both east and west. The pre-Christian population was composed of a wide mixture of tribes, Balts, Celts, Germans, Slavs, along with nomadic peoples such as the Scythians, Sarmatians, Huns and Mongols. The Poles date their history to AD 966 when Duke Mieszko I converted himself and his people to the Roman Church. Pagan Prussian tribes and the Teutonic Knights launched frequent attacks, eventually capturing most of the Baltic coast. In 1308, Gdańsk fell and was renamed Danzig. Casimir the Great finally made peace with the Knights in 1343 and proceeded to consolidate the Polish state. At the time, Russia was a weak, minor power, sapped by unending invasions of the Mongolian hordes. Kraków became the capital in 1304. The city gleamed with the soaring Gothic and Renaissance towers of St. Mary's Church, the Cloth Hall, the Wawel Royal Castle. In 1364 the University of Kraków was founded.

Poland's "Age of Glory," a brilliant era of power and prosperity, opened. During the fifteenth and sixteenth centuries, under the Jagiellons, Polish nobles built fine palaces and mansions, the Polish astronomer Copernicus made his revolutionary discovery that the earth is not the center of the universe and, perhaps most important, a rudimentary system of democracy was established. The assertive nobles founded the parliamentary Diet and limited royal powers. For the first time in Europe, a king was elected. A union was formed with Lithuania, the capital moved from Kraków to Warsaw, and Polish power reached its zenith. The Polish army pushed Ivan the Terrible's Russia away from the Baltic and held off the Swedish invasion in front of the Częstochowa monastery. The monastery's "Black Madonna," a small, dark painting credited with the victory, became a national shrine. Then, in 1683, King Jan Sobieski succeeded in making a daring rescue of besieged Vienna. He surprised the encamped Turks from the rear and routed them.

From this glorious peak, Polish fortunes deteriorated. An insistence on the equality of every Polish gentleman, the system of electing kings – so "democratic" for its time – weakened the state's ability to take decisions. Parliamentary resolutions needed to be unanimous. The princely families began to quarrel and seek support from foreign powers, who in turn saw Poland as an easy target. By buying one parliamentary vote, they could paralyze the legislature. Torn by these internal rivalries, Austria, Prussia and Russia divided up the country between them. After three partitions, in 1772, 1793 and finally 1795, the name of Poland was erased from the map. A small Polish kingdom managed to resurface at the beginning of the nineteenth century, but the Prussians, Austrians and Russians soon smothered it. The solution looked permanent. At the beginning of the twentieth century, French playwright Alfred Jarry set one of his pieces in "Poland, that is to say, nowhere."

The trauma left deep scars on the national conscience. During the long partition period, Poland existed only as an idea, embedded in a language, a religion and a historical consciousness. Culture became embodied in the continuation of the Polish language, and literature played a key role in nationalism. The Roman Catholic Church represented the nation, in its opposition to German Protestantism and Russian Orthodoxy. A tradition of skepticism towards authority, planted by the tender feudal democracy, blossomed into a deep rejection of authority and a tradition of conspiracy, both of which persist today. Three times in the nineteenth century, in 1830, 1848 and 1863, Poles rose in revolt. Each time, they were crushed. A fleeting dose of freedom was won only in 1918, when World War I had left both Germany and Russia exhausted. It was lost again in 1939.

At the end of World War II, Stalin demanded a large chunk of pre-war Poland, and at Yalta the United States and the United Kingdom agreed to give it to him. Ever since, the "betrayal" at Yalta has been burned into the Polish soul. In their anger, Poles describe three old men – one a bloodthirsty tyrant, one a terminally ill politician with little knowledge of the issues, and the other a statesman from a declining empire – sitting around the Crimean resort deciding the fate of Europe. Their frustration is understandable, given that Stalin, Roosevelt and Churchill discussed Poland's future without the presence of a single Pole. Yalta symbolized Poland's impotence. Little wonder that the Poles now insist on being present at the Great Power talks concerning German unification.

Under the border agreements made at Yalta, Poland was moved several hundred miles westwards. Poles from the Soviet-occupied section in the east were moved west, taking the place of German inhabitants of Pomerania and Silesia who left for Germany. In geographic terms, post-war Poland formed a compact rectangle compared with its crooked pre-war shape. The vulnerable corridor through German territory to Gdynia was replaced by a clear outlet to the sea. But the new borders were no more defendable than the jagged pre-war ones. They made Poland reliant on Russia for protection against potential German revenge. Historian Joseph Rothschild noted:

> A war which had begun to preserve Poland's authentic independence from Nazi Germany ended with its being doubly dependent on Soviet Russia. Poland was to be governed by a cadre determined to match its social, economic, and political life to the Soviet model; Poland's international security was to be entirely dependent on Soviet protection of its new western frontier against future German revanchism.

As under the nineteenth-century partition, the Poles refused to succumb to overwhelming odds. The Catholic Church once again proved a strong rallying ground for nationalism. Gone were the large pre-war populations of Germans, Jews, Ukrainians, Belorussians and other ethnic and religious minorities. Before, these internal divisions were played upon by outsiders. Now Poles stopped fighting among themselves and united against what they considered an alien regime. Regular outbreaks of worker unrest, in 1956, 1970, 1976, 1980 and 1988, gradually loosened the Soviet stranglehold.

By 1989, the cycle of repression and upheaval had swung

around. The independent trade union Solidarity was legal. The country's freest elections in fifty years had been held. The first non-communist Prime Minister – the first in a communist Soviet Bloc country – was installed. A formidable task lay ahead. As the new Solidarity government executed a dramatic transition to the free market, it had to energize a dispirited society. Given the exciting transformation, I was surprised to find when I visited at the end of the year that most people didn't radiate enthusiasm. They looked sullen and resigned – exhausted.

Part of the problem was the sheer pace of change. People were disoriented. All their old parameters had fallen away. Beyond that, the disintegration of daily life was terrifying. Prices were soaring and many could no longer afford to buy meat or gasoline. Everybody remembered how hopes had been dashed in 1981, how democratization can always be rolled back. Sure, Gorbachev may be a nice guy, they would say. But what about his successor? Sure, you in the West may offer nice words, but what about some hard cash? Through indifference, many feared that the West would abandon Poland again, just as it had done at Yalta.

Until now, it had been easy for Poles to say that nothing would improve until the Russians set them free. That convenient scapegoat no longer existed. Poles were forced to replace their penchant for defiance with order, to add concrete, step-by-step action to their traditional romantic heroism.

Near the end of my stay, I went to a final Mass at the Holy Savior Church in Warsaw. Monsignor Bronisław Plaseck made an impassioned plea for patience. "Solidarity will be able to help us only when we help ourselves," he said. "We must begin to help ourselves." The heroic Poles had achieved the impossible. Now they were left to focus on managing the possible.

Like the Poles, the Czechs and the Slovaks lived long under foreign domination: the Czechs labored under German Hapsburg rule, while the Slovaks suffered under Hungarian domination. Czechs, Slovaks and Poles speak similar languages and, with a little effort, can understand each other. The similarities end there. For neighbors with so much in common, Poland and Czechoslovakia have rarely enjoyed good relations. Their temperaments are too different. As the westernmost of Slavic lands, the most influenced by the Western Renaissance and Enlightenment, the Czechs share almost none of the romantic Polish spirit of wild passion, soaring emotional highs followed by deep lows. They are the most sober, stolid Slavs. When Solidarity burst upon the scene, Czechs showed their skepticism in biting, black humor.

"A Polish and a Czech dog meet at the border," goes one of the better jokes. "The Polish dog runs right over to the Czech side and the Czech dog runs over to the Polish side."

Why?

"The Polish dog wants something to eat."

And the Czech dog?

"He wants to bark."

When Czechoslovakia won independence on October 29, 1918, it emerged from the ashes of the Austro-Hungarian Empire better prepared for independence than any of the other new Eastern European states. As the most advanced, industrially developed of the Hapsburg lands, the country of 13.6 million inhabitants benefited from a large, well-off middle class. World War I spared Prague's symphony of Gothic and baroque churches and gold-tipped spires, ancient cobbled squares and modern art-nouveau buildings. Czechoslovakia is a beautiful land. In the west, the rolling Bohemian countryside inspired poets, as well as producing some of the world's best beer. Moravia, in the middle, is a gentle, welcoming place, home to fine vineyards. Slovakia, in the east, enjoys a rugged beauty of pristine Alpine mountains and lakes. The climate is temperate, continental. For the two brief decades between the wars, these advantages were brilliantly exploited. While the other new Eastern European nations succumbed to violence and authoritarianism, Czechoslovakia prospered as a successful Western-minded liberal democracy, an island of freedom amidst an ever-widening sea of fascism.

There were some problems. Historically, the Czechs and Slovaks had never had a tradition of unified nationhood, and the First Republic revealed unresolved tensions between the less-developed Slovaks and the better-developed Czechs. The Nazi-influenced ethnic German minority in the Sudetenland proved an even worse wound. When outside forces set a match to these weaknesses, they produced an immense fire. In 1938, after the West had abandoned the country to Hitler at Munich, Czechoslovakia refused to stand alone. It fell to the Nazis without a fight. In 1948, the country again gave up its democracy without a struggle, this time to the communists.

These tragedies pose a profound dilemma, common to all Eastern European countries. Americans and British see the world from the vantage point and aspiration of a Great Power.

From this perspective, small nations look like objects, pawns to be gained or lost in the conflicts or deals of the superpowers. Small nations don't have the luxury of error, they have only some room for maneuver. The great question is how well they use it. In the 1930s Czechoslovakia had a well-trained, well-equipped army. When President Edvard Beneš decided not to fight against the Nazis, was he mistaken? If he had resisted, as the Finns resisted the Soviet Union in the Winter War of 1940, would Czechoslovakia have kept her freedom? Or would she have been crushed and dismembered like Poland when that country decided to stand up and fight?

History offers no clear-cut answers. Twice in their past the Czechs resisted foreign oppression – only to end up crushed. The first instance was Jan Hus's martyrdom in 1415. Son of Bohemian peasants, Hus studied at Prague University before becoming a preacher at the Bethlehem Chapel. In his sermons he attacked the corruption of the ecclesiastical establishment, an issue which Martin Luther would later raise to spark the Reformation. Hus won great popularity among the powerless Czech peasants, oppressed by a German-speaking clergy who owned much of the land. The German Church leaders responded with excommunication. Hus ignored their ban and continued to preach, though he never renounced his ties with Rome. When the mayor of Prague and some city council officers tried to break up a Hussite demonstration, the enraged people stormed the town hall and threw them from the windows to their deaths. The Hussites set up a type of utopian settlement in Tabor. Full-scale battles ensued between them and the Hapsburg Crown. Hus was arrested, condemned and burned at the stake on July 6, 1415.

The second Czech martyrdom came in 1620, at the Battle of White Mountain. Hus's legacy had left Bohemia ripe for the Reformation, and Protestantism made quick advances. The Catholic Hapsburgs resolved to restore their grip. In 1618 two Imperial envoys were sent from Vienna to Prague. The Czechs received them at the Hradčany Castle. Hearing the Hapsburg demands, they became enraged and, like the Hussites two centuries before them, threw their aggressors out of the window. Fortunately, the Austrians were not killed. Unfortunately, Vienna sent an expedition to punish the Czechs. On November 8, 1620, at White Mountain not far from Prague, the Hapsburgs won an overwhelming victory. Their revenge was cruel and swift. The uprising's leaders, twenty-seven nobles, were executed in Prague's Old Town Square. Twenty-seven small white crosses mark the spot. A thorough Germanization program was launched. The Czech gentry lost its land to German landlords. Czech as a language survived only as a provincial patois in backward villages.

By the time Mozart conducted the première of *Don Giovanni* in the Tyl Theater in 1787, Prague had become a thoroughly German city, with German as the dominant language. German and Jewish businessmen turned Bohemia into an industrial powerhouse. Czech locomotives spearheaded the extensive development of European railways. Czech firearms armed the Austro-Hungarian Empire. The Czech lands became known for luxury and style; Czech crystal was prized and Czech spas at Karlsbad and Marienbad attracted royalty from all over the continent. Czech nationalism did not begin to revive until the mid-nineteenth century, led by intellectuals, philosophers, writers, musicians. Their aim was not to provoke a revolutionary uprising, only to revive Czech culture and restore battered Czech pride. Tomáš Garrigue Masaryk, a philosophy professor, won independence in 1918 with clever use of diplomacy.

Where the Poles confronted, the Czechs engaged in passive resistance. In 1942 an underground resistance unit parachuted in by the British ambushed and killed the German governor Reinhard Heydrich. The Germans retaliated by razing the nearby village of Lidice, killing 184 and deporting 235. The brutality taught the Czechs a lesson they would not forget. In 1944 Slovak Partisans launched an uprising against the Germans, tying down large numbers of Nazi troops, and on May 5, 1945, the people of Prague rose against the retreating Germans. But neither the Czechs nor the Slovaks could liberate themselves. They needed the American and Soviet armies. General George Patton reached Plzeň, within striking distance of Prague. His superiors, concerned about following previous agreements with Moscow, forbade him to liberate the capital. Soviet troops arrived there on May 9, 1945. Czechs still recall Patton's army with a mixture of admiration and anger. Before the revolution, a small clandestine demonstration in Plzeň marked the Americans' presence. In May 1990 the new democratic government sponsored an official celebration and more than 100,000 people attended. But to most Czechs the lesson was clear: when it mattered, the West would not stand up for them. They had to stand up for themselves.

Unlike the Poles, the Czechs and Slovaks looked upon the Soviet Union as a friend and ally, the only power that in 1938 had declared its readiness to come to the aid of Czechoslovakia. When Soviet troops entered Prague, red flags of joy flew. Once again, the Czechoslovaks would find their trust abused. After the war, the democratic government-in-exile returned to power from London. President Beneš reoccupied his position. Some omens were good. Just as after World War I, Czechoslovakia emerged from the titanic struggle almost unscathed. Unlike other European capitals, Prague had not been bombed. Beneš hoped to balance East and West, and for a while it looked as if he might succeed. Soviet troops were withdrawn.

The Czechoslovak Communist Party was the strongest of any of the indigenous Eastern European Parties. It won about 40 per cent of the vote in 1948's free election. Communists participated in a government, holding only eight out of twenty-five posts. Slowly and surely, however, they increased their pressure. Stalin forbade the country to take aid from the Marshall Plan. What happened next is a matter of dispute. Did Moscow order its Czechoslovak comrades to take over? Or did the Czech communists act themselves? The communist Minister of the Interior launched a purge of the police. In defiance, the non-communist ministers resigned. Beneš accepted their move and let the communists name replacements. Czechoslovak democracy was doomed.

In the years that followed, Czechoslovakia turned into a hardline, loyal Soviet ally. Only once, in the famous 1968 Prague Spring, did it break the mold, moving towards greater freedom. Communist Party leaders themselves, led by Alexander Dubček, promised "socialism with a human face." Their ideas proved a precursor of Gorbachev's *glasnost* and *perestroika*. But in 1968 it was not Mikhail Gorbachev but Leonid Brezhnev who occupied the Kremlin, and on August 21 Soviet troops invaded and occupied Czechoslovakia. Faced with overwhelming odds, the Czechoslovaks once again offered little resistance.

Ever cautious, the Czechs watched the Poles, Hungarians and East Germans achieve freedom before rising up in their marvelously peaceful revolution of November 1989. After that, Czechoslovakia looked set to become a reform model. Unlike Poland, its economy was not saddled with a crippling foreign debt, so a true market could be established with less pain than in its bankrupt neighbors. Its skilled workers boasted a long industrial middle-class tradition. All they needed was incentive. The country's deep democratic tradition offered fertile ground for planting pluralistic seeds. While an ever-present possibility of social explosion plagued Poland, the sober Czechs showed few signs of letting their aspirations run wild. Calls for revenge against the former communist rulers, common elsewhere, were almost non-existent.

Of course, the twenty lost years cannot just be forgotten. Many of the philosophers, scientists, journalists who spent that time in manual labor now say they are too old to pick up the threads of their earlier professional lives. One night during the revolution I went to a concert featuring artists who had been banned since 1968. Singers such as Jaroslaw Hudra and Karel Kryl, forced into exile, performed. The highlight was a set by Marta Kubišová, one of Czechoslovakia's most popular singers in 1968, who had not been allowed to appear in public since shortly after the invasion. The crowd was in rapture. Kubišová was overwhelmed and found it difficult to speak. A girl presented her with flowers, "one for each lost year." Her voice hoarse, she whispered "Thank you" into the microphone before launching into a final song: "The Times They Are A' Changin'." Although there was something bittersweet about hearing the songs of the 1960s in the 1980s, the pure, unadulterated joy of the crowd washed away my misgivings – at least temporarily.

Like the Czechs and Poles, the Hungarians struggle with the legacies of a checkered history. Elastic borders, stretching like a belt between East and West, reflect their mixed success. A century ago, Hungary encompassed most of the Danube Basin from the western foothills of the eastern Alps to the Carpathian Mountains. After the break-up of the Austro-Hungarian Empire in 1918, the country emerged as a rump limited to the Pannonian Plain. This amputation had meant that about 3 million ethnic Hungarians continued to live in neighboring Czechoslovakia, Yugoslavia, and above all Romania. Hungary today counts about 10 million people. It is a homogeneous country, with only small minorities. At its heart is the spectacular Danube Bend, where the mighty river breaks through a knot of hills and turns dramatically south. Except for a few hills in the north-east and some undulating landscape in the west, the rest of the country is dominated by the *Puszta* – the Great Plain – flat cowboy country, home to herds of cattle and, above all, splendid horses and their riders. The climate is temperate, continental.

A Hungarian born in 1900 grew up in a country which co-led a vast Austro-Hungarian Empire. He entered manhood living in a right-wing kingdom allied to Germany, governed not by a king but by an admiral, Miklós Horthy. By the time he became a father, Hungary had turned into a People's Republic allied to the Soviet Union. As he became a grandfather, his country began dismantling the centrally planned communist system. If he manages to live long enough, he could see Hungary become a neutral Western-style democracy.

Hungary's ability to survive these shifts derives from a distinctive identity. Unlike the Poles and Czechs, the Hungarians are not Slavs. They call themselves Magyars, descendants of an Asian tribe which emigrated from east of the Urals and reached the Danube Plain in the ninth century AD. The people retain a slightly oriental look, speaking a strange language which is a member of the Finno-Ugric linguistic group, sharing the same grammar as Finnish (the Finns also emigrated from beyond the Urals). But not even the Finns can understand their Hungarian cousins. To a Western ear, Hungarian sounds alien, Asiatic, a long string of syllables spoken in strange monotones without any common roots with Romance, Germanic or Slavic tongues. Look at a street-sign elsewhere in Europe and a few basic words always seem decipherable. Not in Hungary. Entrance is *bejárat*; exit is *kijárat*; vacant is *szabad*; occupied is *foglat*.

Since their arrival along the Danube, the Hungarians have survived countless conquerors by alternating confrontation with conciliation. The Russian occupation was only the latest, and the Hungarian fashion for dealing with it was typical. Thousands were killed in the Hungarian Uprising of 1956. After a period of repression, the Hungarians showed their conciliatory side. Under János Kádár, they massaged a compromise with Moscow. In return for subservience in foreign affairs, Kádár won an end to many of the stifling restrictions built into the Soviet-style economies. He encouraged a modest consumerism, along with a modicum of free-thinking.

The first great Hungarian king, Stephen, resembled Kádár in his tactics. Stephen ruled from 997 to 1038, converting the country to Roman Catholicism in order to join the Holy Roman Empire and gain its protection. By arranging astute marriages, Stephen and his successors managed to connect the Árpád dynasty first with the French house of Anjou and later with Poland. No amount of diplomatic maneuvering, however, could stop the mighty Turk, and a powerful Ottoman army overran the country, conquering Budapest in 1526. For the next century and a half, the Hungarians lived under Turkish sovereignty. They stayed on good terms with the sultan and managed to gain significant autonomy, while cajoling and conspiring with the Western powers of Austria, France, even

England, to expel the Turks. In 1655 the Hungarian nobles named the Austrian Hapsburg Leopold as their king, though it took the Austrian army two decades more to drive the Turks out of the country. Even today the Ottoman influence is visible in Budapest, from the swirling, curved arches on Castle Hill to the famous oriental-style steam baths, derived from the Turkish bath. The Hungarians continue to think of themselves as a bridge or pendulum between East and West, connecting the two traditions and swinging between them.

Once liberated from the Turks, the Hungarians soon turned against the Austrians. For eight years, from 1703 to 1711, they fought against overwhelming odds. By the time Austrian control was firmly established, the Hungarians had switched to the second, conciliatory side of their character. They worked to gain autonomy. The freedom they won proved a mixed blessing. It kept Hungary within the Western sphere of influence – certainly a better fate than that reserved for the Balkan nations under the decaying Ottoman Empire; but, unlike the Czechs who were beaten into submission, the Hungarian nobles enjoyed enough leeway to avoid the full impact of the Enlightenment. Feudal rule, collapsing elsewhere, was kept in place. Peasants eked out a living on the potentially fertile land. The nobles meanwhile grew richer. The volatile mixture exploded in 1848, Europe's great year of revolutions. On March 15 students demonstrated in Budapest. Within a few weeks the old order was swept away. Serfs were liberated. A representative government was installed, led by the dashing figure of Lajos Kossuth.

The Hapsburgs refused to accept these changes and sent in their army. At first the Hungarians scored some important victories, but they forgot about the great power on their eastern border. Under the agreements of the Conference of Vienna earlier in the century, in 1849 the Russians intervened to help the Austrians. The Hungarians were helpless. Defeat and surrender were followed by bloody repression. Only after a generation had passed would the Hungarians enjoy another opportunity to win their freedom. Austria, weakened by its battles against Prussia and Italy, offered to share power with nationalists in Budapest. A great liberal statesman, Ferenc Deák, seized the opportunity and in 1867 the Austrian Empire became the Austro-Hungarian Empire.

Hungary, and especially Budapest, boomed. The capital took on its present-day look, expanding into a throbbing rival to Vienna in culture, economics and politics, propelled by a New York-style mixing of nationalities, especially the newly emancipated Jewish population. In Vienna the Danube is hidden behind the city's backside. In Budapest the river plunges through the center of the city. For centuries Buda and Pest were two separate towns, Buda on the hills and Pest on the flat plain. The two parts were first connected in 1839 when a British engineer designed the graceful Chain Bridge across the Danube. During the second half of the nineteenth century, a series of broad, elegant boulevards was built, inspired by Haussmann's Paris. Magnificent palace-like apartment buildings, baroque cafés, bustling shopping streets and broad squares gave Pest a strong cosmopolitan flavor. The well-to-do constructed villas and gardens up the steep slopes of Buda, offering spectacular views of the Danube. In 1896 the world's first subway was opened in Pest's Vörösmarty Square. The famous wedding-cake Parliament building rose. It measured one meter longer and one meter wider than the British Houses of Parliament in London.

What shameless, misguided conceit. Here were the Hungarians trying to tell the world what a great empire they ruled and what great democrats they were. In fact neither their empire nor their democracy was stable. The non-Magyar nationalities – Slovaks, Romanians and Croats – received almost no freedom and their opposition to Magyar rule remained strong. While peasants were being liberated throughout Europe, Hungary's large rural population continued to live in poverty and hopelessness, stamped upon by an often backwards-looking landed aristocracy. Starvation was common. Industrialization, meanwhile, was accomplished at the expense of the workers, who were paid pitifully low wages. Throughout this turmoil, the politicians collided on the issue of the country's proper relationship with Austria. The Independence Party derided the Dual Monarchy as a disadvantageous and dangerous arrangement, while the Liberal Party regarded it as the essential guarantee of Hungarian prosperity.

World War I exposed these weak foundations. When Austria went to war, the Hungarians marched alongside the banner of the Emperor to defeat. A shortlived liberal republic was sabotaged by an unholy combination of monarchists, ultraconservatives and revolutionaries. In 1919 a Red Army under Belá Kun seized power. Romanian troops, supported by France, led the counterrevolution and after 133 murderous days the regime collapsed and Kun fled. He was replaced by Admiral Horthy, who was forced to preside over the dismemberment of the old kingdom. Under the terms of the Treaty of Trianon in

1920, Hungary was reduced to its present boundaries, losing two-thirds of its historical territory. Romania won Transylvania, Czechoslovakia took Slovakia, and the new Yugoslavia incorporated Croatia with the Dalmatian coast. Admiral Horthy was left to rule his kingdom with neither king nor seaport.

Hungarian nationalists were shocked. To this day they complain about President Woodrow Wilson's "treachery" in drafting the Trianon Treaty. Wilson held a noble vision of independent, self-governing nations. Hungarians saw it differently. Many of their people, proud to rule over others, were now subjected to foreign domination. Hungary was ripe to join with Germany and Italy to overthrow what it considered an unfair continental status quo. Allied with the Nazis, the Hungarians won back Ruthenia from Czechoslovakia, Vojvodina from Yugoslavia and Transylvania from Romania. Hungarian units fought with the Germans in the Soviet Union. When the tide turned, Horthy tried to switch sides. German troops prevented this maneuver by marching into Budapest in 1944 and instituting a reign of terror. In a few short months, almost the entire Jewish population was rounded up, despite Swedish envoy Raoul Wallenberg's desperate efforts. Leading Hungarian politicians and intellectuals were deported. When the Russians drove through to Budapest in 1945 they met stiff German resistance and the capital was liberated only after two months of desperate fighting. The city was heavily damaged.

The Allies showed little sympathy. The truncated pre-war borders were reimposed. Elections were held in November 1945, with the communists winning only 17 per cent. The victorious liberal-democratic Smallholders meanwhile won a smashing 57 per cent. A shocked Stalin never again permitted free elections in areas occupied by the Soviet army. In Hungary Communist leader Mátyás Rákosi ignored the election results and proceeded to consolidate control, using what he called "salami" tactics, dividing and conquering all opposition. A purge was launched, which denounced Yugoslavs as Titoist agents, Jews, suspected nationalists, social democrats and army officers. The star victim was Foreign Minister László Rajk, who with two other loyal communist leaders, was hanged in 1949. Others were tortured, including future leaders Imre Nagy and János Kádár.

After Stalin's death in 1953, the survivors of the purge began to be released. Kádár and Nagy were readmitted to the Party and given important posts. Nikita Khrushchev's liberalization encouraged discontent in Budapest. In July 1956 Rákosi was forced from the leadership. In October students organized a march to the statue of Jozsef Bem, the nineteenth-century Polish hero who had fought with Hungarian rebels in 1848. Someone suggested marching on to Parliament. By the time the demonstrators reached the grand building along the Danube, they numbered hundreds of thousands. Calls went out for Imre Nagy, the most reform-minded communist leader. Part of the crowd proceeded to topple the huge statue of Stalin. After secret police fired on a crowd in front of the radio building, soldiers joined the demonstrators and distributed arms to workers.

Nagy was made Prime Minister, and Kádár First Secretary. Both promised democratization. Pushed by the enthusiastic crowds, they promised to disband the secret police and declared neutrality. The Soviets responded on November 6, 1956, by sending in 200,000 troops backed by tanks. Suicide squads lobbed Molotov cocktails, paving stones, even sticks at the invaders. Sniper fire rained down from the top floors of buildings in the city center. Soviet tanks responded by destroying entire buildings. Soldiers used automatic gunfire to cut down many other Hungarian patriots. A puppet government led by the turncoat Kádár was put in power.

Over the years Kádár managed to craft a clever compromise known as "goulash communism." From the mid-1960s, a series of economic reforms freed the country from many of the stifling restrictions built into other Soviet-style economies. Collectivization of the land was ended and a limited amount of private enterprise encouraged. Shoppers and Western tourists filled the same squares which in 1956 had been covered with bodies and blood. Elegant cafés tempted customers with groaning pastry stalls. Street-singers sounded strains of gypsy music.

In the mid-1980s, however, this post-war communist order crumbled. Even though the Hungarian forint enjoyed a good reputation against other Eastern European currencies, a thriving black market persisted. Superficially, the city looked capitalist, full of colorful boutiques, appealing restaurants and comfortable cafés. On my first trip in 1985, I stayed in the Forum Hotel in Budapest, a shining, spotless, Western-style luxury hotel built with Western credits. A few blocks away, however, the gracious old nineteenth-century apartment buildings were falling apart. One night in the Forum cost an average Hungarian's entire monthly salary.

Hungarians put up with this flawed bargain for a long time. Better to have stores full of tempting goods, even without the money to buy them, they reckoned, than to have empty stores and lots of worthless money. Better to have the possibility to speak out, even if that freedom did not translate into the possibility of taking concrete action. But making ends meet became tougher and tougher. People took second, then third jobs. The strain was visible in their faces – and in appalling alcoholism, drug and suicide rates. Ferment mounted. In 1988 the longtime leader János Kádár was deposed. Censorship was ended. The martyrs of the 1956 revolution were rehabilitated. Free, multi-party elections were scheduled for March 1990, and the nationalist Democratic Forum took power. Neutrality became an acceptable political topic.

The country's future now hangs in the balance. It could explode in a wild burst of emotion as in 1848 or 1956, or it could carve out a compromise as in 1867. In his baroque turn-of-the-century office, the former communist Justice Minister Kalman Kulcsar understood the difficult path ahead. A mild-mannered law professor, he spoke softly and precisely, with the charm and polish of an elegant Hapsburg aristocrat. He had just returned from traveling throughout Western Europe, talking with constitutional scholars and studying the successful democratic transformations in Spain and Portugal. But neither Iberian country faced an economic crisis like Hungary's. And neither tried to dismantle one-party control over the economy as well as over the political system. "Lots of things which we are doing here have never been done before," Kulcsar admitted. In a quiet moment, he said his only true model was Hungary's own history. It was a choice between going too far, as Lajos Kossuth had done in 1848, or fashioning a compromise, as Ferenc Deák did in 1867. "Deák was our greatest statesman," Kulcsar said. "This is an exceptional moment in Hungarian history, with an international context rarely so favorable to real change. That is why we must move fast and have the new constitution accepted. Who knows how long this exceptional situation will last?"

Like Hungarians, Romanians have always felt surrounded by alien, hostile nations. Alone in Eastern Europe, theirs is a nation speaking a language which resembles Italian or French. But unlike their Slavic or Magyar neighbors, who are Roman Catholics with strong links to the West, the Romanians received their Orthodox Catholic religion from the East. This unique Latin–Orthodox mixture never quite jelled. In the Middle Ages, Romania suffered successive onslaughts of Goths, Slavs, Avars, Bulgars and Magyars, before the Ottoman Turks won control.

In recent times the Romanians managed to get rid of the Soviet troops and establish a foreign policy sometimes at odds to that of Moscow. The achievement came at a high cost. Long after the other Soviet Bloc countries realized that concessions were necessary to adjust strict Stalinist doctrine to reality, Romanian leader Nicolae Ceausescu resisted and substituted a despotic "cult of personality." It took Eastern Europe's bloodiest revolution to overthrow him.

Horror stories abound about Ceausescu's rule. They are not exaggerated. When I first visited Romania in the winter of 1986, the country's 23 million people lived like cold, starving beggars. At night Bucharest's boulevards became deserted and dark. Private cars were banned due to a fuel shortage. Streetlights were kept off because of an energy shortage. People hurried home to unheated, unlit apartments. The last showing at cinemas was at 5 p.m., and television ran for only two hours a night. During the day shoppers scrounged through food markets which were empty except for some pulpy-looking potatoes and carrots. Once I watched a delivery of oranges arriving at the central Unirii market. It caused a near riot. So did the unexpected appearance of shampoo in the dark and damp Unida department store. Still, I heard almost no complaints. Everyone said they expected worse. It was, thank God, a mild winter. Cold weather meant that people shivered all night, huddled together in front of empty stoves.

Romania sits at the crossroads of Europe's East–West division, between Roman Catholicism and Orthodoxy, between Hapsburg legalism and Ottoman corruption. For more than a century it has been regarded as the last outpost of Asian vice on European soil. Even after the revolution, when my train from Budapest arrived at the main station the terminal was the usual Asian jumble, thronged with city-dwellers, farmers, soldiers, all weighed down with cardboard or vinyl suitcases, sacks of fruit, boxes of chickens, bags of laundry. Outside, the spectacle was of decrepit shops, kiosks and "luxury" hotels, all in need of refurbishment. I chose the Capitol, where the hot water came on and off intermittently and the heating was non-existent. The hotel concierge shrugged and said, "It's not my fault."

When the Romans first conquered the lands, donating their language, they created a colony of high culture. The province was so prosperous that it became known as *Dacia Felix*, one of the empire's most agreeable and civilized regions. Modern-day Romania enjoys extensive oil and mineral deposits, along with large amounts of unusually fertile land. In the north, Transyl-vania, the Carpathian Mountains cut through the country, offering Alpine vistas and rustic wooden architecture. Many German colonists settled here centuries ago, and the farmers sport stocky Alpine hats. In Transylvania's low-lying areas, rolling fields speckled with colorful flowers stretch to the hor-izon. Ethnic Hungarians also make up a large proportion of the population. Whether Transylvania is of Hungarian or Romanian origin remains an explosive historical debate. For centuries the region was ruled as part of the Hapsburg Empire, and its main cities, Cluj, Oradea, Sibiu, Braşov and Timisoara, all exude an air of faded elegance.

In the south the Danube plunges through a deep gorge at "the Iron Gates" before emptying out into a delta and the Black Sea. A huge swath of rich, grain-producing fields spreads out from the mighty river. Bucharest stands in the center of the plain. The Turks made this their regional capital in 1659 in order to gain some space from the more vulnerable Transylvania. As in the other Balkan countries, Ottoman rule cut the country off from the European mainstream. Feudal traditions lingered, alongside unhealthy extremes of wealth and poverty. Much of the population remained illiterate well into the twentieth century.

Cruelty, despotism and vice are deep-rooted. All schoolchil-dren learn with some trepidation about Dracula. The horror story is based on the tales surrounding Romanian ruler Vlad IV. His real name was Vlad Tepes, son of Vlad Dracul. During the fifteenth century he led the final burst of Catholic resistance to the Turkish advance. While the lurid legend of his savage ritual practices cannot be verified, he was given the nickname Vlad the Impaler because of his habit of impaling his foes. Romanians seem to cherish his memory. Near Braşov, the Bran Castle has been turned into a tourist attraction, billed as Dracula's Castle. The connection with Vlad may actually be tenuous, but the heavy stones and narrow corridors do have a forbidding aura. "Vlad was quite courageous," the guide kept insisting. He did, after all, resist the rapacious Turks, and for that courage his crimes can be overlooked.

Romanians don't have many other historical heroes to ad-mire. Under Ottoman rule, the territory developed a reputation for Byzantine despotism and Asian vice which lingered after independence. It emerged on the modern map more as pawn than player. In 1806 the Russians drove the Turks from the land and imposed a severe occupation, complete with deportations to Siberia. The modern Romanian harbors deep hatreds against his powerful Slavic neighbor. The Turks returned for a while, only to be dislodged again in the middle of the century. A German prince, Charles, was installed on the throne in 1866. When he died in 1881 without an heir, another German prince, Carol, was crowned king.

For the first half of the twentieth century, independent Romania fed like a scavenger off the little goodies thrown to it by the Great Powers. In World War I it stayed neutral for two years, inviting bids for its participation from both sides. When the Allies promised Transylvania, it entered the war on their side. The Germans invaded and sacked Bucharest. Romania sued for peace. Two days before the end of hostilities, it again declared war on the Germans. Thanks to their cynical efforts, the Romanians were given control over Transylvania. What was a small kingdom suddenly more than doubled in size and population. Large minorities of Germans, Hungarians, Jews and Gypsies were added, which Romania was ill-prepared to rule.

Political instability and economic failure marked the inter-war years. The traditional conservative parties collapsed. Communists found little support in a country where 80 per cent of the population eked out a living on the land. Crown Prince Carol, a notorious playboy, stepped in. He never managed to establish firm control. A right-wing fascist group called the Iron Guard rose to prominence, its death squads plunging the country into chaos. In 1930 Carol II banned all political parties and proclaimed a royal dictatorship.

During this time, Bucharest became known as "the Paris of the Orient," fabled for its cosmopolitan sophistication as well as its high life and intrigue. The Queen Mother, Marie, of British and Russian royal descent, won global attention for her wardrobes and her love affairs. The aristocrats spoke French, their favorite language, and drank champagne at the Athenée Palace Hotel. There was something obscene about the wealthy class's cavorting and providing the glitter for gossip columnists while the mass of citizens wallowed in poverty and misery. In her famous *Balkan Trilogy*, British novelist Olivia Manning best describes the atmosphere. "Stout, little Romanian women, not noticeable before, pushed their way through the wagon-lit, chattering in French," she wrote about arriving in Bucharest by train. "They gave little squeals of excitement as they chatted to the officials and the officials smiled down on them indulgently." At the train station, the air "smelt of the Orient." In the poorer working-class districts, "in gas-lit rooms no bigger than cupboards, moving behind cleared windows like sea creatures in tanks, coatless men thumped their irons and filled the air with hissing fog."

When World War II broke out, King Carol tried to play off the two sides. Both the Allies and Axis spurned him. With the Nazis and Russians still at peace, the Germans awarded Transylvania to the Hungarians and southern Dobrudja to the Bulgarians. The Russians took Bessarabia and northern Bukovina for themselves. In 1940 Carol abdicated as the country crumbled around him. Pro-Nazi Marshal Ion Antonescu came to power, supported by the fascist Iron Guard, and the new government took the country into the war on Germany's side. Antonescu survived one attempt by the Guard to despose him, but when Germany began to lose the war Carol's son, King Michael, mounted a successful *coup* and tried to switch sides. It was too late. The Russian army occupied the country in 1944.

Stalin still faced a problem. At the war's end the Romanian Communist Party numbered only about 800 members. Within a year, thanks to shady maneuvers, the non-communists were divided and conquered. But the new communist leadership remained dependent on Moscow's support. Over the years, it managed to gain some legitimacy by promoting nationalism and tweaking its finger at Big Brother. Under Nicolae Ceausescu, Romania refused to follow the Soviet Bloc in breaking relations with Israel after the Six Day War in 1967. It was the only Warsaw Pact country which denounced the 1968 Soviet invasion of Czechoslovakia and did not participate with troops, and the only one to take part in the 1984 Olympics in Los Angeles. But these divergences never called into question fundamental Soviet interests, and in the Gorbachev era they were of little value to the West.

Isolated on the international scene, the Ceausescu regime didn't seem to care about the criticism it received. The West lacked influence and, ironically, the Soviets also seemed impotent. They didn't want to find themselves responsible for this Balkan mess. For years, Romanians were too scared to grumble much, even in private. All typewriters had to be registered with the police. Soldiers stood at almost every street-corner. One out of every four Romanians supposedly worked for the secret police; some say the true number was one in three. Whenever workers rose up in defiance – the Jiu Valley miners in 1977, and in Brasov in 1988 – they were crushed. Intellectuals remained isolated. Anyone who dared protest was sent off to the countryside or held under house-arrest, unable to contact potential co-conspirators. Fear reigned.

People had no friends outside their immediate family. "I didn't tell anyone what I truly thought, even my fellow workers at the office," explains Adrian Dascalescu, an editor at the foreign-policy monthly, *The World*. "The only thing I'd ask them is 'How are your children?' and 'Isn't it a beautiful day?' Anything else could have been used against me by informers." One opposition group, the Antitotalitarian Forum, boasted that it was created before the revolution. The group totaled three families. "If we had taken anybody else in," explained leader Viorel Hancu, "it would have exposed the group to infiltration by the Securitate."

This legacy would prove hard to overcome. After Ceausescu fled Bucharest in December 1989, a "National Salvation Front" took control of the country with the help of the army. A new President, Prime Minister and government were installed and recognized internationally as Romania's rightful rulers.

The revolution soon turned ugly. Many Romanians were distressed by how a group of ex-communists seemed to wrestle control of the Front. Students who had played a prominent role in the revolution held anti-Front demonstrations, complaining of their lack of influence. "The Front has stolen our revolution," charged Vlad Enaş, editor of the student newspaper at the Polytechnical Institute. "We've become actors in a play which somebody else writes and directs." Front leaders rejected these accusations. In a power vacuum somebody has to step in and make decisions. The ex-communists, professional politicians, had that experience. "You can't just run a country with poets and students," explained Adrian Dascalescu. "If you have a car, you can't give it to people who don't know how to drive."

The Front abolished the worst abuses of the Ceausescu regime, draconian food and electricity rationing, and committed itself to democratic elections. Some food started to appear in the shops again; there were even some oranges. People began to speak to each other. Unlike on my previous trips, I found it easy to strike up acquaintances. I was even invited into private homes, something unthinkable before.

Most Romanians I met remained skeptical about the future. Considering the past, the lack of democratic traditions, who wouldn't be wary? But a great load had been lifted. As many people told me, "It couldn't get worse."

Neighboring Bulgaria conjures up similar Balkan images of a backward, luckless, even sinister state, home to the "Bulgarian Connection" and the "killer umbrella." In London in 1978, Georgi Markov, a Bulgarian exile who had broadcast embarrassing news of his homeland on the BBC, was jostled on the street by a stranger who jabbed him with an umbrella. It looked like an accident. Markov fell ill and died four days later. During his autopsy, doctors discovered that he had been injected with a tiny poison pellet. A few years later, the Bulgarian secret service was back in the news when Western investigators charged its secret police with managing arms and drug trafficking. Mehmet Ali Agca, the Turkish terrorist who tried to kill Pope John Paul II, claimed he was acting on Bulgarian orders. Although his testimony was never proved and the Bulgarian official implicated in the plot was eventually released from jail in Italy, the odor of an unsavory, ruthless country lingered.

Given these preconceptions, I was surprised by Bulgaria. Instead of being dirty and ugly, the country is full of spectacular scenery, with its wide Black Sea beaches and the soaring Balkan and Rhodope mountain ranges. The large central valley is a natural garden, supplying the Soviet Bloc with much of its fruit and vegetables. In the famous Valley of the Roses, 70 per cent of the world's rose attar is grown and distilled. Sofia, the capital of one million people, is set in the foothills of snowcapped Mount Vitosha.

Of all the Soviet allies, Bulgaria has the reputation of getting along best with Russia. The relationship resembles that of a good, obedient son with a demanding father. The two nations share the Cyrillic alphabet and the Orthodox Church. Russian troops liberated their fellow Slavs from Turkish rule in 1878. A huge Tsar Alexander II sits high on horseback, dominating one of the capital's central squares. Elsewhere in Eastern Europe, a monument praising a Russian tsar would be spat on. Even in the Soviet Union itself Alexander is out of favor, but in Bulgaria he is revered as "the Liberator."

As in any unhappy family, a good measure of bitterness and insecurity exists on the part of the weak youngster. During the Middle Ages, the Bulgarians created a flourishing, prosperous empire, spreading from the Black Sea to the Adriatic and the Aegean. After the Ottomans overwhelmed them in the fourteenth century, however, the Bulgarians lived in bondage unequaled elsewhere in Europe. Turkish colonists followed their victorious army, settling on empty lands. Greek priests ruled their Church. When at the beginning of the nineteenth century

Serbia and Greece won their independence, the Bulgarians remained sullen and resigned. As Turkish power waned, the area fell into anarchy, ravaged by roaming armies and corrupt officials. None the less, a literary revival did take shape, rekindling vernacular Slavonic and memories of the medieval Bulgarian kingdoms. A Bulgarian exarch, the Orthodox equivalent of a bishop, was finally appointed in 1872.

Four years later a violent insurrection broke out. The Turks, helped by Bulgarian converts to Islam called Pomaks, suppressed it. About 15,000 Bulgarians were massacred, and many villages and monasteries destroyed. The following spring the Russians invaded. They occupied the country and took over its administration before granting it independence. But during the following decades the new country found it difficult to establish its own identity. In the vicious little Balkan Wars of 1912 and 1913, Bulgaria was forced to cede much of its territory. In both World Wars it allied itself with the losers. King Boris managed to keep some distance from the Nazis, saving Bulgarian Jews from deportation, and never declared war on the Soviet Union. But after an angry meeting with Hitler, who wanted complete obedience, Boris suddenly died at the age of forty-nine, on August 28, 1943. As Soviet armies advanced, the Bulgarian authorities tried to avert an occupation by seeking an armistice with the Allies. The ploy failed, and on September 8, 1944, Soviet troops entered the country. A communist coalition came to power the next day.

The key figure was Georgi Dimitrov, Comintern General Secretary who had lived in exile since 1923. The burly, mustached Dimitrov was Bulgaria's Lenin, Trotsky, Stalin and Tito rolled into one. In 1933 he had been arrested in Berlin and charged with setting fire to the Reichstag to provoke upheaval; actually the Nazis had staged the incident. Dimitrov, defending himself, turned the trial around with fiery, theatrical attacks on the Germans. World public opinion swung to his side and he was acquitted. The Soviet Union offered him citizenship and in 1934 he went to Moscow, where he was greeted as a hero. From then on, he would be a figure of great importance in the world communist movement. At the end of the war Dimitrov returned home and used brutal repression to establish control. People's Tribunals were set up, sentencing more than 2,000 class enemies to death. Many thousands more perished without the window-dressing of a trial.

Soon the Party turned on itself. On Stalin's orders, authentic communists judged too "nationalist" were subjected to show trials. Before the Soviet dictator's death in 1953, a similar process of show trials would take place in Hungary, Czechoslovakia and Poland. Its original aims were to weed out figures judged either too unreliable or independent of Soviet control. But the purges ended up accusing entire groups of people and threatening to consume the Communist Parties themselves. A sinister pattern was established. Trumped-up charges would be lodged: Zionism, nationalism, sympathy to Yugoslavia's Titoist heresy. Confessions would be fabricated or extracted under torture.

The Bulgarian purges were the earliest in the Bloc, beginning in 1947. The most prominent victim was Traicho Kostov, a close friend of Dimitrov's. He was charged with being "an enemy of the Soviet Union" and "an agent of Imperialism." Though he refused to confess and proclaimed himself innocent, he was convicted and executed in 1949. Six months earlier, Dimitrov had died, exhausted and broken. He was buried just across from the shady trees of the Sofia City Garden in a concrete bunker mausoleum – a copy of the Lenin Mausoleum in Moscow. The purges continued to swell, eventually encompassing more than a quarter of Party members. Anybody who wasn't a "Muscovite," who hadn't spent the pre-war years in Moscow, was suspect.

Home-grown Party leaders were allowed to rise in the hierarchy only after Stalin's death. In 1954 Todor Zhivkov became Party First Secretary. He would rule for thirty-five years, fond of repeating how "the Soviet Union and Bulgaria breathe through the same lungs." When Khrushchev fell in 1964 Zhivkov adapted to the new line of Leonid Brezhnev. In 1968 he joined in the Warsaw Pact invasion of Czechoslovakia. In the 1970s he supported *détente* and in the 1980s he tried to embrace *perestroika* and *glasnost*.

Key economic ministries were dissolved and individual company managers were told to take over from the bureaucrats. The number of regional administrative districts was reduced from twenty-eight to nine, and multi-candidate elections for local officials and factory managers were encouraged. Chaos, not greater efficiency, ensued. Frightened managers refused to take initiatives. Threatened bureaucrats fought back. The mass media failed to clear up the confusion. After being encouraged to attempt more critical reporting, Bulgarian television began singling out cases of mismanagement. For Zhivkov, that went too far. The Communist Party daily, *Rabotnichesko Delo*, called for discipline. Adventurous journalists were reprimanded, often losing their jobs.

To be fair, Bulgaria made some significant progress under Soviet domination. Thanks to its backwardness, it avoided the worst distortions of Stalinist-style heavy industry. Some industrialization was attempted, without falling into the fallacy of grandiose plans. Instead, investment was concentrated on agriculture, and today the country is an efficient producer of grain, tobacco, fruits, wine and vegetables. Moscow subsidized this prudent plan by providing a ready market which absorbed a large trade deficit on the part of its faithful ally.

Unfortunately, the cost of this caution kept piling up. Gorbachev began to show himself less indulgent to Bulgaria's perpetual trade deficit, demanding better-quality goods. The country's technocrats responded in the late 1980s by obtaining infusions of Western capital. The debt load ballooned to around $11 billion, and since 80 per cent of Bulgaria's current trade remained within the Soviet Bloc, even the best managers had little room to maneuver by seeking out lucrative Western markets. By 1990 Sofia suffered from daily electricity black-outs. Gas queues stretched around corners. Shoppers said that such basics as eggs and meat were in short supply. Western bankers refused further credits and Bulgaria stopped payment on its loans. "The country is bankrupt; no one will give them even a $20 million loan," one said. "I just don't see what they can sell abroad to pay the money back."

Zhivkov was ousted in November 1989. Though his replacement, Petar Mladenov, Foreign Minister for seventeen years, never enjoyed the reputation of a reformer, he moved to undo his predecessor's legacy. After becoming Communist Party First Secretary, he authorized independent associations, restored to ethnic Turks their religious and cultural rights, and promised free elections.

But compared to the rest of Eastern Europe, Bulgaria's revolution seemed cold and half-hearted. It lacked the heartfelt joy of Czechoslovakia, the heavy emotion of East Germany, the explosive rage of Romania, or even the cool, calculating logic of Poland and Hungary. It was a revolution of little steps, directed from top to bottom, often with only faint echoes around the country. Where hundreds of thousands demonstrated in Prague and East Berlin, a large expression of popular discontent in Sofia consisted of a few tens of thousands gathering in front of the Parliament. Leaders of the budding opposition lacked the tough schooling of the Czech or Polish dissidents. "No real revolution has come here," lamented Yanko Yankov, leader of the Social Democrat Party. "We dream of being like the Czechs and fear being like the Romanians."

Admidst the uncertainties of the new post-Cold War world, Bulgaria again appeared as a young, immature son terrified of being forgotten by his Soviet father. Moscow's offer to arbitrate the dispute with Turkey over the treatment of the ethnic Turks created a Cyprus complex, a fear of being abandoned to a Turkish invasion. At one of the angry anti-Turk demonstrations, pretty twenty-six-year-old Nelly Dimitrova told me that "With the Soviet Union weakened, the Turks could come back." While all small Eastern European countries live under the shadow of potential foreign occupation and domination, this insecurity seems almost apocalyptic among the Bulgarians, even among the country's leaders. At a recent meeting with Soviet Prime Minister Nikolai Ryzhkov, Mladenov reportedly asked whether he could count on Russian support if Bulgarian–Turkish relations deteriorated. Ryzhkov stayed silent. "The Bulgarians don't expect the Russians to arbitrate, they expect them to be on their side," one Western diplomat says. "They are very, very frightened."

If Bulgaria is uneasy and unsure about its identity, Yugoslavia suffers from an even worse identity crisis. Bulgarians know they are Bulgarians. What is a Yugoslav? The name means "South Slav." But almost no one admits: "I am a Yugoslav, I am a South Slav." Instead, they assert: "I'm a Serb," "I'm a Croat," "I'm a Slovene," or one of the other various groups which make up the country's national maze. "How many European countries will there be at the end of the century?" Yugoslavs like to joke. "One Western Europe, one Eastern Europe – and six Yugoslav republics."

The 23 million Yugoslavs indeed look as though they come from different countries. They speak different languages. Some use the Cyrillic script, others the Roman one. Some are Roman Catholics, others are Orthodox, and others are Muslims. Most are Slavs, but there are also a significant number of non-Slavic Albanians. Before 1918 these peoples had never lived within a common state. Their land is unsparing. Except for verdant valleys that cool the north, the terrain is rugged right down to the turquoise Adriatic.

Even by Eastern European standards, the Southern Slavs' history is marked by extraordinary suffering and humiliation. For centuries the north-western half of Yugoslavia seethed under Austrian domination, while the south-eastern part slumbered under Turkish rule. In Niš, near the Bulgarian border, a gruesome memorial marks the spot where Turkish authorities built a tower from the skulls of Serbian peasants who rebelled in 1804. Austrian rule could be just as brutal. In Zagreb a stone stands where Matija Gubec, leader of a Croat peasant revolt, was executed. The Austrians forced him to sit on a burning throne while they crowned him with a red-hot iron crown.

Besides a deep memory of such atrocities, the two occupations left separate, very different legacies. Under Turkey, the south sank into oriental darkness, never experiencing the Renaissance or Enlightenment. Politically, it favored authoritarianism; economically, it retained feudalism. Under Austria–Hungary, the north kept its connections with Western European civilization. These divisions persist and, if anything, the differences today between Slovenia in the north and Kosovo in the south are larger than the differences between the United States and Yugoslavia. In Slovenia, unemployment is less than one per cent. In Kosovo it is close to 50 per cent. Slovenia is straining to enter the First World, while Kosovo is struggling to escape from the Third World.

Stereotypes abound. Slovenes are sober, serious. Macedonians are moody, oriental in temperament. Both are small nations, numbering fewer than 2 million each, who joined the Yugoslav federation for protection from outsiders. Croats are the second largest nationality, with a population of 5 million, and perpetual rivals to the 9 million Serbs. Ever since the Croats lost their freedom in the twelfth century, they have burned to express their identity. By comparison, the Serbs seem swashbuckling. Their medieval kingdom was destroyed by the Turks in the late fourteenth century, but along with their tough Montenegrin cousins they later became the only South Slav people who managed to gain independence by themselves.

When national revivals swept Europe during the nineteenth century, the idea of Yugoslavia was born. Its adherents believed that the oppressed South Slavs were tribes of the same people, who, once united, would merge into a common national existence. The nationalists were mistaken. After Yugoslavia was created in 1918, political parties were built around ethnic blocs. The Serbs dominated Parliament and ran the country in alliance with a Slovene Clerical Party. In 1928 a Serb deputy assassinated Stepan Radić, leader of the Croatian Peasant Party. Croat extremists responded by assassinating King Alexander I in 1934.

When Hitler invaded, the country split apart. The Nazis created an independent state of Croatia and placed at its head

Croatian fascists led by Ante Pavelić. Croatian police proceeded to cooperate with the Gestapo in murdering, with exceptional cruelty, Jews and Serbs. Serb nationalists, led by Colonel Draža Mihajlović, retaliated by carrying out massacres of the Croat population. The suffering was terrible. It was the worst possible type of tribal and religious conflict, with both sides trampling over innocent people. At the war's end, some 2 million Yugoslavs had perished, only one-fifth of them soldiers who died in battle. The total number of dead reached one-tenth of the entire population.

Out of this terror, the communists emerged as the most genuine resistance group. They were the only organization committed to the Yugoslav ideal of a nation of South Slavs. Their membership came from all the nationalities and from all social classes. Their leader, the charismatic Josip Broz Tito, was able and clear-sighted. While Mihajlović's Chetniks made deals with the Germans so that they could concentrate their firepower on the communists, Tito was not tainted by collaboration with the Germans and Italians. Some evidence has emerged in recent years about the communists arranging truces with the Nazis, but such truces were temporary and tactical. Gradually, the Western Allies, and particularly the British Prime Minister Winston Churchill, became convinced that Tito was doing most of the fighting against the Germans, and in 1943 Western aid started flowing to the communist Partisans.

When the Red Army entered Yugoslavia in 1944, it did not stay on as an occupying force. Tito's Partisans liberated most of the country themselves, including the capital, Belgrade. Everywhere else in Eastern Europe, the Soviet army installed the communists. The Yugoslav communists earned a unique legitimacy as an authentic nationalistic force. While other Eastern European countries first took part in multi-party coalitions, the Yugoslav communists gained total control; and in the immediate post-war years, Tito and his comrades pursued their goals with single-minded determination. They moved away from the wartime alliance with the United States and Britain. Industry was nationalized. Land was collectivized. Tight censorship was installed. A vicious purge claimed thousands of supposed Croatian fascist sympathizers. If anything, the Yugoslavs seemed more Stalinist than Stalin.

Slowly, however, the two sides headed for a confrontation. In 1947 Tito stopped the proliferation of joint ventures with Soviet companies, declaring them exploitative and discriminatory. He became annoyed when Stalin tried to temper their revolutionary enthusiasm in helping the communists in the Greek Civil War, and was shocked when Soviet diplomats tried to spy on the Yugoslav Party. But it was Stalin, demanding absolute fealty, who finally broke with Tito. On March 18 and 19, 1948, Soviet military and civilian advisers were withdrawn, claiming that the Yugoslav Communist Party was riddled with British spies and that its leadership was illegitimate. On June 29 the international communist agency, the Cominform, announced Yugoslavia's expulsion. A Soviet embargo was placed on the country. Stalin believed that all he needed to do was "shake my little finger and there will be no more Tito." But Tito resisted. Eventually, economic and military aid came from the West, and his position stabilized.

After the break with the Soviet Union, Yugoslavia was free to experiment more than any other communist regime. Tito declared neutrality and joined with India's Nehru and Egypt's Nasser to found the non-aligned movement. He took care – more than other "non-aligned" states such as Cuba – to tread a careful balance between East and West. At home, censorship was eased, Church freedoms relaxed and travel freed. Millions of Yugoslavs left to find work in Western Europe. A novel system of worker self-management was devised to give factories some independence and workers a voice. During the late 1950s and 1960s, the combination produced high economic growth, making Yugoslavia a model for idealists in both East and West. French socialists such as Michel Rocard, later the pragmatic Prime Minister, envisioned workers owning and managing companies. Czechoslovak communists who later launched the Prague Spring looked to Yugoslavia as proof that a more pluralistic and prosperous communist society could exist.

During his lifetime Tito managed to contain national rivalries. The stout, barrel-faced leader commanded such authority that no one dared cross him. Born in 1892, the seventh child of a Croatian peasant, he fought in the Russian Civil War with the Red forces. In the 1930s he organized the Yugoslav Brigade which fought on the Republican side of the Spanish Civil War. He survived six years in Yugoslav jails, and Stalin's great purges in Moscow. These experiences, along with his wartime resistance, hardened him, and if need be he could be unbending. In 1973, when he suspected the Croatian communist leadership of nationalism, he purged it.

Tito could also be flexible. In 1974 he gave up trying to run a unitary country from Belgrade, devising instead a new constitution which established the far-reaching autonomy of six republics and two autonomous provinces. The different Communist Parties in each of the six republics acted as checks on each other. Nicolai Barovič, a Belgrade-based civil-rights lawyer, explained how the strict Bosnian authorities tried to forbid free expression. Writing an article or singing a song deemed "nationalist" could mean up to five years in jail. But you could sing the same song and publish the same article in more freewheeling Serbia. "In Yugoslavia, there are lots of groups fighting for power," Barovič told me. "That creates room for freedom."

Unfortunately, the decentralized power structure produced economic absurdities. Each republic built its own steel, chemical and textile industries. Each kept its own foreign-exchange account and borrowed abroad, carrying out its own monetary and trade policy, which meant that the federal authorities had no power to repair the faltering economy. When the foreign-debt crunch came, nobody knew the total of Yugoslavia's debt.

Once Tito died in 1980, the republics found themselves in open battle, which sharpened to the point of violence. The explosion came over Kosovo, the poor autonomous republic within Serbia. Under the new constitution, the Albanian majority had gained significant power over their own affairs. This angered the Serbs, who pressed to incorporate Kosovo into their republic. When that goal was achieved in March 1989, Serbs sang and danced in Belgrade – and thousands of Albanians took to the streets around Kosovo. Helmeted riot police in armored personnel carriers restored a sullen truce which could explode at any time in renewed fighting.

The only positive sign was that the ethnic quarrels produced no superpower jitters. In 1914 Balkan hatreds plunged the Great Powers into World War I. In 1948 the superpowers came close to another confrontation over Yugoslavia. Now Washington and Moscow shared an interest in not aggravating the inherent instability of Europe's underbelly. "This hasn't become a focus of superpower rivalry like Nicaragua or Afghanistan," an American diplomat in Belgrade commented. "No one thinks it is profitable to meddle."

The Cold War began after the Soviet Union imposed its will on Eastern Europe. It is ending because Eastern Europe is free. Although the origins and causes of the superpower conflict remain a matter of dispute, everyone agrees that Germany was the focus of that confrontation. During the war, the Allies decided to divide their former enemy into occupation zones.

Stalin professed to want a unified Germany, but he had already made secret plans for the establishment of communist rule in his portion of Germany.

On April 30, 1945, just hours before Adolf Hitler shot himself, ten men boarded a DC-3 in Moscow. Their destination was Bruchmühle, a small town nineteen miles east of Berlin where the Soviet military headquarters was located. The ten men were all German communists who had lived out the Nazi regime as émigrés in the Soviet Union. Walter Ulbricht, the man who would rule East Germany until 1971, was their leader. The youngest was Wolfgang Leonhard. He fled to Yugoslavia in 1949, and ended up at Yale. In his classic autobiography, *Child of the Revolution*, Leonhard recounted how the ten men had been hand-picked by the Soviets for their loyalty. All were Comintern-trained agents. They had detailed instructions on what to do upon their arrival in Germany, including the seizure of Gestapo records so that new police spies could be recruited by blackmailing them with their Nazi pasts.

Initially, the Communist Party denied any intent to impose a Soviet-style regime and promised to work to create a parliamentary democracy. Christian Democratic, Social Democratic and Liberal Democratic Parties were authorized, just as in the West – with one big difference. The new parties were required to join together in an "anti-fascist democratic bloc," forcing a permanent coalition with the communists.

As hostility between Moscow and Washington mounted, occupied Germany split. In the Western sectors, a far-reaching currency reform and extension of Marshall Plan aid launched a spectacular economic recovery. Russia responded to these moves with mounting bitterness, culminating in the blockade of Berlin. The dramatic airlift through the severe winter of 1948 –49 saved the city. By the time the blockade ended, the situation of Germany had been altered. The three Western zones had come together economically and politically, under the prosaic title Trizonia, while the Soviet zone had taken on more and more of the shape of other "popular democracies."

The Socialist Unity Party, which had been formed in 1946 in a merger between the communists and Social Democrats, ended all vestiges of pluralism. Soviet-style "democratic centralism" prevailed, with authority flowing downward from the leadership. The principle of equal representation for Social Democrats and communists was abandoned. A Politburo under Ulbricht held power, Marxist-Leninism became a compulsory course on all school curricula, censorship was instituted and an elaborate police apparatus established. In 1949 fraudulent elections were held and, on October 7, the People's Congress approved the formation of a German Democratic Republic.

East Germany was born a somber, irascible little state. Though it was the Germany of Martin Luther, of Johann Sebastian Bach, of Humboldt and Bismarck, governed from the traditional capital, Berlin, it never escaped the shadow of the much bigger and more populous West Germany. While West Germany began life in 1949 with 49 million inhabitants, encompassing an area roughly the size of England, Scotland and Wales – or Connecticut, Pennsylvania and New York – East Germany was half as large, home to 17 million souls living in 41,000 square miles – about the size of Indiana. It is a flat land, with many historic sites but little natural beauty. Before the war it was the agricultural, Protestant part of Germany. Some indigenous light industry existed, such as porcelain in Dresden and optics in Jena, but it had none of the heavy-industrial base of the West, with its Saarland and Ruhr Valley. Worse, the industries depended on resources from the West.

The northern half of the new state contained a section of the German plain and the Baltic coastal regions. This was the old Brandenburg heart of Prussia. To the south were the hilly province of Thuringia and the historically important lands of Saxony. Dresden was long one of Europe's richest cities thanks to its silver mines and the discovery of the technique for producing porcelain. Dresden and the smaller town of Meissen are still famed for producing fine porcelain.

The communist regime's relationship to the larger German nation always remained ambiguous. While West Germany accepted the heritage of the Third Reich, East Germany affirmed that Nazism was the natural consequence of capitalism, and by rooting out capitalism it had no moral responsibility for Hitler's crimes. But the East German leadership sometimes described their state as a provisional arrangement which could provide the basis for a government of all Germany – if the West German state was abandoned. To reinforce this German identity, it adopted the black, red and gold flag of national unity, just as West Germany did, adding only the hammer and sickle in the middle.

The new state remained an embattled outpost. Its overriding problem was its relation to its western neighbor, whose economic miracle soon propeled it to prosperity and a certain self-confidence. In 1953, when a 10 per cent rise in work quotas was proclaimed in East Germany without a corresponding rise in pay, masons and carpenters laid down their tools and started a march on Communist Party headquarters. Hundreds joined them. They began shouting for a cancelation of the new work norms and for free elections. As the strikes spread across the country, Soviet tanks were called in. For one glorious day the workers fought with rocks and Molotov cocktails. Officially, twenty-nine died; unofficially, hundreds perished. Some 1,500 people were imprisoned, and a vast purge removed tens of thousands of doubters from the Party. Bertolt Brecht wrote a poem which described the terrible irony of the situation:

> After the uprising of the 17th June
> The Secretary of the Writers' Union
> Had leaflets distributed in the Stalinallee
> Stating that the people
> Had forfeited the confidence of the government
> And could win it back only
> By redoubled efforts. Would it not be easier
> In that case for the government
> To dissolve the people
> And elect another?

In the following years, that happened. Walter Ulbricht and his communist cronies implemented repressive policies, nationalizing most industry, collectivizing the land and imprisoning anyone who showed opposition. The people left. The stream of emigrants became a flood in 1961, after President John Kennedy and First Secretary Nikita Khrushchev held a stormy summit in Vienna. By August 1961 almost 2,000 people were leaving each day. Altogether, between 1949 and 1961 some 4 million Germans had moved West. It was a costly, humiliating drain on the fragile state, setting the stage for the construction of the Berlin Wall, and in the early morning of August 13, 1961, workmen blocked the many street-crossings between the two sections of the city with barbed wire and bricks.

The Wall achieved its short-term goal: it ended the population hemorrhage. For the first time, the East German regime could make plans without having to deal with the constant loss of skilled workers. A "New Economic System" was announced. It loosened the rigid bureaucratic structure of the economy and encouraged some individual initiative and innovation. The "other German economic miracle" took place. Throughout the 1960s and 1970s, *per capita* income rose and the country became, in terms of productivity, the strongest in the Soviet Bloc. East

Germans became better dressed and enjoyed more leisure time. Some artistic freedom was permitted, exemplified by the publication of Christa Wolf's novel *Divided Heaven*, which expressed the painful dilemma of honest, hard-working East Germans in deciding whether or not to flee to the West.

Any assessment of these achievements must be qualified by a comparison with West Germany. Compared to the neon super-abundance of the West, the East continued to appear drab, dull, dark, shabby, scruffy and somber. No wall could hide the difference. East Germans began to own televisions, which brought increased exposure to broadcasts from the West, and *détente* brought an increasing number of West German visitors. It was a vicious circle. The regime craved international acceptance, but the more it opened up to the world, the more the disparity with the West undermined its legitimacy. Good relations with Bonn were needed, both for the prestige and for essential West German marks. But the more Western visitors who came, the more pressure was put on the regime to justify itself.

One desperate attempt to seek foreign and domestic recognition focused on sports. A program for spotting talented children and then relentlessly training them vaulted East Germany past the West Germans in the number of Olympic gold medals, and even past the American team in 1976. In another attempt to gain legitimacy, the leadership rehabilitated the Prussian and Saxon past. East Berlin's monuments, which had been left as eerie skeletons from the war, were restored. The statue of Frederick the Great of Prussia was returned to its place of honor on the Unter den Linden, restored to its original name from Stalinallee. In Dresden the Zwinger Palace and Museum, home to King Augustus II, was re-opened in all its original baroque glory, covered with a new golden shine. In 1983 a year-long commemoration of the 500th anniversary of Martin Luther's birth in Saxony was sponsored. Long portrayed by the atheistic regime as a religious fanatic, Luther suddenly became the champion of progress. Even Bismarck was accorded new respect. Instead of being considered a reactionary *Junker*, he was celebrated for making Prussia the first industrial country to adopt extensive welfare legislation.

The new rendering of the past, designed to implant a true East German patriotism, was incomplete and half-hearted. Traditional animosity increased between Prussians and Saxons. Although Bismarck was rehabilitated, little mention could be made of his role in unifying Germany. That would have provoked unwanted thoughts about an all-German future. As the country opened up, mention of reunification disappeared. The official line became that East Germany was a separate nation as well as a separate state. The 1968 constitution declared it to be "a socialist state of the German nation." By a revision of 1974, it became "a socialist state of workers and farmers."

This assertion created ever more dependence on the big socialist brother, the Soviet Union. The constitutional amendments of 1974 proclaimed, "The German Democratic Republic is for ever and irrevocably allied with the Union of Soviet Socialist Republics." East Germany's young people were told to learn from the Soviet Union. When Gorbachev came to power, they would turn his name, and the Soviet example, against their rulers, shouting, "We want Gorbachev." As the world economy plunged into recession at the beginning of the 1980s, living standards fell and the state's weaknesses worsened. The need for West German marks and good relations with Bonn increased, the ranks of would-be opposition activists swelled and the number of would-be emigrants soared. The eventual explosion of 1989 surprised many with its power, as did the quick move to unification. In retrospect, what seems more surprising is that the revolution took so long to come.

East Germany was always a strange, special case. Its lack of self-confidence, its fear of being gobbled up by a stronger neighbor, its permanent, relentless quest for identity and legitimacy – all these represented problems common to Eastern Europe. But there was one crucial difference. Whereas other Eastern Europeans could stand up as a coherent nation, East Germany was never more than a state, representing less than half a country. It could not obtain true legitimacy. After the Wall fell, some intellectuals talked of a Third Way, between capitalism and communism, a "socialism with a human face." But the attraction of such a Third Way was limited. Without Soviet protection, with only the bankrupt communist ideology for protection, East Germany found itself naked and sick alongside a powerful, well-clothed neighbor. The diagnosis was fatal. Before World War II, it was part of Germany, and as the Cold War ended it prepared to become part of a new Germany.

<u>People</u>

Chapter Three

The Founding Fathers:

Communism's Aging Leaders

The moment someone breaks through in one place,
when one person cries out, "The emperor is naked!"
– when a single person breaks the rules of the game,
thus exposing it as a game – everything suddenly
appears in another light and the whole crust seems
then to be made of a tissue on the point of tearing
and disintegrating uncontrollably.

Václav Havel, The Power of the Powerless

Until 1988, five of Eastern Europe's six Communist Party chiefs
were gray old men, each more than seventy years old: Erich
Honecker in East Germany, Gustáv Husák in Czechoslovakia,
Todor Zhivkov in Bulgaria, János Kádár in Hungary, and
Nicolae Ceausescu in Romania. Each had been in power for
decades. By the end of 1989, all were gone, either dying or
dead. Their passing meant more than the end of an era. It
symbolized the bankruptcy of the entire communist system,
the diagnosis of its terminal illness. No new communist
leader would find it possible to pick up the system's shattered
remains.

The Founding Fathers dominated their countries' entire post-
war histories. The ideology they espoused once seemed attractive and worthy, not stagnant and corrupt. These communists
joined the Party out of genuine commitment, to fight for a Brave
New World. They were idealists, bony puritans with ascetic
features. They were tough. They hoped. They dreamed. The
world around them was filled with injustice, masses of impoverished workers and peasants groveling before a well-off few.
These communists, who believed in a better world, sacrificed
and suffered for their beliefs. But power corrupts, and these
men wielded absolute power for decades. In the end, their faces
were etched with deep lines, their sad eyes and drooping

lids reflecting both their personal and their countries' tragic experiences.

Most of the Founding Fathers had at one time been jailed by right-wing regimes for belonging to an illegal "subversive" organization. Hitler's SS arrested Erich Honecker in 1935, when the future leader of East Germany was twenty-three years old. Sentenced to ten years in prison in 1937, Honecker was released only at the end of the war in 1945. Born to a family of poor coalminers, as a young man he had developed a hatred for capitalism's inequalities. He met his future wife, Margot, in the Party. Both proved excellent organizers and climbed up through the hierarchy together. Erich joined the Central Committee in 1946, the Politburo in 1950, before taking over as First Party Secretary in 1971. Margot became a member of the Central Committee. Because of his deep-seated belief that the communist end justified any means, Honecker defended his crucial role in building the infamous Berlin Wall in 1961, describing the hideous edifice as "an anti-fascist barrier" against West Germany. Given his experiences under Nazism, he believed the lie. All his life, he maintained that the Nazi epoch was a direct, natural consequence of the evils of capitalism, and that, in spite of its flaws, the communist system represented a historic advance.

Honecker understood that East Germany had to strengthen its economy and that a social contract must be struck with the people. On taking control in 1971, began to forge a somewhat less rigid relationship in which West German economic support helped him weather the deterioration of the world economic climate. He also relaxed restrictions against the Protestant Churches, and let more of his citizens visit relatives in the West. These measures helped him preside over the country's transformation into an industrial and military power, second only to the Soviet Union in the Warsaw Pact. But when Mikhail Gorbachev came to power and began toning down ideological warfare, Honecker just couldn't adapt. He continued to compare capitalism and communism to "fire and water." Gorbachev recognized that the communist economic system was a failure, but Honecker refused to abandon central planning and expensive subsidies on basic consumer goods. "When I go and see Honecker, he's very much aware that 85 per cent of West Germans have a higher living standard than us, but he also knows that 15 per cent live much worse," said Jürgen Kuczinsky, one of his economic advisers. "He believes we must take care of that remaining 15 per cent, whatever the cost."

When thousands of the best and brightest young East Germans fled the country in the fall of 1989, and thousands more inside the country demonstrated for freedom, Honecker closed his country's borders. He compared the situation to that of China in the early summer of that year and ordered the police to fire on demonstrators. But younger Politburo members rejected his stance and ousted him as Party leader on October 18. A few weeks later, the Berlin Wall was opened, and Honecker's legacy was shattered. Along with eleven top associates, the Party which he had helped found expelled him, placed him under house-arrest, and indicted him for corruption and abuse of power. His once austere image collapsed under accusations of having Swiss bank accounts, country estates and hunting lodges. His cancer worsened. He was expelled from his villa in the posh Berlin suburb of Wandlitz and the only place he could find to live was a two-room apartment in a church rectory, offered by a generous pastor. Crowds jeered him, holding up a poster showing him dressed in barred black-and-white prison clothes. For Hitler's former prisoner, the pathetic, pitiful end proved devastating. "He finds it difficult to understand the events taking place," his doctor said.

In Czechoslovakia Gustáv Husák's career took a similarly tortuous, tragic path. Husák was born near Bratislava in 1913, a year after Honecker. Educated as a lawyer, in 1924 he joined a small group of left-wing intellectuals to form a literary review, *DAV*. Most of *DAV*'s founders were communists, who combined an ardent nationlism with their socialism; all these young men would rise to great importance within the communist movement.

By the mid-1930s, Stalin had done his best to see that all Eastern European Communist Parties were bolshevized. Any members with the slightest pretension to bourgeois ideology, who refused to accept the Soviet dictator's strictures without questioning, were weeded out. But Stalin could not touch *DAV* because the Slovak group was only loosely affiliated to the pre-war Czechoslovak Communist Party. When the Slovak communists defied the Soviet Big Brother and formed a new party in 1939, Husák and his friends from *DAV* stepped into the leadership.

Husák proved impetuous, independent and flexible. After the Molotov-Ribbentrop Pact of August 1939, Stalin decreed that the Eastern European Communist Parties should make their peace with the Nazi dictator. Husák refused. He helped establish an underground resistance against the Germans. Under his leadership, the Slovak communists organized minor acts of sabotage and contrived to steal small supplies of arms which they hid in the hills for the "inevitable" armed struggle against the fascists. Importantly, Husák struck an agreement with the Social Democrats to work together in the underground. He managed to have the Slovaks accepted as full and equal partners, not just as an inconsequential offshoot of the more numerous Czech resistance groups. This "nationalism," contrary to the sacred doctrine of democratic centralism, infuriated Stalin. But it won Husák the leadership of the Slovak National Council.

In 1944, under Husák's guidance, the Council declared an armed insurrection against the Germans in Slovakia. A courageous confrontation with the Nazis followed. At Banská Bystrica the Partisans held out for sixty days, even though they were surrounded on all sides by seven German divisions. Even this defeat did not mean the end of the revolt; groups of Partisans fled to the hills and continued their guerrilla activities. When the Red Army arrived in 1945, Husák's partisans had written a glorious chapter in Slovak history. Before World War II the Czechs had stamped on the Slovaks as second-rate cousins. Slovakia now insisted on and obtained the right to autonomy in post-war Czechoslovakia.

Despite this success, Stalin and his loyal Czech communists detested Husák's independence. When the communists took full power in Prague, they began attacking any Slovak who showed the slightest inclination to question the central authority. At the Ninth Party Congress in 1950, Husák was thrown off the Slovak Board of Commissioners, arrested and charged with the dread crime of "bourgeois nationalism." He received a life sentence in 1954. Released only in 1960, he was readmitted to the Party in 1963 and fully rehabilitated later that year. In 1968 he emerged untainted by sinister Stalinism. He supported the Prague Spring reform and was named the country's Deputy Prime Minister.

After the Soviet invasion, Husák switched camps. He attacked his fellow Slovak Dubček for dithering and called for a "new Party and state leadership which will be able to guarantee peace and security." On April 17, 1969, Dubček himself recommended that Husák replace him. Many Czechoslovaks approved the choice in the hope that Husák would show himself willing and able to stand up to the Russians. He did little to justify their trust, directing a huge purge from the Party of Prague Spring reformers. Husák was a complex personal tragedy. A revolutionary and humane Marxist intellectual, he ended up forcing his hero Dubček into a menial job. After Gorbachev's ascension to power, Husák paid lip-service to *perestroika*. He was tired and old. During the youthful Soviet leader's first visit to Prague, he strolled with him down Na Příkopě Street. Gorbachev plunged into the crowds, shaking hands and smiling to the cries of "friendship, friendship." The white-haired Husák walked well behind him, stiff and stern, a stubborn relic from another era. "Husák was a gifted man, with a very high IQ," insisted his former colleague Vladimir Kadlec, Minister of Education in 1968 and himself purged after the Soviet invasion. "But he had little real intellectual courage."

When Czechoslovakia's revolution came in November 1989, Husák was ensconced in the Hradčany Castle as President. The crowds below in Wenceslas Square demanded his resignation. Husák refused. He clung to power even as his communist comrades gave it up. Alexander Dubček was brought back to head the National Assembly. Posters went up calling for Václav Havel, Husák's nemesis, to become the new President. Husák resisted. The opposition Civic Forum threatened to hold a mass demonstration at the castle and, if necessary, carry Husák out of office. Husák finally gave up, pleading for clemency in a resignation speech full of pathetic self-criticism. "If there were mistakes," he said, "these were the mistakes of people, not the mistakes of ideas." His last official action was to swear in the new ministers of the anti-communist government. It was a surreal scene. Husák drank champagne with the men whom he had harassed and imprisoned, assigned to menial labor and deprived of such small freedoms as vacation trips even to other communist countries. "It was fantastic," Jiří Dienstbier said afterwards. "Even Husák was talking about democracy."

Of all the Founding Fathers, the Hungarian János Kádár proved the strongest, most powerful personality. He started out the least popular Eastern European leader, proceeded to become the most popular, then finally plunged again into unpopularity. Soviet tanks brought him to power in 1956 after crushing the daring and bloody uprising. Even then the forty-four-year-old Kádár cut a curious figure. Only days before, he had praised the rebels for their "glorious uprising," and voted in favor of a multi-party democracy and Hungarian neutrality. Now a Soviet armored car delivered him to Budapest's extravagant Parliament building, where he declared the uprising a "counter-revolution." Executions, show trials and furious repression followed. The revengeful Red Terror turned Kádár into Hungary's most hated man, nicknamed "the Butcher of Budapest."

Cleverly, craftily, Kádár managed over the years to refashion his image. Without challenging Moscow, he installed a series of market-oriented economic reforms and relaxed the political atmosphere. As long as Hungarians didn't cross the line into outright dissent, they enjoyed significant personal freedoms. Where Stalin once said, "He who is not with us is against us," Kádár reversed the doctrine, proclaiming, "He who is not against us is with us." In gratitude, Kádár's countrymen gave their leader a new nickname, "Uncle János."

"Kádárization" depended on political and economic reforms. But it also rested on Kádár's unique authority, skills and personality, a triumph of his dogged, tenacious style. These traits were developed in youth. Kádár was born an illegitimate child in 1912 in the twilight years of the Austro-Hungarian Empire, in what is now Yugoslavia. His mother was a peasant woman. His father was a young soldier from a family of prosperous farmers, one of the so-called *kulak*s who were later hated and despised by all good communists. Disowned by his father, young János's earliest memories were filled with the poverty of the Hungarian village of Kapoly, where he spent his first six years in a foster-home. He never forgot being called a "bastard" by other peasant children. This injustice formed his early understanding of Marxism. "My knowledge of the class struggle consisted of little more than repeating, 'Son, the gentry are crooks!' " he later recalled. " 'They are tormenting the poor, but they cannot be defeated because they are stronger.' "

At the age of six János was reunited with his mother and moved with her to Budapest. In the city he developed passions for soccer, chess and reading, devouring everything from Hungarian poetry to Greek classics. But as much as he read, he never took on intellectual airs. Abstruse Marxist ideology did not appeal to him, and in public appearances he never got caught up in fine points of theory. His stories, anecdotes and metaphors were always simple and straightforward, easy to understand. When he first occupied high positions in the Party and government immediately after World War II, he was intellectually outclassed by widely read, cultivated Moscow-trained communists. Ironically, his lack of formal education proved a blessing. While the cultivated communists trained abroad soon lost contact with the ordinary Hungarians, Kádár never lacked the common touch. However many books he read, however famous he became, he continued to identify with the working class and with the lessons of simple socialism. As the country's leader, he frequently visited factories and workers' apartments in Budapest's working-class 13th District, where once he was Party chief. He always wore a tie; if he did not, he once explained, workers might think he lacked respect for them.

The Depression and the backward-looking right-wing Horthy regime gave him his vision of socialism. Young Kádár joined demonstrations of workers protesting against unemployment in 1930. Police beat him into unconsciousness. Soon afterwards, he joined the Young Communist Workers' Federation. For the next decade and a half, he lived in a shadowy, clandestine world of hide-outs and secret passwords. Despite several arrests, he rose through the Communist Party ranks, becoming secretary of the illegal organization's Central Committee in 1943. After the war, he became Minister of Internal Affairs. In this post from 1948 to 1951, he showed himself able and willing to implement the early purges, some of whose victims he knew were innocent. He stayed on until his own arrest in 1951. Tortured and sentenced to four years in prison for conspiring against the state, he was freed in 1954 after Stalin's death. He and his friends would never forget the Terror. "It was worse, worse than anything during the Horthy times," György Aczél recalled, his former cellmate and longtime Politburo colleague. "We were being arrested by our own friends." The totality of the destruction still astounds him. "It was shocking, brutal. Of the 10 million people in Hungary, 640,000 were imprisoned during the early 1950s."

This injustice did not prevent Kádár from consolidating his own rule after 1956 with death sentences against his former colleague Imre Nagy and seventy other leading rebels. But Kádár never used imprisonment and terror in the same personal or indiscriminate way as his predecessors. In 1961 he declared, "Seven or eight years ago everyone in Hungary was suspected and spied upon. One chose a man by chance and told him, 'You are suspect; you are flirting with the Imperialists!' At first the man was afraid. Then he spent his days trembling. The former leaders of the Party pushed men towards our enemies to such a degree that at the end certain of them in fact did find themselves in the enemy ranks."

Even as Party First Secretary, Kádár continued to live in a modest three-roomed villa in the Buda hills. Each morning he would drive himself to Party headquarters, with only one security guard. He never permitted a personality cult to develop. Whenever his image appeared on television news reports, he would leave the room. No pictures of him were displayed in public buildings. When Gorbachev visited him in Budapest and took his walkabout, Kádár strolled about without bodyguards, chatting with bystanders, while the Soviet leader was surrounded by security men.

Kádár could never escape his original sin of opposing the 1956 uprising. When his successors set in motion the rehabilitation of its martyrs and granted them a public funeral in June 1989, one name went unmentioned in all the speeches. It was János Kádár. The traitor-turned-hero, praised for pulling his country back to its feet, was once again derided as the man responsible for the execution of the uprising's leaders. János Kádár had become King Lear, a lone tragic figure, spurned by his former friends. He was known to be ill and no longer appeared in public. Rumors spread that he and his wife had committed suicide. He died three weeks later, on the same day that the Hungarian Supreme Court finalized the decision formally to rehabilitate the leaders of the 1956 uprising. "In his last days, Kádár was an incredible personal and political tragedy," admitted his close comrade György Aczél. "In 1985 he could have won a free election with 80 per cent of the vote. Three years later, he couldn't have got 8 per cent."

"National" communists like Kádár were always forced to balance domestic and Soviet pressures. After the war, Stalin never trusted home-grown Eastern European communists. He recruited and trained his own men to Sovietize the region. These "Muscovites" were dispatched to the satellites. Their task was to impose the Stalinist Soviet system at any cost. They understood that they were mere "frontier guards" of Soviet Russia. Their purpose in life was not serving their own working class so much as the international proletariat, and by "international" Stalin meant the various nations of the Soviet Bloc. He stressed homogenization. All the satellites launched ambitious programs to build up heavy industry. Huge uneconomic steel mills were built. Agriculture was collectivized, and even though this led to food shortages almost everywhere, the Muscovites blamed war and the enemies of socialism for the failure. By the early 1950s every major city in Eastern Europe had named its main street for Stalin, and almost all the capitals erected a huge statue of the Soviet leader.

This determination to impose unpopular but loyal leaders on his satellites was strongest in Poland, the country with the deepest anti-Soviet feelings. Stalin once compared imposing communism on Poland to saddling a cow. As early as 1938 the Soviet dictator dissolved the original Polish Communist Party. When Soviet troops occupied half of Poland the next year, many of these former Party leaders who opposed the invasion were sent to Siberia. Sneering sycophants were installed in their place. The original post-war Minister of Defense, Marshal Konstanty Rokossowski, was a Russian citizen of Polish origin.

The leaders who followed Soviet footsteps soon found themselves destabilized from within and without: by Yugoslavia's show of independence in 1948, by Stalin's death in 1953, and by Khrushchev's revelations about the Terror in 1956. When Polish workers in Poznań revolted, the Polish Communist Party managed to bluff Khrushchev into accepting Władysław Gomułka as their leader. Instead of spending the war years in Moscow, Gomułka had stayed at home and fought as a guerrilla. After the war Stalin denounced him for "right-wing deviationism" and suspended him from the Party. His re-emergence as the Party leader in 1956 headed off unrest. Gomułka admitted communist mistakes of the past, pleaded for sacrifice from workers and promised significant changes. The crowds cheered. But this "nationalist-style" communist could not deal with the fundamental problems of a bankrupt economy. In 1968 Gomułka allowed a campaign against student activists to turn into a full-scale anti-Semitic campaign, and by 1970 another generation of workers had taken to the streets to protest over food prices. When the army fired and killed scores, Gomułka's rule collapsed.

The new Party leader, Edward Gierek, sought to appease and reassure an alienated nation and rebuild a weakening Party with consumerism. In Czechoslovakia, Husák managed to buy his citizens off with houses and cars. In Hungary, Kádár spiced a productive food market with a dose of tolerance. Gierek borrowed heavily from the West to fulfill the consumerist yearnings of his public. He didn't touch the faulty central planning system. The Polish economy remained in incompetent hands. When the West demanded its money back, there were no longer enough cars or summerhouses to buy anyone off.

Solidarity's formation in 1980 touched off a mass exodus from the Party. By the time martial law was declared and Solidarity crushed the following year, the Party couldn't find any credible slogans. At its head was General Wojciech Jaruzelski. Jaruzelski, with his ramrod-straight military bearing, evoked some sympathy from a weary public for his ascetic lifestyle. He lived in a simple Warsaw villa. But he broke communist rules in two fundamental ways. Communist generals are supposed to serve the Party, not lead it. No Communist Party anywhere has been headed by a professional army man. To an orthodox Marxist, Jaruzelski's leadership must have smacked of something South American. Instead of "Mr. First Secretary," he was addressed as "Mr. General." Perhaps even worse, Jaruzelski was not the son of a worker or peasant. He was born into a family of land-owning gentry, whose heraldic crest was a blindfolded crow. To the first-generation communist, this general-at-the-helm represented everything of the hated old order: the aristocracy, the military, sentimental patriotism and archaic chivalry. Before the war all Poland's heroes had come from the gentry – Tadeusz Kosciuszko, who fought for American independence, and Józef Piłsudski, who won the country its independence in 1918. The post-war egalitarian communist working-class order had never sunk deep roots. The old class-ridden aristocratic order had outlasted it.

If Poland's flirtation with "national" communism ended in disaster, the formula took on a bizarre and outrageous shape in Romania's Nicolae Ceausescu. Ceausescu was born into a peasant family in 1918 at Scornicesti in the south of the country and joined an illegal communist youth movement in 1933. From then until 1944 he spent most of his time in prison. After the war he worked in the Party's organizational department. He became a candidate member of the Central Committee in 1945, Deputy Minister of Armed Forces in 1950, a candidate member of the Politburo in 1954 and a full member in 1955. In 1965 he succeeded Gheorghe Gheorghiu-Dej as First Secretary.

Ceausescu's subsequent career can be divided into three phases. Between 1965 and 1968 he consolidated his position and was no more than first among equals. At the time, he cut a profile as a youthful, energetic leader, with a strong commitment to change. He extended his predecessor's policy of fostering Romanian nationalism and stressed his country's independence from the Soviet Union. Between 1967 and 1971 he ruled as the pre-eminent leader and Romania's great reformer. He kept diplomatic relations with Israel after the Six Day War in 1967 and the following year refused to send Romanian troops to participate in the invasion of Czechoslovakia, the only Warsaw Pact leader to do so. At home, he condemned the violations of legality of the Stalinist era. In 1971, however, Ceausescu switched course and promoted a hardline policy of discipline and heavy industrial growth.

During this phase, he began building his infamous personality cult. A small man, he took pains to appear large by being photographed in the midst of children or standing above people around him. Portraits showed him always smiling, though his face looked cold and reserved. His books filled the windows of every bookstore, quotations hung on billboards on every road and were chiseled into stone on every monument. A miniature replica of the Arc de Triomphe in Paris was erected near the Bucharest Convention Center to honor the "Ceausescu Epoch." His face dominated Romanian television, which broadcast for only two hours each night, and the front page of every newspaper printed his holy words every day. At the National History Museum in Bucharest, a permanent exhibition was mounted paying him homage. Walls were covered with photographs of him opening factories, surveying fields of wheat, visiting the Queen of the United Kingdom and the King of Spain, and greeting the Presidents of Canada, the United States and France.

Writers, poets and lyricists churned out Ceausescu literature. He was described as a "far-reaching, rigorous and profound thinker." He was a "scientist who opened new horizons," "an inexhaustible source of ideas," a man of historic action, of peerless humaneness, a prominent personality of the contemporary world, the people's most beloved son, "the architect of our grandiose times." It was even written in Romanian history books that Ceausescu's small hometown, Scornicesti, was the place where man first lived in Europe. No matter that history books elsewhere in the world disagreed: such things didn't matter to Ceausescu. As the cult took hold, hagiographers even used religious imagery. Ceausescu became "the luminous beacon," "the Helmsman who guides," and ultimately "our lay God."

Ceausescu promoted his family into positions of influence. His wife Elena became Deputy Prime Minister and the second most powerful person in the country. One of his sons, Nicu, ran the Communist Youth apparatus. The President's brothers, numerous in-laws and cousins also ranked high in the Party system. Radio Free Europe researchers carried out a "Who's Who" study of the Ceausescu dynasty, only to concede at the end, "There may be other in-laws and distant relatives who are still not known as such."

A certain strange Machiavellian logic lay behind this madness. Ceausescu moved around his ministers like yo-yos, up and down, back and forth. Nobody outside the family managed to build up a power base. Beyond coercion, the Ceausescu personality cult was constructed upon two persuasive pillars: cries of nationalism and promises of prosperity. His independent stand within the Warsaw Pact made him a hero at home, and for a long time won him kudos abroad. The American press hailed him in 1984 when he refused to follow the Soviet boycott of the Los Angeles Olympics. Ceausescu hypnotized his people with a glorified vision of backward Romania rushing headlong into industrialization, even though his obsession with huge prestigious projects, such as a dam over the Danube, and his insistence on paying back international debts left a crippled economy.

Romanians may have recognized the fraud, but Ceausescu continued to believe in his policies. Living in isolation, he didn't see his people's sufferings. While Romanians froze in unheated apartments lit by a single 40-watt bulb, he plundered his country, building across it *nouveau riche* palaces which he visited once or twice a year. After his death the new government accused him of salting away more than $1 billion in foreign bank accounts. His power-hungry wife had a passion for furs and jewelry, and his son Nicu for women and whiskey. Every morning Bucharest's streets were cleared of all traffic so the President's car could pass. Before he visited a village, it was spruced up. Sometimes the leaves of withering trees were even painted green.

Some said he was just a poor peasant who found himself out of his milieu. Others said he was deranged, deluded. Doctors I talked to after his death insisted he was "paranoid." Whatever the exact diagnosis, the poor peasant boy was insecure about his origins and may have held many deep-rooted prejudices of ignorance. Romania's Chief Rabbi, Moses Rosen, believed he was anti-Semitic. "Ceausescu wanted good relations with Israel," he said, "because he believed American Jews controlled all the world's finances."

There is no rational explanation for Ceausescu's monstrous personality. One similar figure was Stalin, and in fact Ceausescu identified with the Soviet despot. "In twenty years Stalin raised Russia from an underdeveloped country to the second most powerful country in the world," he told *Newsweek* in his last interview before he was toppled from power. "Of course he made mistakes," he added. "But he won the war. He built nuclear weapons. He did everything a person should do in his job."

Not long after returning to Boston, a Romanian émigré, Liviu Turku, visited me. He said he had defected six months before from the "research" services of the Foreign Ministry. At that post he had direct contact with Ceausescu. "Is he crazy?" I asked. My visitor sighed. "Everybody asks me that," he said. "A psychologist might say he suffers from some delusions. But I think he is sane. In his view, Romania is now on the map. People must suffer to build a glorious future."

Whenever reality intruded upon the utopian absurdity, Ceausescu just shrugged it off. In 1987 Gorbachev visited Bucharest and was taken to see the Unirii market. For the occasion, it had been specially stocked, with overflowing shelves of fruits and vegetables and meat. As the motorcades of the two leaders prepared to leave, a small riot broke out. In Ceausescu's full view, hungry bystanders broke through the police perimeter and started storming the store. Luckily for him, the rioters shared no political motives. They just wanted to buy the food.

As the people's pent-up anger mounted in December 1989, Ceausescu responded by calling a mass rally in the center of Bucharest. He came out on to the balcony of the Central Committee headquarters and began denouncing the pro-democracy demonstrators as "fascists." Shouts of "Down with Ceausescu" rang out. Television showed his face twisting in genuine shock. Elena, standing next to him, yelled, "Give them something." Ceausescu announced a rise in wages. It was too late. The crowd kept on screaming, and Ceausescu fled inside. A helicopter picked up him and his wife from the roof. Some say they were trying to flee to North Africa, others that they were aiming for a hide-out in the Transylvanian mountains from where they could rally followers. The plans were bungled. The next day, December 22, at 2:15 p.m. a small, white helicopter was forced to land near Tirgoviste, fifty miles north-west of Bucharest. The couple and a bodyguard commandeered a red Dacia automobile and kept on trying to escape. But at a roadblock, a rebel soldier recognized them. Arrested, they were held for three days, given a two-hour show trial and executed by firing squad on Christmas Day.

To the end, the Ceausescus did not yield. Throughout the trial, admittedly a parody of military justice, Ceausescu sat behind a lunchroom table in a dark topcoat and scarf, reacting with contempt to the court's charges. "I will answer only to the working class," he insisted. Asked about a Swiss bank account containing $400 million, he retorted, "I don't know anything about it." He dismissed his ousting as "a *coup d'état* provoked by fascists." Elena Ceausescu displayed similar anger. At one point she challenged the judges by saying, "Is it possible to say this to the President of the Scientific Academy?" referring to one of the titles she had acquired during her husband's rule. Facing the firing squad, she told the soldiers that she had been like a mother to them. One soldier told her to think of the mothers who had been killed under her husband's rule.

The provisional government justified the execution as necessary to end resistance from the Securitate. After Ceausescu's bullet-riddled corpse was shown on television, the violence did calm. Nobody I met in Romania showed any sorrow over their dictator's fate. Nobody disputed the legality of the trial. Later, it was revealed that the execution had resembled an orgy of violence: soldiers in the firing squad began shooting before the orders were given and thousands of bullets were pumped into the couple's bodies.

Within hours of their deaths, Ceausescu's books were being taken from stores and burned. The placards praising the "Genius of the Carpathians" were pulled down. On my previous visit they had been placed every couple of hundred yards along the road between Oradea and Cluj. By December 26, the day after the executions, all were gone. It was as though Ceausescu had never existed. At long last, Romania had begun to exorcise its ghosts.

Next door in Bulgaria, Todor Zhivkov built a much more orthodox, benign Balkan personality cult. Born in 1911 to a peasant family in Pravets, a village near Sofia, Zhivkov's early biography is typical of a Founding Father's: a child from a poor, rural background who went to work in the city where he became a selfless, devoted communist. Young Zhivkov studied at a technical school in Sofia, then worked as a printer. "I remember meeting Zhivkov when he was a printer in the underground," recalled Alexei Sheludko. "He was a clean, strong force, who believed in the fight against fascism." Before the war he was imprisoned and tortured for his political activities. During the war he joined the Partisans, rose to the rank of colonel and participated in the 1944 Sofia uprising.

Soon Zhivkov would be corrupted. For his zeal and loyalty, he was rewarded with the post of chief of the People's Militia.

Under his direction it conducted a bloody purge against anti-communists. As a loyal Stalinist, he continued to rise through the Party's bureaucracy until he became First Secretary in 1954. Over the next three and a half decades, Zhivkov consolidated power and appeared to win a certain public popularity. His formula consisted of ingratiating himself with successive Soviet leaders and portraying himself as a paternal father-figure. The Zhivkov image included a modest personality cult, one well suited to this Balkan country used to gentle authoritarianism. His photos were not plastered on buildings, and superhuman or godlike imagery was not used to describe him. He never assumed intellectual airs. He preferred the image of "man of the people," who understood their needs and assured order and stability for them.

Zhivkov's home village, Pravets, was turned into a model village. A sparkling four-lane superhighway was constructed from Sofia to reach it. A new glass-and-steel House of Culture soared in the central square. The apartment blocks for the 4,200 inhabitants were new and clean. Stores sold Swiss chocolate. But when I visited in 1988 there was no adoring Stalinist-style statue to the Great Leader. In an attempt to adopt *glasnost*, Zhivkov had declared a ban on state rituals and political imagery carrying the "superficial pomposity" and "ostentation" of the past. He decreed a more "natural, simple and businesslike" style.

The trick failed. If old-style Stalinist-style adulation was out of fashion, new Gorbachev-style admiration was in. A large banner dominated one side of the square: "Perestroika Is Our Destiny." The presidential home, a thatched hut, stood off the main street. Here the young Zhivkov had lived until he was fourteen with his parents, Kristo and Marutsha. Parents and children slept on the floor in the same room. The house had been restored and turned into a sort of museum. Visitors were handed a book entitled *Todor Zhivkov: A Biographical Sketch*. It ran to 450 pages.

"What about the new anti-personality cult?" I asked the guide.

"I don't know about that," she answered. "We have 200,000 visitors every year."

As his reign dragged on, Zhivkov's innate crudeness and cruelty resurfaced. Police harassed and beat up dissidents. A vicious policy was decreed to change the names of Bulgaria's one million Turks.

In January 1989, *Le Monde*'s Sylvie Kauffmann obtained what turned out to be the last interview with the leader while he was in power. The appointment was scheduled for 10 a.m. Zhivkov opened it by offering his guest a brandy. She refused. He took two shots. During the interview which followed, he was often incoherent. "It was embarrassing," Kauffmann recalled. "Whenever he meant to say 'Gorbachev,' he would say instead 'Brezhnev.' The translator tried to correct him, saying 'Comrade Zhivkov, you must mean 'Gorbachev.' Zhivkov didn't even listen, and just repeated 'Brezhnev.' "

In November 1989, Zhivkov was finally fired. Needing a scapegoat, Bulgaria's new leaders turned against him with a vengeance, charging him with corruption and putting him under house-arrest in a villa outside Sofia. State-run television showed pictures of his luxurious homes, filled with riches unobtainable for ordinary Bulgarians. His slavish followers suddenly became critics. "He ruined our country," said his former comrade Sheludko. "He was an ignorant peasant."

When the Founding Fathers left the scene nobody could pick up the pieces. Two of the successors, Egon Krenz in East Germany and Karel Urbanek in Czechoslovakia, lasted only a few weeks in power. The others, Petar Mladenov in Bulgaria, Ion Iliescu in Romania and Rezsö Nyers in Hungary, struggled to hang on. Everywhere, the new leaders disavowed any ties to the discredited Communist Parties of their predecessors. The tactic seemed doomed to failure. The newcomers were just too compromised. "Mladenov is trying to blame Zhivkov for everything, but he is a creature of Zhivkovism," argued Dimitar Tomov, vice president of the Independent Society for Human Rights. "It's genetic and there's nothing he can do to escape."

Unlike their predecessors, the second-generation leaders joined the Communist Party after the war, less out of idealism than ambition. Membership meant privileges and power. Once the going got tough, their lack of strong beliefs left them too weak to sustain deep, far-reaching reforms. "The new generation has a no-risk apparatchik mentality," speculated Jiří Dienstbier. "They just look for the open door on the train and jump on."

Alexis de Tocqueville would have recognized the pattern. In a classic pre-revolutionary situation, the French philosopher described how the ruled lose their fear while the rulers lose their will to rule. The second generation lost just that necessary conviction during that long gerontocratic twilight of the Found-

ing Fathers. Watching and listening to these colorless apparatchiks, one feels they had doubts, that deep down they knew
their communist system was bankrupt. When the moment came
to take over, they did not have the nerve. None tried the
Ceausescu route of using force. They just succumbed. "Whenever we met with the communists," explained Petr Pithart, a
leading Official of Czechoslovakia's Civil Forum, "they appeared confused, unsure of what to do."

The Communist Parties they ruled crumbled amid their confusion and hesitation. In Poland, Hungary and Czechoslovakia,
the parties dropped their old names in favor of new "democratic" socialist ones. In Romania the Party was even outlawed.
Elsewhere, young fresh faces were promoted to leadership
posts, men like Gregor Gysi in East Germany and Vasil Mohorita
in Czechoslovakia, both in their thirties. Gysi was a lawyer who
had made a career defending dissidents. Party memberships
continued to decline in 1989 until the once formidable organizations collapsed. In both countries, more than half a million
members handed back their cards within weeks. "Gysi's a nice
guy, he means well," said Peter Jastrow, one member who
relinquished his card. "But the Party's problems go beyond a
leadership change. After all Honecker did, I'm too ashamed to
call myself a communist any more."

Even in Hungary, home to Kádár, the most talented and
flexible Founding Father, the communists struggled under a
new leader, Rezsö Nyers. When Nyers was seventeen, he
joined the Social Democratic Party, which was soon absorbed
by the communists. Later, he would insist that he had remained
a Social Democrat. Nyers became an economist, whose ability
Kádár appreciated. In 1968 he fathered the ground-breaking
"New Economic Mechanism," which injected market mechan-
isms into the stultifying central planning system. When a Soviet
backlash in the early 1970s forced a slowdown in the reforms,
Kádár dropped Nyers, first from the ruling Politburo and then
from the Central Committee; he retained only a position at the
Institute of Science where he could continue to develop his
economic ideas. "Kádár's greatest quality was his ability to
avoid grudges," Nyers told me. "He could have destroyed me.
Instead he saved me for a more propitious time."

With Gorbachev in power, the time came. At the special Party
conference in 1988 which ousted Kádár, the sixty-seven-year-
old Nyers joined the Politburo. Less than a year later, with
preparations for free democratic elections well advanced, the
Party needed a leader who inspired confidence among the

general public. Along with reformer Imre Pozsgay, Nyers was the obvious choice. He enjoyed a well-earned reputation for sincerity, geniality and honesty. Polls showed that more than half the opposition sympathizers trusted him. As rumors spread that he would be named Party First Secretary, Hungarian journalists tried to track him down. Nyers was returning home from a Socialist International meeting in Stockholm. The journalists staked out the VIP exit at the Vienna airport where he was changing planes. They never found him. "He's such a modest man," one journalist later said in amazement. "He just passed through the ordinary passport queue."

Once in office, Nyers's only purge was of old-fashioned, outdated communist ideology. He dropped all references to Marxist-Leninism. The Red Star on top of the Parliament building came down. The Hungarian Socialist Workers' Party became the Hungarian Socialist Party. The people's militia was disbanded. Nyers agreed to full, democratic elections and approved a constitution guaranteeing full Western-style human rights and an independent court system. He even changed Hungary's name from "People's Republic" to the simpler, more democratic "Republic." At a Party Congress in October 1989, Nyers was elected Party President.

Ironically, many radicals in the Party protested. They complained that the new President refused to expel every last member of the old guard. Bearing grudges and depriving people of Party membership had never been Nyers's style. This same lack of vindictiveness, which not long before had assured him widespread popularity, now turned against him. He was seen as weak and indecisive. By 1990 Budapest standards, the longtime radical reformer had become a "conservative."

Jiří Dienstbier *(right)* always kept his wry sense of humor, even through long years of imprisonment and manual labor. Here, on the day after his appointment as Czechoslovakia's Foreign Minister, he cuts open the Austrian border with Austrian Foreign Minister Alois Mock.

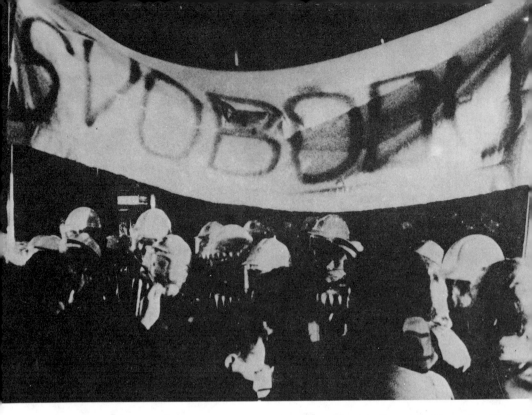

Posters from the Revolution. The police beating of students *(above)* in Prague on November 17, 1989 sparked Czechoslovakia's peaceful revolution. Pictures of the incident were turned into posters and pasted all over the capital.

chodźcie z nami!

Solidarity swept Poland's June 1989 election with its distinctive red lettering and simple message: "Come With Us." The campaign for the Hungarian referendum *(below)* on direct presidential voting in November 1989 was much more divisive.

NÉPSZAVAZÁS AZ ÚJ MAGYARORSZÁGÉRT

1989.november 26-án

ELŐSZÖR MEGYEK SZAVAZNI

ÉN IS, PEDIG 40 ÉVE VAGYOK NAGYKORÚ

IGEN   IGEN   IGEN   IGEN

Revolutionary kisses. Two gleeful East German refugees weep with joy after receiving permission to emigrate in October 1989. In Bucharest *(below)*, amid street-fighting in December 1989, a soldier and student found time to fall in love.

The Founding Fathers. At a Warsaw Pact meeting in 1986, the youthful Soviet leader Mikhail Gorbachev *(center)* stood out among the aging Eastern European leaders, left to right: Todor Zhivkov of Bulgaria, Nicolae Ceausescu of Romania, Gustáv Husák of Czechoslovakia, János Kádár of Hungary, Wojciech Jaruzelski of Poland and Erich Honecker of East Germany.

Bearded intellectual Bronisław Geremeck *(left)* formed an effective team in Poland with his alter ego, charismatic Lech Wałeşa *(right)*.

Václav Havel never felt comfortable addressing large crowds. But he stood up in front of hundreds of thousands of demonstrators in Prague in November 1989, and led Czechoslovakia to freedom.

iritual leaders of the revolution. Czechoslovakia's priest Václav Malý *(above left)*, Romania's Pastor szló Tökés *(above right)*, Romania's Rabbi Moses Rosen *(below left)* and Poland's parish priest nisław Waszyński *(below right)*.

Politicians of the revolution. Czech peasant petition writer Augustin Navrátil *(above left)*, Polish philosopher–activist Adam Michnik *(above right)*, Hungarian reform communist Imre Pozsgay *(below left)* and Hungarian opposition leader Miklós Haraszti *(below right)*.

Chapter Four

The Nomenklatura:

Apparatchiks Under Siege

The heroic era of communism is past. The epoch of
its great leaders has ended. The epoch of practical
men has set in. The new class has been created. It is
at the height of its power and wealth, but it is without
new ideas.

Milovan Djilas, The New Class

Ivan Krempa was born in 1927, a poor peasant's son in rural
Slovakia. Under Czechoslovakia's pre-war democracy, his
father never received an education beyond grade school. Young
Ivan could look forward to a similar sad future, struggling
to make a living on the mountainous family plot. When the
communists took over, he trooped towards the Communist
Party. His ideological profile fitted. A victim of the capitalist
landlord, he became the beneficiary of the new ruling class.
The Party gave him an education, sending him to study in
Moscow. It guaranteed him a comfortable apartment. It set
aside for him a comfortable country retreat for his weekends
and vacations. It even assured his children a bright future, a
college education followed by important Party responsibilities.
In return, Krempa repaid his benefactors with unwavering
support.

When Communist Party chief Alexander Dubček proclaimed
"socialism with a human face" in 1968, Krempa did nothing to
oppose the changes from his comfortable perch as a lecturer in
Marxism at the 17th November University. Later in the year,
Soviet tanks invaded Czechoslovakia. A grisly process called
"normalization" ensued. The most prominent Prague Spring
participants found themselves cut off from their jobs and futures. Dubček was expelled from the Party and given the lowly
post of forester in Bratislava. Krempa was brought before a
Party committee and asked his opinion of the invasion. Did the

Prague Spring represent a counterrevolution? He nodded yes. This loyalty was soon rewarded with an appointment to the Institute of Marxism and Leninism in Prague. In 1977 he became Deputy Director of the prestigious Insitute and was elected to the Central Committee.

Throughout Eastern Europe there are millions of communist Krempas. Sons of workers and peasants, originally recruited for ideological reasons, they were promoted for their loyalty. Where others might question, they obeyed. Their loyalty was not won through the revolutionary spirit or utopian dreams of equality. It came from their desire to step up the social ladder. Not wanting to lose these privileges, they long opposed *glasnost* and *perestroika*. Even after the democratic revolution, many of these apparatchiks maintained a tight hold on the state apparatus. They make up the so-called "Nomenklatura," the list of people approved by the Party to important posts in almost every walk of life: central and local government officials, managers in industry and commerce, publishers, newspaper editors, senior army officers, judges, trade-union leaders, university rectors, headmasters, leaders of youth and women's organizations, bankers, fire-brigade commanders.

How to dismantle the Nomenklatura represents a key problem in the wake of Eastern Europe's revolution. Their incompetence can no longer be tolerated. But a witch hunt could veer off into all-consuming, destructive violence like the angry score-settling in East Germany and Romania. The new non-communist-led governments must tread a fine line between reform and revenge, overhauling a system which, by its very nature, bred Krempa-like mediocrity. Under the Nomenklatura system, lists of positions and of people judged fit were maintained at the Party's central, regional and local committees. If you weren't on the lists, you had no chance of succeeding. The system promoted docile yes-men and penalized outspoken individuals. Unquestioning obedience and loyalty to the Party were rewarded, individual initiative and innovation discouraged. When political analysts in Prague tried to discern potential reformers within the ruling Party, they came up empty-handed. "All potential Czech Gorbachevs were purged twenty years ago," one friend told me. "Only careerists join the Party now."

On the twentieth anniversary of the 1968 invasion, I met Krempa at an official press conference. Then only sixty-one years old, he looked much older. He wore a stodgy gray suit. A bulging belly protruded from his off-blue shirt. He talked like a tape recorder. Yes, he admitted, the Prague Spring had started

88

out with a historic chance to "renew socialism." But it had veered out of control with the emergence of independent groups challenging the communist monopoly of power. "The process of renewal was taken over by those who didn't want socialism to get better," he maintained. "They wanted to destroy socialism." The Soviet invasion became necessary to uproot this "counter-revolution." "We had no other way to beat back the bourgeoisie," he said, his voice rising. "I don't want them ruling me again."

At the end of the press conference he agreed to an informal talk. He sat back, loosened his tight tie and, in a much calmer, controlled voice, began to outline his life-story. It was the archetypal communist version of the rags-to-riches drama: a rise from poverty and obscurity to material comfort and social prestige, based not on talent and hard work but on loyalty and political reliability. In theory, he stood at the top of the world. The Czechoslovak Communist Party reigned paramount. It ran everything. It steered the nation, controling the present and determining the future through its selective interpretation of the past. In practice, the story was different. Krempa and the Party were fighting a rearguard action to preserve their privileges. If the Party could be wrong about the 1968 invasion, further questions would follow. Did communist rule represent the will of the Czechoslovak people? Or did it result from the strength of the Soviet Union? The wrong answer could undermine the Czech comrades' legitimacy – along with Krempa's privileges.

Czechoslovakia's aging rulers came to power under the umbrella of Leonid Brezhnev. Their wooden style didn't fit the era of *perestroika* and *glasnost*. Mikhail Gorbachev began to nudge them towards reform. If they didn't jump on, he warned, they could miss the train of history. Little wonder Krempa seemed scared. In the past, he could always count on Moscow to shore him up. Now Moscow was reforming, arguing that reviving communism meant ending Party privileges, indeed the entire Nomenklatura system. As he talked, Krempa's face swelled and flushed a deep red. With passion – the only passion I saw him show – he lashed out in private against his once-loved Soviet comrades. "All four of my brothers were helped by the Party," he said. "I don't think what Mr. Gorbachev is doing now is positive."

When I was in Prague a year later covering the November 1989 revolution, I followed the news of the successful Malta summit, of Gorbachev's subsequent meeting with Warsaw Pact leaders in Moscow, and of his separate meeting with the Czechoslovak communist leaders. The five Warsaw Pact states which had invaded Czechoslovakia in 1968 formally renounced and condemned the invasion as an intervention in another country's internal affairs. I thought of Krempa. The next morning I telephoned him at the Institute. He told me that he had just returned from a spa, where he was being treated for nervous tension.

"No, no, I can't talk now, we have so much work and I'm feeling terrible," he said.

"What work?" I asked.

"We have to rewrite the document on 1968."

The conversation was surreal: here was the man who had once defended the invasion dreaming up ways of condemning it.

Krempa was switching his position because in the traditional world of communism the job of the Nomenklatura was to carry out orders. The Party's Politburo, a body with ten to twenty members chaired by the First Secretary, set policy. The Nomenklatura asked no questions. Undoubtedly, Eastern Bloc communists are divided into fundamentalists and modernizers, hardliners and softliners, ideologists and technocrats, conservatives and liberals. But these frictions were set aside by a common interest in keeping afloat a system which guaranteed them both power and privilege. The Nomenklatura was like a feudal ruling class. Its members enjoyed their positions because they belonged. They did not individually own the means of production. They collectively controlled them. They were the "owners" of the People's Democracies. Like other class systems, this "Red Bourgeoisie" was self-perpetuating. Nomenklatura children enjoyed the same automatic advantages, as long as they played by the system's simple rules: loyalty to the Party comes before anything else.

Before Solidarity took over the running of Poland, one Western specialist, Alexander Smolar, estimated that some 1.5 million people depended directly on the Party monopoly for their jobs. He also found that their advantages were comparable with hereditary privilege in the West. If you were the son of a loyal Party apparatchik, you had a much higher standard of living, better education and career chances than the non-Party child. In countries where housing remained scarce, a member of the Nomenklatura was assured an apartment. And in countries where consumer goods were in constant short supply, the Nomenklatura enjoyed access to special stores.

The Nomenklatura system of privileges had its protocols: perquisites were parceled out according to rank. Politburo members fared best. Under Edward Gierek, Polish party leader from 1970 to 1980, the corruption took on grandiose proportions. Gierek received from the office of the Council of Ministers a two-family house, complete with greenhouse, in Katowice. His sons, Adam and Jerzy, each received a house plus a country villa. In the mid-1980s, when the Party created a secret commission to investigate corruption among former Politburo members, the existence of an immense recreation estate high in the Carpathians was revealed. There Gierek organized huge hunting expeditions. In the evenings he entertained guests with generous amounts of Western liquor, Western films and "hostesses."

The Gierek system expanded the number of positions reserved for Party members. When a retired teacher wanted to open a clubroom for retired people in Warsaw, he was told that the directorships of all such clubs were reserved for Party members. Bureaucrats in the Building Ministry obtained gifts such as Western washing machines, tape recorders, stereos and radios from the Pewex stores. Another conspicuous sign of rank was a chauffeur-driven car. Most Poles felt lucky to have access to a cramped Polish-made Fiat; the waiting list for this most meager of cars stretched to several years. Top communist officials were chauffered about in Western luxury cars. Cabinet-rank officials used French Peugeots or Italian Fiats. Lower-ranking officials made do with the Polish-made sedan Polonez.

Given the affront of communism's proclaimed ideal of social equality, the extensive system of perks inspired widespread public anger. In August 1980, at the moment of the Solidarity strikes, an official poll reported that 85 per cent of the respondents thought social inequalities were "great or very great," and 61 per cent thought it "unfair" to link privileges to high positions. They demanded a leveling of incomes as well as limits on access to goods in short supply, like apartments and cars, and to privileges such as special stores and vacation homes. The poll concluded: "an acute sense of social injustice" was fueling the current crisis.

In 1981, after martial law was declared and Solidarity outlawed, the Party could find no effective arguments to lure former members back. None of my Polish friends would admit to being a Party member. It was simply too shameful. Mothers prayed in church, crying, that their infant sons would never become Party members. Only the most cynical and corrupt would join, and it was little wonder that the quality of Party chiefs was appalling. Poles nicknamed them "concrete." When I visited the famous Lenin Shipyard in Gdańsk, I met the shipyard's Party chief, Henryk Ludynia. He wore an ill-fitting striped suit with no tie and short socks. A big bull of a man, his reddened face showed signs of heavy drinking. He had difficulty putting together coherent sentences. In the course of a choppy half-hour discussion, I managed to discover that 900 of the 3,300 Party members before 1980 had resigned or been expelled by 1982. Even after martial law was declared, Party membership lagged. Throughout the whole of 1984 the Party recruited only twenty-one new members. In 1985 the figure reached twenty-five. During the rest of the decade it did not improve. Looking at Ludynia, it wasn't hard to understand why. When we left, my translator Krystyna Wróblewska became furious. "Our problem is people like him," she said. "He should be a garbage collector, not a manager."

Nomenklatura corruption seems endemic to all forms of communism, even the most open-minded, flexible variant of the system. Poland, it could be argued, was constrained by the Soviet Union's deadening influence. Yugoslavia was different. Under Tito, the Yugoslav communists broke free from Soviet tutelage and promoted a brand of "national" communism which combined an opening to the West with a bold experiment in "worker self-management." Unfortunately, worker self-management only created a new way to join the Party élite: through the Workers' Councils. Non-communists, non-Nomenklatura people, were excluded.

Milovan Djilas, one of Tito's closest associates and a key figure in Yugoslavia's break with Moscow, was the first to comprehend the debilitating effect. After he had turned away from the regime in the early 1950s, he published a scathing indictment of the Nomenklatura under the title *The New Class*. At the time, the infant Yugoslav communism was still trying out its first steps, but Djilas already observed how newly appointed Party apparatchiks appropriated luxurious perks, lavish villas, chauffeur-driven cars, even beautiful buxom young women to complete the picture. He saw the perks as inevitable in any one-party system, especially a one-party communist system which tried to control economic as well as political power. "The roots of the new class were implanted in a special party, of the Bolshevik type," he wrote – a party which labeled a certain set of people as "the avant-garde" and gave them complete control over administration. "The new class may be said to be made up of those who have special privileges and economic preference because of the administrative monopoly they hold."

When I met the intense, white-haired Djilas at his Belgrade apartment and asked him about *The New Class*, he chuckled. How right he had been, he said. Titoism, like all "national" communism, was not able to solve the fundamental problems of communist inefficiency and corruption. By the late 1980s, Yugoslav communism was literally collapsing under the weight of the "new class's" folly.

Djilas and I were speaking just after the revelation of a huge scandal: a Bosnian Communist Party chief had stolen up to $900 million. The scandal centered on the agricultural processing firm of Agrokomerc, which had been turned into the personal fiefdom of its chief executive, Fikret Abdic. From a sprawling villa on the Adriatic coast, Abdic ruled in royal style, attended by a retinue of secretaries and bodyguards. He used his privileges as a member of the Bosnian Central Committee to pressurize the local state-owned banks into guaranteeing a steady flow of unbacked Agrokomerc promissory notes. The guarantees made it possible for Agrokomerc to sell the worthless notes for cash to other banks around the country. When the fraud was revealed in 1987, Abdic and more than a 100 other Party officials were indicted and Agrokomerc was declared bankrupt. Its creditors, many of them normal workers, were left struggling to absorb the huge losses.

Yugoslavs lost all confidence in their system. Not long after covering the Agrokomerc scandal, I visited Belgrade Radio. Its hit show was a daily feature called *Section 101*, which resembles the American National Public Radio's *All Things Considered* or the British Broadcasting Corporation's *The World Today*. Alexander Zigič greeted me. He was only twenty-one years old at the time, but already exuded a rare charisma, a presence which cannot be taught. I wasn't surprised when he told me that he was the host of the show. He spoke in fluent English about his country's problems. After a while we began discussing his own career. "I don't have a future here," he said sadly. I didn't understand. After all, he was obviously talented. "I'm stuck as an announcer; I can't get a better job as a journalist." Why? "Because I'm not a Party member and I don't have the connections." Later he introduced me to the show's editor-in-chief, a wiry man who had a habit of looking at his feet when talking. Unlike Alex, he didn't speak a foreign language and hadn't traveled to the West; but he was a loyal Party member. Alex became so frustrated with his job prospects in Yugoslavia that in the end he emigrated to the United States.

Of all the Eastern European Communist Parties, Hungary's managed to attract the most talented people to its ranks. György Aczél, the longtime Politburo member and cultural tsar, directed this successful policy. While in power, Aczél would invite writers over to his apartment for dinner and use flattery to advise them about the acceptable and unacceptable. Don't question the Communist Party's "leading role." Criticize anything else, he would say – except the Soviet Union. And perhaps, he would suggest, ever so gently, you don't have to be so direct about this particular failure. Otherwise everything is all right. It was a paternal system, where right and wrong were clouded. Although it didn't destroy the Nomenklatura system, it did avoid a Czech-style purge and allowed less-than-committed Marxists to rise. For Aczél there was no other way to survive in the stormy world of Eastern European politics. A compact man with a mischievous mustache, he greeted me in his comfortable office. He was dressed informally, with an open-collared checked shirt. Speaking with candor, without rancor, he recounted his long career, its ups and downs. He displayed no regrets. "After the Soviet invasion here and the Soviet invasion in Czechoslovakia," he said, "the Hungarian people understood our situation, even the most primitive layer of society."

János Barabás was a star Aczél protégé. He went to the prestigious Budapest District Six High School in the 1960s, along with future dissident Miklós Haraszti. Barabás and Haraszti make for an interesting comparison. Both are Jewish, intellectual and ambitious – and both saw themselves working for a democratic, Westward-looking Hungary. But while Haraszti turned against the system after the Soviet invasion of Czechoslovakia in 1968, Barabás believed it would be more constructive to work within the communist power structure. "I became convinced that Kádár was much wiser than Dubček," he explained. "The only way to reform a communist system was slowly, from within."

When the Soviets forced a halt to the ambitious Hungarian economic reform in 1972, Barabás went along and took a job in the Central Committee as an assistant to hardline ideology chief

János Berecz. Ever since, a scent of opportunism has lingered around him. Barabás is bald and jovial, his youthful face ruddy and his belly suggesting a love of creamy Hungarian cooking. But he liked to receive Western correspondents and always offered frank answers to tough questions. At that time – the mid-1980s – no other Central Committee official in any Eastern European country offered such useful briefings. As Hungary's problems mounted, his views radicalized. "The old Kádár compromise no longer worked," he admitted. "A mere reform of communism no longer sufficed." Gorbachev's ascent to power gave him an appropriate moment to act, and Barabás embraced the radical goals of junking the entire one-party rule and the state-run economy. The only model of socialism which he saw working was the Western one – as practiced in Scandinavia or neighboring Austria. "When I think of socialism," he told me, "my model is Austria or Sweden."

In June 1989, he became the Party's ideology chief. His task was to turn his party into a Western European Social Democratic Party. At the next Party Congress, the Hungarian Socialist Workers' Party became the Hungarian Socialist Party. The changes were not just semantic. The new Socialist Party declared a readiness to fight free democratic elections. Under Barabás, the Party's strategy seemed to be that the best form of advance is retreat, that by transforming itself into a Western European Social Democratic Party, the Hungarian Socialist Party could win some 15 to 35 per cent of the vote in a genuine election, opening the way for a coalition government – and reborn respect for the Party. That goal proved to be optimistic. In the elections of March 1990, the Party received less than 10 per cent of the vote. "Perhaps it's good if we go into opposition," Barabás told me in our last talk. "I look at Social Democrats in West Germany. They are in their eighth year of opposition and still earn respect."

The admission, stunning as it was, did not suffice. Reformers within the Party led by Imre Pozsgay argued that all former hardliners should be forced from power. Only by making a complete break with the past, they said, could the Party regain credibility with disillusioned voters. Their arguments doomed Barabás. After the Party Congress, the position of ideology chief was eliminated. Barabás was proposed as Ambassador to Moscow, only to have the Party's parliamentary committee reject the nomination. He still received some "assignments," from time to time, but he finally decided to leave politics and enter business. "I would like to work as a management consultant," he said. "When I was in America I met many management consultants. It sounds like a fascinating field."

Following Barabás's departure, the Hungarian Party promised to dismantle the system of bureaucratic privileges. Party buildings were put on the market and the Party stopped receiving government funds. Even the conspicuous fleet of black Mercedes, which had been reserved for the Politburo, was sold off. Party members were asked to hand in their cards and take out new membership forms adhering to the Socialist Party. The results were shocking. Before the Congress, the Party numbered 750,000 members. Afterwards, it came crashing to the ground. Only 25,000 people chose to take out Socialist Party membership.

Hungary's Nomenklatura problem persisted. The new Socialist Party, small as it was, remained more numerous than any of the budding opposition parties. Incompetents were left over from the previous regime, particularly at the middle levels of bureaucracy. Zsigmond Járai, Deputy Finance Minister, told me that he found himself stymied at every turn by "our slow-moving elephant of a bureaucracy." A modest, soft-spoken man, Járai gives an impression of quiet competence. He speaks fluent English and trained at the London and New York stock exchanges. When we first met, he was setting up the Budapest Bond Market, the first bond market behind the Iron Curtain. When that venture became a great success, Járai took the logical next step and in 1989 inaugurated the Soviet Bloc's first stock market.

As a reward, the reform-minded communist government promoted him to a top-ranking position at the Finance Ministry. There his new task was to win foreign investment. Under a new law, foreign investors now could buy 100 per cent of Hungarian companies. But as he went about his work he found himself confronting big obstacles. His Nomenklatura underlings at the Ministry could not discern the "value" of companies in Western-style accounting terms. Company managers – key members of the Nomenklatura – meanwhile began selling their companies to themselves for a pittance. Others resisted selling to foreigners unless they were kept in their present positions – a condition which put off most investors. "The gap between what the government wants to do and what it is able to do is immense," Járai complained. "The Nomenklatura is like a mafia – we just can't break its power."

The only solution, he said, was to pension off incompetent

apparatchiks. Under this solution, existing company managers would be offered a comfortable retirement. The incompetents would be peacefully dislodged, while competent managers rose to the top. This would take years and cost a lot of money, but it would be worth it. "After Franco, the new democratic Spanish government pensioned off the old bureaucrats," Járai explained. "Everyone was offered early retirement. It took them five years and it cost them a lot – but it worked."

To the people of East Germany, "buying off" the Nomenklatura was not a fair solution. As the revolution picked up steam, revelations of corruption fueled their resentment. Few of them were prepared for the tales of venality which spilled out. Television beamed images of Wandlitz, the sealed compound north of Berlin where the top leadership resided. In a country where people waited years for a two-room apartment and where the law forbade citizens from taking more than about $7 across the border, stories surfaced of hunting retreats stocked with deer and spacious houses fitted with expensive tiles and wood, purchased abroad. The wife of one Party official was even said to have ordered an Italian tile floor only to have it ripped up again and redone. Another Party official reportedly used a government jet to fly his family abroad on holidays – to the United States. Often the revelations were not overwhelming by Western standards, but in East Germany the public was shocked. "We really didn't expect this corruption, we really thought these people were kosher," said Irene Runge, a Jewish sociology professor at East Berlin's Humboldt University. "It's like having twenty-five Watergates all at once."

Outcry rose as the people learned that the funds to pay for these luxuries had been embezzled from state industries. Public ire focused on one Central Committee member, Alexander Schalck-Golodkowski, who ran a little-known Central Committee operation called the Commercial Coordination Office. It was connected with a weapons-exporting firm and other companies that had extensive hard-currency dealings abroad. Accusations were also lodged that 372 works of art had been stolen from state museums and sold to collectors in the West. Just before the East German authorities issued a warrant for his arrest, Schalck-Golodkowski turned himself in in West Berlin. His deputy was jailed in East Berlin on suspicion of having siphoned off $110 million.

Elsewhere in the capital, a crowd of 100 or so citizens led regular police to the offices of the hated secret police, the Stasi.

They wanted to prevent files from being destroyed. How to dismantle the secret police soon became a major problem throughout the Bloc. Post-revolutionary governments were determined to dissolve their domestic spy agencies, but encountered resistance. The worst fight came in Romania, where the vast Securitate openly waged war against the army and the population. Even in Hungary, non-communist political groups gathered evidence that the police were still bugging their telephones.

Eastern Europe's secret police used to be a law unto themselves, reporting only to a handful of top leaders. There was no accountability, and when the old system collapsed the new leaders found themselves as ignorant as anybody else about the extent of the police apparatus. Both East German and Czechoslovak leaders said they did not know how many people were employed by the police or how many informers they had. Eastern Europeans knew about the spying and assumed that even their office colleagues could be reporting on them, but no one knew for sure who was guilty. "If we start putting all the police on trial, we could end up persecuting almost the entire population," one skeptical Romanian told me. Even though the Securitate had been abolished, he insisted on anonymity. "They haven't just vanished," he explained. "They could come back."

In Poland, Solidarity almost didn't take power because it was initially so divided on plans for dealing with the Nomenklatura. Three weeks before he took office, Tadeusz Mazowiecki published an article outlining his fears. A Solidarity Prime Minister would not have control over the army, he argued. He would not be able to command allegiance from the hundreds of thousands of apparatchiks in the ministries and factories around the country. He would find himself at the mercy of an enemy bureaucracy. "A Prime Minister and a few ministers can't wipe away forty years of misrule in a few minutes," explained Solidarity Senator Andrzej Machalski. "We risk taking all the responsibility without having the real power."

But the communists had been humiliated and could not form a coherent government. As the country's economic situation worsened and strikes began to break out, Lech Wałęsa decided that the country faced chaos unless Solidarity stepped in. He acted. Without telling anyone, including his closest advisers, he typed out a telex from his Gdańsk headquarters calling on the former communist puppet parties to join him in forming a government.

Some Solidarity leaders clamored for firing half of the Nomen-klatura – up to a million people. Mazowiecki accepted the need to make symbolic changes. Pro-Solidarity writer Andrzej Drawicz was appointed head of the crucial Committee for Radio and Television Affairs, long the key propaganda tool of the communists. The new chairman's first act was to fire the three national news anchormen, who were identified with the com-munists. But Mazowiecki ruled out any "witch hunt." Soli-darity, he explained, didn't have qualified people to man all the vacated posts. It must also avoid frightening the commu-nists, who still controlled the army and police. Mazowiecki called together the staff at the Council of Ministers. "I will not fire you," he told them. "I expect you to behave in a civilized, professional fashion." The communist staff members were shocked. "I was sure he was going to bring in his own people," one said. "He's up there all alone, with all these communists. It's strange."

Strange as it sounded, the strategy made sense. To prove his goodwill, the communist Minister of the Interior agreed to dismantle the hated Zomo paramilitary units. The Zomos, with their dirty gray-blue fatigues and long white nightsticks, had for years been considered by Poles to be no better than organized hooligans, playing a detested role in imposing martial law in 1981. A small force, Ogpo, was created as a replacement, numbering only 5,000 officers, compared to the 12,000 Zomo officers. Their deployment came under the control of the Prime Minister's office rather than the provincial police chief. The task of monitoring dissidents was abolished. Among the force's main new duties was crowd control at soccer matches.

Reports trickled in of massive communist defections. In Gdańsk I went to see Bogdan Borusewicz, who had been at Lech Wałeşa's side in the Lenin Shipyard in August 1980. Now, instead of fighting the communists, he was receiving frequent visits from panic-stricken Party-picked managers of state-run companies, all important communists. "It's become a pilgrim-age," he joked. "The managers come to talk about the situation of their companies, to establish relations with people who will take over power." So far, Borusewicz said, they had not renounced their Party membership and asked to take out Soli-darity cards. But he predicted that they soon would do so. "If the Party cannot distribute power and privileges for a year, it will collapse," he concluded. "The people in the Nomenklatura will be loyal to any power – including Solidarity."

Chapter Five

The Workers:

Workers Against the Workers' State

They pretend to pay us. We pretend to work.

Eastern European factory saying

He was a child of post-war Polish communism, born in 1943. His father eked out a living on seven acres of mediocre land in Popowo, a backward hamlet on the Vistula about halfway between Warsaw and Gdańsk. His early life was tragic. After his father died of privations suffered in a Nazi prison camp, his mother married her late husband's brother. Soon the new family totaled seven children. They lived in a two-roomed wood-and-daub hut. One room was the kitchen where sausages were hung. Outside, a little cowshed housed a cow, some pigs and chickens – the family's entire worldly wealth. Often bread ran short; sometimes two months could go by without a crumb.

Under the post-war communist regime, conditions improved. The young boy became the first in his family to receive an education. Aged sixteen, he became a boarder at the vocational school in Lipno, the district capital of 15,000 people. The school was designed to prepare a new generation of workers to build Polish socialism. In three years, the highly-strung, insecure country lad learned the rudiments of the electrician's trade. He forgot about his family's backward village. "As soon as I left home, all that once bound me to my family and to the village of Popowo, where my ancestors had settled and lived, and where I myself was born, withered away," he later recalled. "I've never really tried to preserve any ties with the past."

The budding young socialist worker was none other than Lech Wałęsa. In August 1980 he would scale the twelve-foot-high Lenin Shipyard gates and lead striking workers in their epoch-making struggle to form the communist world's first free independent trade union. His exploits are shrouded in myth and legend, and little wonder. Here was the simple electrician from a shipyard named for Lenin challenging a system which claimed to rule in the name and interest of the proletariat. Here was a worker overthrowing the workers' state.

Like millions of peasant youth across Eastern Europe, Wałeşa abandoned rural life for a job in a newly expanding industrial center. He felt the same frustrations of being a worker in a workers' state that millions of others felt. Just as he was a child of communism, he was also a product of communism's failure. What set him apart was his genius for expressing these frustrations and fashioning a concrete response to them. Through an independent, self-governing trade union, Polish workers took control of their own future. They looked beyond their immediate economic wants, setting their sights on higher political and moral issues.

Marx prophesied that workers' states would emerge where capitalism had run its course and done its historic work. Instead, Marxists came to power in rural, agricultural societies, first Russia, then Eastern Europe. Except in Czechoslovakia, which boasted a strong working-class tradition, the new communist rulers faced the task of creating socialism from an underdeveloped base, of creating workers to justify a workers' state. They succeeded. In one quick generation, millions of peasants like Wałeşa left the land to man expanding steel factories, coal mines and shipyards.

Today, throughout Eastern Europe, workers constitute the largest social class – often outnumbering the peasantry and white-collar groups. While the advanced capitalist West moved on through the "second industrial revolution," turning old blue-collar workers into white-collar or service employees, Eastern European workers retained a strong, antagonistic nineteenth-century class consciousness. Western European workers became bourgeois, but Eastern European workers remained workers.

Their role in the revolution was crucial. Strikes took on immense power because there are few other ways of showing public dissatisfaction. When workers go off the job in the West, their action is considered normal. When workers went off the job in the East, they precipitated a deep political crisis. Strikes in the West are resolved through compromise. Strikes in the East turned into open confrontation.

For the communists, betrayal by the workers represented cruel revenge. The construction of a new society based on proletarian myths and symbols was designed to create a solid base of support for socialism. But workers took these promises at face value. They began to expect the benefits of socialism. When these proved a mirage, the new working class turned against its rulers in a series of bitter confrontations. The first initial test came in Czechoslovakia. On June 1, 1953, in Plzeň, workers revolted against a sudden and sweeping currency reform that changed 50 old crowns overnight into one new crown. Hundreds of men from the Škoda automobile works broke out of the plant, ramming the gate with a heavy truck and engaging in a running battle with the plant's People's Militia. "We want free elections," the crowd shouted. They began tossing busts of Stalin and Czechoslovak communist leaders out of the windows. A Soviet flag was set on fire. An American flag was raised – the Americans had liberated Plzeň in 1945. At noon, many of the demonstrators went home to eat. Soldiers sealed off the main city square. Agents from the state security police checked the plant and began to round up the demonstrators. The shortlived revolt was soon crushed; it never grew into anything more than an isolated incident.

More worker uprisings marked the crisis year of 1956, in both Hungary and Poland. Workers at the Zipso Locomotive Factory in Poznań in Poland took to the streets protesting against price rises and salary cuts. They held makeshift placards blaring "Bread and Freedom" and "Russians Go Home." Security forces put down the rising in two days of street-fighting, in which fifty-three died and hundreds were injured. A Wałęsa-like figure emerged from the workers' ranks, a young man named Lechosław Gozdźik, who was secretary of the Party group in his factory. The other national hero to appear in 1956 was Communist Party leader Władysław Gomułka. Irony of ironies, Polish workers waited in their factories in October 1956, ready to defend the "reformist" Gomułka leadership against the Red Army.

In Hungary the intellectuals at first paid little attention to the working class. But as the unrest swelled, an array of Workers' Councils sprang up. When the Russians invaded in November 1956, the bitterest fighting took place in Budapest's working-class district. Even as the Soviets wrested control of the streets, a general strike took hold of the entire country. The independent Workers' Councils radicalized. They began to organize an entire political system based on their councils. A National Workers' Council was established, demanding direct rule over the factories. Even here, Hungarian workers did not protest against communism. Instead they demanded true communism. The Greater Budapest General Workers' Council demanded negotiations with the Russians and the new Kádár regime. As November dragged on, the strikers continued in their defiance. But the odds were hopeless. In January 1957, the main strike leadership was arrested and the last Workers' Council dissolved.

In Czechoslovakia, twelve years later, most workers watched the Prague Spring's cultural and social reawakening with indifference. Accustomed to living secure, comfortable lives, they made no demands of their own for independent political parties or free self-governing trade unions. Reform-minded Communist Party leader Alexander Dubček realized that this apathy was dangerous. Conservatives within the Party might be able to mobilize the working class against economic reforms, which might mean factory closures and wide pay differentials. Accordingly, Dubček decreed a workers' self-management system. Directly elected "Enterprise Councils" were established, with powers to supervise management and its financial strategy.

After the Soviet invasion, these councils gained real authority, rallying to resist the Russian troops. Thousands of workers helped to produce and transport protest literature, to set up clandestine broadcasting networks and to subvert Soviet military supplies. While Soviet tanks patrolled the streets of Prague, workers at the ČKD works in Vysočany gave shelter to Dubček and his fellow reformers to hold the Fourteenth Congress of the Czechoslovak Communist Party. Still, an indigenous workers' movement never emerged. The Enterprise Councils were planted from above. When they came under attack after August 1968, their shallow roots dissolved. By the middle of 1969, the councils had been abolished.

Of all the Eastern European workers, the Poles were the first to organize themselves into a politically potent force. Everywhere else the initial pressure for revolution came from intellectuals, with workers providing back-up support. In Poland the workers organized themselves and then extended a hand to the intellectuals.

Lech Wałeşa graduated from his vocational high school in 1961 and took a job repairing electrical machines in a POM agricultural cooperative at Lochocino. The POM symbolized the regime's attempt to communize the countryside by building industrial-size farm cooperatives out of small private holdings. These cooperatives controled access to tractors and other farm machinery, which peasants lacked. Along with machinery, the system brought a vast transformation of the traditional social structure. "A new type of peasant laborer had made his appearance, who belonged neither to the town nor to the country," Wałeşa discovered. But the peasant–worker proved an unfortunate graft. "Country people reacted to the 'new' in their own way – traditionally – and the POM employees devoted a good part of the timetable reserved for the upkeep of the tractors and state farm machinery to work on their own projects." To Wałeşa, the corrupt POM seemed "a dead end, suffocating, eventually unbearable."

In 1967 Wałeşa quit and moved to Gdańsk, where the expanding Lenin Shipyard needed new young workers to meet ambitious shipbuilding targets. Within a few days, Wałeşa became employee 61 878. Assigned to Shop 4 in the Mosinski Crew, his job consisted of laying cables on large factory fishing boats. The yard was one of Poland's prides, the type of place where visiting heads of state were taken to see the joys of constructing socialism. By Polish standards, the training and pay were good – especially in the 1960s, a decade of relative economic smooth sailing. Single workers received their own rooms in a dormitory. Most married workers soon managed to find their own apartments. Plentiful social and sporting activities, even a yacht club, were offered.

Wałeşa appeared set to become a pillar of the Socialist Workers' State. Though small in stature, his square, muscular physique and rugged features made him look like one of those stocky Stakhanovites who could boast about laying a record number of bricks or a record length of cable in a shift. Ideologically, he fitted the profile of a poor peasant son moving up in the brave new world of industrialized Poland.

But something went wrong. In the rush to fulfill ever larger targets, the shipyard's atmosphere deteriorated. Work shifts were extended and production quotas raised. Whereas twenty hours of work to make one table once brought 1,000 zlotys, the time allotted was reduced first to fifteen, then to ten hours – a 50 per cent wage cut. Changing rooms, lockers and lavatories deteriorated. Worst of all, a reduction in housing investments forced Wałeşa and his bride Danuta to spend the first two years of their married life squeezed into a cramped room on Beethoven Street. "The hostel provided a metal bedframe with a lumpy mattress, a floor and four gray walls, all in a filthy state and reeking of mildew, a rickety table, and two chairs, each missing at least one leg," he remembered. "A man could drink and sleep at the hostel, but he couldn't really live there."

In the final months of 1969 and the early part of 1970, management kept repeating how production quotas were not being met. Tension mounted. Then on December 12, 1970, the radio announced a series of steep and unexpected price increases, particularly of food items. Flour rose by 16 per cent, sugar by 14 per cent and meat by 17 per cent. On the following Monday 3,000 workers from the shipyard marched on provincial Party headquarters. It was Wałęsa's day off. On Tuesday he showed up for work at 6.30 a.m. Men began urging him to follow them to the management offices. He followed. He was twenty-seven years old, and for the first time in his life he had gone out on strike.

The strikers moved on to the militia's headquarters on Swierczewskiego Street. A crowd massed and began throwing stones. One shattered a window-pane. Police opened fire on the demonstrators and men were killed on both sides. In the fighting, the Party building and the main railway station were burned down. Wałęsa watched in horror. Workers were being murdered by the workers' state, Poles killed by Poles. In the ensuing years, he would never forget those images of fallen comrades. The more the authorities attempted to suppress the memory of the December dead, the more he remembered. It became an obsession. He helped raise money for the families of the victims; he argued for a monument in their memory.

The new Party leader, Edward Gierek, promised a reform of the official trade unions. Toughened and hard bitten by the recent events, Wałęsa none the less took him at his word. He joined the union and was elected as a representative at the Health and Safety Office. There he argued with management for more protective clothing, more soap, more towels, anything to improve the workers' ever tougher existence. His efforts achieved nothing. Higher-ranking union officials, all of them Party members, blocked his demands. "The union, such as it was, merely served as a driving belt – the shortest route for communicating Party directives to the workers," he discovered. His anger mounted. During trade-union elections in 1976, he stood at a meeting and launched into a fiery tirade. "The official trade unions," he announced, "are an instrument employed to eliminate every possible influence of the world of workers on public affairs, and that in a country supposedly run by the proletariat!"

The response was swift. He was summoned to the director's office, where the secret police were waiting. They told him to keep quiet in public. He refused. The shipyard guards were then called and dragged him to the gate. His dismissal notice came a month later. For the next four years he endured a succession of odd jobs and frequent forty-eight-hour arrests. The once-model socialist worker had been transformed into an enemy of the socialist state.

By the time the rebellious Lech Wałęsa scaled the fence of the Lenin Shipyard on August 14, 1980, he no longer saw himself fighting to reform the socialist system. He wanted to destroy it. When Wałęsa arrived, the strikers were wavering. Director Klemens Gniech had promised negotiations on condition that the strikers went back to work, and men were drifting away. Wałęsa scrambled up on to the podium and tapped the large director on the shoulder.

"Remember me?" he said. "I worked here for ten years, and I still feel I'm a shipyard worker. I have the confidence of the workers here. It's four years since I lost my job."

He declared an occupation strike. The crowd erupted in agreement. Under Wałęsa, the workers made five demands, including the construction of a monument to the victims of December 1970. On this point, they would not budge. The director promised wage increases. He promised a new super-market. Wałęsa and the workers wanted their monument. The director finally had no choice but retreat. He promised that they would get their monument.

Even after Wałęsa had become a worldfamous figure, a Nobel Peace Prize-winner, he was still no traditional, predictable poli-tician. He wore dark checked suits to lend himself a cosmopoli-tan air, but they hung stiffly on him. He looked more comfortable in worker's blue overalls. Where other politicians spoke in measured tones, Wałęsa shouted. Where others im-plied, he pleaded; where they demanded, he insisted. When-ever he had to give a written speech, he would mumble the words in a boring monotone. But as an off-the-cuff, impromptu public speaker, he was mesmerizing. Before thousands, he could stand up and charge along like a verbal express train, using rich, juicy metaphors and streetwise anecdotes. It didn't matter that often his rhetoric wasn't crystal clear. His passion was overwhelming, irresistible. Wałęsa talked the language of the average Pole, and he expressed the emotions of the average Pole.

Like other Polish workers, he was raised a devout Roman Catholic. Outside their shack in Popowo, the Wałęsa family treasured an open-air statue of the Virgin Mary, before which their mother led hymns and prayers. "My faith can be said to have flowed into me with my mother's milk," Wałęsa recalls. Later, as a trade unionist, he never forgot to wear a pin of the Black Madonna on his lapel. When the Lenin Shipyard was on strike, one of the most moving scenes was of workers taking Mass, and after martial law and the banning of Solidarity, Wałęsa set up his office in the basement of Gdańsk's St. Brygida's Church. Father Henryk Jankowski, his confessor, became one of his key advisers.

If the Church nurtured skepticism about godless communism, Polish patriotism spurred hatred of the alien Russian doctrine. As a child, Wałęsa's mother read him nationalist authors such as Henryk Sienkiewicz. He and his fellow workers could never consider themselves warriors in the international proletariat: they were first and foremost Poles. This point became clear just before Wałęsa signed the agreement ending the 1980 shipyard strike and creating Solidarity. There he stood, holding in his hand the outsize plastic ballpoint pen decorated with a photograph of the Pope. "There are no victors and no vanquished," he stressed. "We have settled 'as Pole talks to Pole.' " The phrase "Pole talks to Pole" would become a rallying cry for the first glorious eighteen months of Solidarity's legal existence.

In the late 1970s, several currents fused these religious and patriotic sentiments into a powerful political movement. Within the Church, a brilliant group of philosophers and writers associated with the Kraków weekly *Tygodnik Powszechny* and the Warsaw monthly *Więz* formulated a new Catholic social philosophy suited to the needs of the new communist working class. They no longer just asked for the right to build more churches and seminaries; they demanded more respect for the human rights of all Poles, believers and non-believers. Such language from the pulpit had a direct influence on workers like Wałęsa. "The priest was always telling me, 'Don't believe what you hear on the radio,' " one shipyard worker told me when I visited Gdańsk. " 'Believe what you see.' "

Through the Church, workers like Wałęsa made contact with opposition intellectuals in a group called KOR. The intellectuals preached that the only way the people could defend their God-given human rights was to form their own "self-defense" committees. From this nugget emerged the idea of free trade unions. On the eve of May Day 1978, a "Founding Committee of Free Trade Unions on the Coast" announced its existence in Gdańsk. Lech Wałęsa was among its earliest members. The group began producing its own newspaper, *Robotnik Wybrzeza*

– the *Worker on the Coast*. Wałeşa distributed it at factory gates and outside churches after Mass, dodging the secret police at every step. In September 1979, *Robotnik Wybrzeza* published an entire issue devoted to "A Charter of Workers' Rights," for better wages, shorter working hours, improved safety precautions, promotion by merit, abolition of police privileges and, above all, new trade unions.

By 1980 the seeds had been planted, the tactics and goals set. Workers, intellectuals and the Church formed an implicit alliance, unknown in the West and unique in the Soviet Bloc. It combined a religious vision of human rights with a secular vision of self-defense committees and the workers' deeply felt sense of injustice.

When Lech Wałeşa vaulted over the shipyard gate on that fateful August day, he still feared that his Free Trade Union "needed a year or two more of hard work to prepare." The demands presented to the management were very specific: "We wanted to keep things simple, avoid unnerving the mass of workers who had joined our strike with complex arguments."

The workers were more sophisticated than he suspected. "Why risk our necks for a couple of thousand zlotys?" they demanded. Management looked ready anyway to meet these material demands. As news arrived of other factories stopping work, Wałeşa called for the shipyard workers to continue their own strike in support of strikers elsewhere. The workers agreed. They no longer focused on pay increases. They demanded instead free self-governing trade unions.

While Polish workers mounted a frontal assault on the system, other Eastern European workers, discouraged by the failures of their own revolts, devised tactics to combat the system through subtler, more private means. They slackened off. "We pretend to work," the saying went, "and they pretend to pay us."

Czech workers were once the pride of Europe. Before the war, their workmanship produced a wide variety of sophisticated products, from the worldfamous Moser crystal to sleek Škoda automobiles, rivaling Mercedes and BMWs. Now Škoda cars and Java motorcycles are considered cheap, obsolete, poor-quality goods. In the West they are sold at discount. This low quality and inefficiency did not just result from absurd mistakes in planning or from too many bureaucrats. It came from poor effort. Once I was researching a story on the renovation of Prague's historic Old Town Square, where work had begun on the famous spiked Tyl Towers. I first arrived at 9 a.m. The workers should have begun their shift at 7 a.m., but already they were taking half an hour's "coffee break." They asked me to come back and see them afterwards. When I returned at 11 a.m. they were off again, this time on their one-hour "lunch break." I returned for the final time at 1 p.m. The workers had gone. "It's Friday," the foreman explained. "They like to begin their weekends early."

On Friday afternoons Prague seemed to empty of life as cars jammed the roads, the citizens heading for country cottages. Helicopters were called in to monitor the traffic. Residents joked that only East Germans spent Sundays in Prague. In theory, the workers were fleeing the stress of their jobs in order to relax under apple trees. In reality, most spent the weekends doing their hardest work – fixing up their cottages and gardens. When they returned to work on Monday they were ready to rest. In 1984 a study showed that workers in many industries wasted up to 20 per cent of their time on the job by arriving late, leaving early and taking long breaks. "People have retreated into their private lives," Jiří Dienstbier said. "They don't see anything to be won by doing a good job at work. So they get rid of their frustration by fixing up their cottages."

Similar frustration existed everywhere in the Soviet Bloc. Miklós Haraszti, the Hungarian dissident, once spent a year working at the Red Star Tractor Factory in Budapest. He found workers focusing on hitting "homers." A "homer" is an object made for the worker's own purpose using the factory's machines and materials. "By making homers we win back power over the machine and our freedom from the machine; skill is subordinated to a sense of beauty," Haraszti wrote. "They are created out of junk, from useless scraps of iron, from leftovers, and this ensures that their beauty comes first and foremost from the labor itself."

Imagine! Instead of "workers of the world unite," Haraszti postulated a new slogan: "Only Homers Fulfill You." The Hungarian title of Haraszti's book about Red Star translates as *Piece Work*. (In the English translation, the book is called *Workers in a Workers' State*.) At Red Star, employees were paid by the piece, and management tried to increase anticipated output by lowering piece-rates, time-rates and supplementary payments. Communism promised job security. Instead it produced "insecurity." Workers chased piece-rates in a world of the hare and hedgehog – "Them" and "Us." "They" were the smirking boss, foreman, rate-fixer, inspector. "We" were the abused workers.

When Haraszti finished his manuscript, he sent it to a publishing house that had asked him to write about working conditions. The publishers returned it with a note saying it was "hostile." Haraszti circulated copies to other publishers and friends. The authorities were alerted; Haraszti was arrested. He faced an eight-year jail sentence for "inciting hatred of the state." At his trial, the prosecution charged that the description of the Red Star Tractor Factory represented a generalized attack on the entire communist system. Haraszti claimed that the book was a sociological study of a single workplace. To take the book as a general attack, his lawyer argued, the court had to regard the "piece-rate" system as basic to socialism. Haraszti was convicted. On a strict legal basis, even he now admits that the court's decision made sense. "Of course *Piece Work* is an indictment of working-class conditions in a so-called workers' state," he told me. "My lawyer accepted unjust laws as valid."

In November 1989 the book was finally published in Hungary. It received widespread acclaim and sold out its first printing of 50,000 copies. Whenever Haraszti went on the campaign trail, workers pleaded for autographed copies.

Worker alienation seems endemic to communism. In Yugoslavia, Tito tried to avoid the authoritarian ills of centralized communism by creating a unique worker self-management system. Enterprises were owned and managed by their employees. For his labor, a worker received wages – and the right to participate in enterprise decisions. Departments and subdepartments each elected their own Workers' Council, which managers consulted before making major decisions. "In state socialism as in Czechoslovakia, workers are alienated because reform can only come from the top," claimed Damir Grubisa, a leading Croatian communist. "Here workers feel they participate, that the decisions are in their own hands."

I visited the Lek Pharmaceuticals factory in Ljubljana, the capital of Slovenia and the most prosperous of Yugoslav cities. Vice president Metod Dragonja received me, looking like a Western European businessman in his stylish Burberry shirt and jacket. Dragonja described how Lek wanted to build a new chemical plant. The Workers' Council refused the investment. It wanted to spend more money on improving the bus service to the old plant. The battle dragged on for months. The workers wanted a bus service every fifteen minutes. Such frequent service, Dragonja insisted, would cost too much. After a long debate, the workers agreed to accept service every half-hour and finance the new factory. "While we needed a better bus service," Dragonja admitted, "we should have focused on the more important decisions."

Worker self-management was too democratic. It made business decisions unwieldy and inefficient. In a large factory, managers had to gain the approval of as many as fifty councils. At the ATM engineering plant in Zagreb, managing director Ljubomir Zubcic told me how he needed approval from three councils – one representing production, another assembly and a third engineering – to launch development of a new measuring device. "Let's just say," he explained, "that I needed a good argument to justify my plans."

The most serious drawback was that workers put short-term gains ahead of their company's long-term health. When there were profits, they more often voted for higher wages than for new equipment. This tendency explained much of Yugoslavia's high inflation and low productivity. "Worker self-management puts politics over sound business decisions," Milovan Djilas told me. In his opinion, the major problem concerned ownership. Under worker self-management, the firm belonged neither to the staff nor to the state. Its owners were the "community." Few understood this vague proposition. Djilas believed that only capitalist incentives would force workers to stop acting selfishly and adopt a long-term perspective. He proposed making the workers "shareholders." "Under worker self-management, workers don't actually own anything," he explained. "As shareholders, they would become responsible."

Official Communist Party newspapers blamed workers as Eastern European economies fell further and further behind their Western counterparts. Prague's *Rudé Pravo* criticized their "formalism and passivity." Communists began discussing the dreaded "U" word – unemployment. Yugoslavia had long accepted the inevitability of joblessness, and in some areas of the country unemployment reached 30 per cent. But until 1988, guaranteed lifetime employment was assured everywhere else in the Soviet Bloc.

Hungary then became the first country to break the taboo on unemployment. A few weeks after the lay-off notices were mailed to 2,000 workers at the Ganz-Mavag Engineering Company, I visited the firm's factory in Budapest. The reaction was surprising. Few workers complained. "If I'm fired, I can find another position," one worker told me. "None of those who have left have encountered any problems."

Since the communist system had long overemphasized heavy industry, Jozsef Bognár, director of the Institute for World Economics in Budapest, argued that Hungary had 20 per cent too many workers engaged in manufacturing and 20 per cent too few in the services. Unemployment was needed to make this "structural" and "psychological" transition; communism, which had always revered the strong coalminer and rejected the weak desk-worker, would have to reverse its priorities. Of course, any structural change brings dislocation, and this one was no exception. Most of the unemployed came from north-western Hungary, where large mines and steel factories faced closure. Scattered strikes were reported in the region. Many workers could not find jobs near their homes: they had to come to Budapest.

At Ganz-Mavag one welder explained how he had lost his job at a steel mill in the north-west. He had been offered the choice of a job in Budapest at the railway-carriage factory or no job. So he had become a "guest-worker" in his own country, living in a dirty workers' hostel during the week and commuting several hours back home each weekend. "Americans also have their Pittsburgh," reminded Iván Berend, president of the Academy of Sciences. "Workers here have to understand that they are not guaranteed a job in the same place for ever." In Berend's view, the problem was one of principle. "For forty years we guaranteed workers their jobs as a principle," he said. "Our problem isn't unemployment. It's breaking the principle of full employment."

The workers at Ganz-Mavag rejected any notion of a strike. They didn't seem interested in creating their own version of Solidarity. "We're not like Poles – we want to work," one young welder said. "We don't think a strike will solve our problems. It won't create work or get us higher pay." A group of intellectuals from research institutes did however form their own independent trade union, the Democratic Trade Union of Scientific Workers. I attended its inaugural meeting in the small Metroklub Theater. It looked more like a gentle coffee-table discussion than a rough-and-tumble union meeting. The new union leaders acknowledged that they enjoyed few links with the working class inside factories. "We won't become a mass movement like Solidarity," admitted Pál Forgács. "Our workers aren't interested."

Forgacs and other intellectuals misjudged the workers. In the end, they proved unwilling to accept communist rule. In Czechoslovakia, workers unleashed the crucial blow against the old regime on November 23, 1989, holding a two-hour strike which attracted widespread support. Until that moment, the communists still thought of Civic Forum as a fragile collection of intellectuals and students. When the workers went out – millions of them, in every part of the country – it was an overwhelming display of the breadth of the opposition's support. "For the opposition, it was fantastic that workers became so active and politicized," recalled journalist Jana Smidová. "They understood so well the demands of Civic Forum, and they refused to be afraid."

A few days after the strike, I drove to Kutná Hóra, a medieval town marred by the construction of a huge ČKD heavy-machine plant. The once gorgeous streets were covered with soot. Smoke belching from the factory chimneys produced a curious time-warp, transporting me back to early Victorian days.

In Kutná Hóra I met the strike leader, Karel Polivka. Like most of his fellow Czech workers, he cut a solid, sober figure. Worker revolts and independent trade unions such as Poland's Solidarity didn't interest him. The Poles, he scorned, are lazy, and look what happened to them – they endured grinding poverty. So for almost all of his forty-eight years he had ignored politics and lived life for small pleasures: the comfortable apartment, the yellow Škoda sedan, and big, full glasses of superb Pilsner beer. "We never had strikes here before because people were satisfied – and scared," he explained. "The police, the cadre officers, the personnel officers could all fire us the minute we stepped out of line."

Polivka himself enlisted in the Communist Party in 1962 while completing military service. "The army Party organization defended common soldiers against officers," he explained. In 1968, however, he quit, disgusted by the Soviet invasion. New courage came only two decades later, after he had seen East Germans rise up in revolt. He joined Kutná Hóra's budding Civic Forum group, and on strike day led 2,300 workers from the ČKD factory through the front gate, past the banner reading "Along the Lenin Road to Socialism," then on across the high-way, through the snow-covered fields into the medieval town square. It was his first time out on strike. "The workers are no longer separated from the intellectuals," he said. "I respect Václav Havel as my leader."

I wondered whether this new alliance could be maintained as different class interests began to clash. Civic Forum's ministers pledged to close aging, money-losing heavy industries such as the ČKD plant in Kutná Hóra. Polivka told me that he would turn his factory Civic Forum group into an independent trade union. While such a union cannot be expected to stand idle as its members are put out of work, he said that Czech workers remember their prosperity under capitalism and are ready to trade job security for the prospect of a more prosperous future. "I'm not frightened of losing my job," he said. "People who like to work, people who are skilled – they will find work in the new Czechoslovakia."

In Poland, the strikes started again in 1988, soon after May Day. First, the 200 bus drivers of Bydgoszcz stayed at home and paralyzed traffic. They demanded higher wages to compensate for rising food prices. The authorities caved in and gave them a huge 60 per cent increase. This settlement increased the appetite of other workers. As the bus drivers returned to work, other strikes were mounted across the country. Once again, the cry of "Solidarity" was heard. Once again, flowers, banners announcing "Occupation Strike," and pictures of the Polish-born Pope John Paul II and the Black Madonna were pasted on the much-photographed Gate No. 2 at the Lenin Shipyard. And once again, Lech Wałeşa was out in front.

Within a few months, the communist authorities were negotiating with the man they had once derided as "a simple electrician" or "the former head of a former union." Within a year, Solidarity was once again legal. One disappointment accompanied these remarkable developments: Solidarity's return kindled little enthusiasm in the workplace. Back in 1980, the independent free trade union counted 10 million members. Five months after its rebirth in 1989 the reconstituted union numbered fewer than 3 million. Even at the Lenin Shipyard in Gdańsk, union leader Alojzy Szablewski told me that membership was off. "People today are much more careful. They don't believe. They are afraid. They don't join." Shipyard workers worried about their jobs. With Poland's economy crumbling, Solidarity leaders talked openly about the necessity of closing down or at least cutting back employment in the bankrupt shipyard. "It's nice to have Solidarity back," said one angry worker. "It would be much nicer to have a good job with a good salary."

The crisis at Solidarity's birthplace represented only the beginning. Solidarity leaders planned to privatize many other large state-owned enterprises. Economists estimated that if inefficient Polish industries were suddenly exposed to market forces, about half of them would go bankrupt. Millions of workers would be put out of work, while private entrepreneurs would be given new freedoms to pick up the slack. Divisions between a new white-collar class and the old blue-collar class would rise. On the streets of Warsaw, Polish yuppies already cruised around in shiny new Mercedes and BMWs while the impoverished masses rushed from supermarket to supermarket in search of flour.

Solidarity confronted a second squeeze between its two largest constituencies, farmers and workers. Rural Solidarity, the farmers' wing, pushed for increased prices of food products. Workers' Solidarity demanded wage-indexing to make up for the increased food prices. "We don't have a coherent economic policy," admitted Andrzej Machalski, a Solidarity senator. "We are divided between two wings: the union side, which thinks you can repair the socialist economy, and the entrepreneurial side, which thinks you should change the whole system."

Moving from opposition to government is never easy. In opposition, the target was clear: the coercion of a totalitarian state. Once that target vanished, politics became, as French political scientist Jacques Rupnik noted, "an expression of competing interests, of differing opinions about the conditions of freedom, about the allocation of resources, about how the pie gets cut up." Solidarity's former broad basic goals – freedom, democracy, prosperity, no longer sufficed. "If we have pluralism, Solidarity cannot exist like this for long," Wałeşa told me. "It's a matter of time – five, ten years."

Wałeşa himself loomed as a larger-than-life figure, a legend – and like all legends, the reality is a mixture of myth and reality. When I first met him in 1985, he was in eclipse. Solidarity's ranks seemed to be shrinking and union activists were criticizing their leader for not being more active.

He lived in a cramped apartment in a faceless gray block of a housing project in Gdańsk. "No," he said, answering the doorbell, "I don't want to talk. I don't give interviews on Sunday." Then he stuck out his right hand and smiled. Never mind, he would talk. The child with him disappeared into another room. Wałeşa sat down on a couch in the living room with one of eight offspring straddling a knee. The aroma of dinner came from the kitchen. He lit up a cigarette and plunged into politics.

His message was simple, straightforward. "Our possibilities are limited," he said. Solidarity would have to marshal its resources in preparation for more propitious omens from the Soviet Union. His presence and charisma were overwhelming;

he dominated the entire room. He stabbed in the air for emphasis, he slumped in the chair to express disgust. His mile-a-minute language was expressive, colorful, full of metaphor. Poland's geopolitical situation, he explained, resembled "a bird fluttering on the back of an elephant." His wife Danuta interrupted him: "Dinnertime." Her husband, wound up with the discussion, continued talking. Danuta gave us a dirty look. I finally had to excuse myself.

The next time we met, the new strike wave had propelled Wałeşa back on to the front pages. With funds won from international awards, he had just moved with his family out of their cramped apartment into a handsome stucco family house on tree-lined Polanki Street in the city's swank Oliwa section. He drove around in a big, blue Volkswagen van, donated by West German trade-union leaders. He still dominated any room he entered; he was still capable of the unique verbal pirouette. But the union firebrand had vanished; in its place stood a budding statesman, a man striving to become the patriotic hero uniting all Poles.

His model was clear: Józef Piłsudski, Poland's leader between the wars. A drawing of Piłsudski's proud mustached face hung in Wałeşa's office. Historians consider Piłsudski an ambiguous figure. Like America's George Washington, he was Poland's Founding Father, winning its independence in 1918 and saving the new state by routing the Russians in the 1919–20 Russian–Polish War. In some ways, his political vision was generous: he believed in a Poland in which the country's Catholic majority would live in peace with its numerous minorities – Jews, Germans, Ukrainians, Lithuanians. But Piłsudski was also a populist, even something of a fascist. When Poland's democracy faltered, he engineered a *coup d'état* and ruled as an autocrat until his death in 1935.

Wałeşa's critics have long accused him of being both too moderate in his politics and too dictatorial in his methods. In October 1980 his job as national chairman was contested by several Solidarity radicals, including his own deputy in Gdánsk, Andrzej Gwiazda. Pouting like a spoiled child, Wałeşa cut off all free discussion, and almost failed to be re-elected. In 1988, when he entered into new negotiations with the communists, the young strikers protested that he was betraying Solidarity. They again protested when he agreed to partially free elections and permitted the communist Wojciech Jaruzelski to be elected President. Wałeşa didn't even bother to listen. "Look, if I don't make a decision, nobody else will," he justified himself to me.

"Nothing will be solved if we just keep going around throwing stones and stamping feet."

A few months later, he brought the union into government against the counsel of his advisers, pulling off what has become known as a *coup*. Without informing even his close advisers, he sent a personal envoy to Warsaw to strike the deal. Once again Solidarity's parliamentary deputies were furious. They summoned him to a dramatic caucus at which they accused their leader of acting in an "autocratic" and "undemocratic" fashion. Wałeşa shut them up. "I gave you guys the possibility of acting, but you didn't manage to succeed," he said. "I succeeded."

The critics shut up. Nobody could dispute his success. Neither could anybody dispute his popular support. Polls showed he enjoyed 80 per cent support nationwide. To workers, he remained the only public figure who expressed their feelings and spoke their language. "Wałeşa is first and foremost a politician," admitted Alojzy Szablewski. "But he still understands the workers." Among intellectuals, Wałeşa won respect for his pragmatism, his intuition and his courage. Poland's best and brightest congregated around him. "Lech has probably never read a book in his life," says Krzysztof Śliwiński, an editor at the Solidarity newspaper. "But every day I am around him, the more impressed I am."

Wałeşa avoided saddling himself with the tough choices. He could have become Prime Minister. Instead he preferred to give the job to his friend and adviser, Tadeusz Mazowiecki. The tactic was designed to leave more room for maneuver – he would remain someone not directly involved in making unpopular decisions, the person who could shape events and step in if things went wrong. But the solution left Wałeşa feeling frustrated, like a lead actor shunted into a secondary role. He began to criticize the Mazowiecki government for failing to explain the recovery program, warning that high prices could provoke a "civil war." "My house will be the first to be burned down," he told a group of supporters.

Back in Warsaw, his Solidarity colleagues in government were irritated by his behavior. No one questioned that he was an extraordinary politician, pragmatic and decisive. No one failed to admire his courage, how he survived eight long years out in the political wilderness with his image and power intact. What everyone wondered was whether Wałeşa would emerge a dedicated democrat or turn into a dangerous demagogue. In the spring of 1990, he declared his intention to run for President and began pushing for early elections. As President, he would have to learn how to make the sort of trade-offs and log-rolling familiar to lawmakers in the West. He was a brilliant general in wartime, an abnormal, exceptional situation. He may not be a brilliant politician in peacetime.

Chapter Six

The Intellectuals:

No Ivory Towers Here

Beware! Here speaks a rebel, one of that dangerous
breed, the soft and polite.

Heinrich Böll on Czechoslovak President Václav Havel

Bronisław Geremek is a medievalist. His best-known book
focuses on thirteenth-century Paris. Within the narrow field of
French medieval history, he cuts a distinguished figure, writing
not just about the powerful and wealthy, but also about the
poor and uprooted, beggars, thieves, vagabonds, prostitutes,
sorcerers, entertainers, peddlers and even hermits. Whenever
we met in his cluttered, book-filled apartment on Piwna Street in
Warsaw's Old Town, the soft-spoken, gentle, fifty-six-year-old
bearded professor would settle into an easy chair and light his
pipe. Invariably, he was dressed in a rumpled tweed jacket.
He speaks an elegant, flawless French. Once, I saw research
documents for his next paper scattered about his desk. The
topic, he told me, was "medieval witchcraft."

Bronisław Geremek is also a leading Solidarity activist, its
parliamentary leader and one of Lech Wałęsa's closest advisers.
In 1980 he and sixty-four other Warsaw intellectuals published
an "appeal" in support of the striking shipyard workers in
Gdańsk. As an initiator of the action and the owner of an
automobile, Geremek was chosen to deliver it. "We needed
someone with a good car to go to Gdańsk," recalled his
close friend Krzysztof Śliwiński. "Bronek had a Volvo."

The historian arrived at the Lenin Shipyard with Tadeusz
Mazowiecki, later Solidarity's first Prime Minister, on the eve
of the first major negotiations. Timothy Garton Ash, the British
journalist and historian, recalled what happened next. " 'We
are only workers,' Wałęsa told them. 'These government negotiators are educated men; we need someone to help us' – and
together they sketched out the idea of a 'Commission of Experts'

to advise the strike committee and check the small print of any agreement."

Suddenly, the historian found himself making history. Among the "experts," Geremek won a pre-eminent place. Wałeşa respected his lucid, trained mind. Geremek in turn admired the union leader's native intelligence and common sense. The two men served as alter egos. Where Wałeşa acted impetuously, Geremek worked methodically; where the worker was shortsighted, the historian took the long view. Ever since 1980, Geremek had been at Wałeşa's side, his bowed, bearded figure, pipe in hand, advising, calming and cautioning. Wałeşa addresses him, appropriately, as "Professor."

Eastern European intellectuals do not hide away in secluded ivory towers. They have long constituted a separate class in society – the intelligentsia, respected and admired for their wisdom and activism – and in the battle against communist oppression, scholars manned the front lines. Czechoslovakia's Civic Forum and Hungary's Democratic Forum are dominated by writers and journalists. The revolution of 1989 was, in many ways, the victory of culture over power. Most of its leaders would prefer to read newspapers than to make the news. But in their countries' abnormal situations, they felt obliged to plunge into politics. "If I were in the West, I probably wouldn't be involved with politics because it's simply an exercise in power," Geremek himself said. "Here in Poland, however, an intellectual must be engaged, because we're fighting for the very right to think."

Throughout Eastern Europe, the written word – in open letters, manifestos, pamphlets and books – wields a rare power. Reading represents no simple pastime; it plays a vital role in social life, and not just for intellectuals. All classes in society read, from the lowest of manual workers to the most rarefied of specialists. What we in the West express orally, Eastern Europeans put on paper. What we televise, they publish in articles and books. The hunger for books and knowledge is palpable. According to Prague publishers, more copies of William Faulkner have been sold in Czechoslovakia, a country of only 13.6 million, than in his native United States. Books by William Styron and John Updike enjoy print runs of 50–70,000 copies in Czechoslovakia; Styron's *Sophie's Choice* sold a whopping 100,000 copies there. Even a volume of esoteric poetry by John Ashbery enjoys a first printing of 10,000 copies. A Polish publisher, PIW, put out 100,000 copies of James Joyce's *Ulysses;*

within days they were gobbled up. Adam Mickiewicz's *Pan Tadeusz*, the nineteenth-century epic poem celebrating Poland's fight for independence during the Napoleonic Wars, was first published in 1834. In 1986, a century and a half and hundreds of printings later, another reprint was issued. It has sold more than one million copies.

In Prague, one of my favorite haunts is Arbes, the crowded bookstore which sells more than 400,000 books a year. Every Thursday eager customers begin queuing at 5 a.m., waiting for the weekly shipments of new books to arrive. A good book sells out within minutes. I once hunted through Warsaw bookstores, talking to the browsers. Anna, a young woman, told me this was the tenth bookstore she had visited the same day. She was looking for science fiction, a volume of Isaac Asimov or Ray Bradbury. Despite high print runs, a terrible shortage of books frustrated her. She found few of her favorite authors in official bookstores. A shortage of paper was responsible for much of this problem. But politics were also to blame; the Party favored publishing propaganda to literature. Sometimes a friend who worked as a salesgirl put aside a copy when it arrived. Sometimes, Anna went to private flea markets. Asimov and Bradbury were available there, but at prohibitive prices – more than ten times the official rate. "I read thirty books a month," she said. "I'll read anything I can find."

Anna and other Eastern Europeans prize words for the flavor they inject into an otherwise drab daily life. Eastern European television is boring, public cinemas reek of filth, and the private supply of video recorders remains inadequate. People therefore treasure an unusual poetry reading, talking about it for months afterwards as a major event in their lives. I will never forget spending long evenings crammed into small apartments as guests gathered to discuss their latest literary find or to tell rich stories about their experiences. These evenings transformed drab cities like Warsaw and Belgrade into venues teeming with life, full of seething arguments and uninhibited passion. But beware! If you hadn't read every volume of Dostoyevsky, if you couldn't shed light on Hemingway's characters, or if you didn't understand the basics of Freud's psychoanalytic theories, you could be reprimanded and scorned. "Reading is a religion in this part of the world," Tadeusz Konwicki, one of Poland's best-known novelists, told me. "It fulfills a spiritual need."

Writers – of plays, poems, novels, non-fiction and even films – focus on serious subjects, particularly political commentary, moral philosophy or heavy historical themes. Film idols are not glamorous screen stars. They are moral heroes. Little tradition exists of "light novels," "light theater," or "light film." In countries often ruled or dominated by foreign powers, where national survival has meant an act of will, culture has long substituted for politics. During the Nazi occupation, when not only cultural life ground to a complete halt but the entire nation seemed in danger of becoming extinct, underground resistance presses continued to print – along with political leaflets and fighting handbills – poems and short stories, often of considerable subtlety. In the context, they seemed as rousing as direct propaganda.

While World War II presented an extreme situation, the principle of culture as an expression of nationalism represents a much older phenomenon. During the nineteenth century many Poles, Czechs, Romanians, Bulgarians and Yugoslavs were forced to learn the language of the occupier. Often they were forbidden to speak their own languages even at school. In this abnormal situation, writers gained great authority. The entire intelligentsia enjoyed an aristocratic ethos, seeing itself charged with a sacred mission: to guard, treasure and expand national culture. Writers burnished the myths of their national past and kept alive the very idea of the nation. In Bulgaria, for example, a literary revival stirred the long-dormant national spirit. In 1763 a monk of Mount Athos named Pasii wrote *A History of Bulgarian Tsars and Saints*; it inspired the opening of new places of instruction of the Bulgarian language and an entire new school of modern Bulgarian literature. Often writers took direct political action. Poet Sándor Petöfi was one of the leaders of Hungary's 1848 War of Independence and died in battle.

Perhaps the most bitter and courageous cultural war was fought in Poland, where the historic novels of the Nobel Prize-winning Henryk Sienkiewicz or the epic poetry of Juliusz Słowacki or Mickiewicz nourished entire generations. After two armed uprisings failed in the nineteenth century, few Polish nationalists saw the possibility of winning independence through violence. Instead of engaging open politics against the German, Austrian or Russian Empires, thousands kept the cause alive by fighting for Polish culture. Self-education became a craze, secret libraries of banned Polish literature flourished, and a special "Flying University" created an entire curriculum of clandestine courses. Classes changed location each week to avoid detection. Marie Curie was its best-known graduate. As historian Norman Davies put it, "The typical Polish 'patriot' at the turn of the century was not the revolutionary with a revolver in his pocket, but the young lady of good family with a textbook under her shawl."

When Czechoslovakia became independent in 1918, it was dubbed the "Republic of Professors." The republic's first two Presidents, Tomáš Garrigue Masaryk and Edvard Beneš, were both academics by training and temperament. Masaryk made his name as a professor of philosophy at the University of Prague, where he helped revive the dormant Czech language – which had receded into little more than a patois – as a serious subject of study and literature. The struggle for language rights, for the pre-eminence of the Czech language in Bohemia, prompted furious clashes between Czechs and Germans. In 1891, when Prague's German street-signs were replaced by Czech ones, it represented a triumph of considerable emotional impact. Later, Masaryk managed to turn the thrust of mounting Czech militancy away from armed insurrection towards peaceful, broader goals of liberal democracy. After he became President, his intellectual interests never flagged. Every week he continued to attend a literary salon held by the writer Karel Čapek. It's hard to imagine an American politician participating in a weekly literary salon!

Even though they ended up leading the crusade against communism, the intellectuals' deep patriotic tradition first served the communist oppressor. In the wake of World War II, many intellectuals joined the Party. Liberal Western values had not stood up to Hitler. During the war, the communists often led the resistance. The chiefs of the bourgeois Home Armies were often pre-war officers with much of the ideology of their caste. To the rank and file – young teenagers who wanted to fight the enemy effectively – they appeared out of touch. War proved a great leveler; privileges attached to age or class ceased to have meaning, and the possession of wealth raised doubts about one's sincerity and staying power. After the war, the young resistance cadres wanted to find some way of expressing the equality and comradeship of the wartime underground movement.

The surge of genuine admiration for the Soviet Union's victory compensated for Eastern Europe's deep sense of cultural superiority over Russia. Amidst the devastation, many young intellectuals saw the Soviet Union as a successful model of rapid modernization and industrialization. This infatuation was not limited to the eastern half of the continent. Many of the most talented Frenchmen, Italians and other Western Europeans also flocked to the cause. Neal Ascherson, the British writer, describes the pro-communist sentiment as a "huge revival of political energy," like "the continental wave of revolutions in 1848." As had happened a century before, there was a

confluence of armed struggles for national independence with ideologies of social and economic change. Socialism, in the broad sense that encompasses more than Leninist or Marxist interpretations, took the place that romantic liberalism had occupied in the nineteenth century.

The new communist religion seduced the most unexpected of figures – from the Polish Catholic nationalist writer Jerzy Andrzejewski to conservative exiles such as poet Antoni Slonimski. In his celebrated book *The Captive Mind*, Nobel Prize-winner Czesław Miłosz described how these fellow Polish artists, normally rational, unsentimental men, were swept away before a Soviet Union which radiated power, while the democratic West equivocated and temporized. They joined the Party to take a turn at the steering-wheel of history. Miłosz himself, even as he lambasted the new communist religion, saw a sense of historical "inevitability" behind Soviet control over his country. To him, the only viable escape looked like emigration. He asked for political asylum in France, and in 1953 published *The Captive Mind*.

Time soon proved Miłosz wrong. Much of the initial intellectual enthusiasm for communism was channeled into the stultifying arena of the political bureaucracy, the Nomenklatura. This transformation from idealist youth into corrupt middle age is portrayed by two Hungarians, György Konrád and Ivan Szelényi, in their book *The Intellectuals on the Road to Class Power*, written between December 1973 and December 1974. Konrád is a distinguished novelist who was once a social worker, and Szelényi a sociologist who was fired from his job for attempting to publish a genuine account of factory life. Under capitalism, the two men argued that power was controlled by anyone who possessed capital. Under communism, where the state possessed the capital, this power was conferred upon a corps of planners and technicians. Bolshevism, Konrád and Szelényi wrote, was a corrupt system set up by intellectuals for intellectuals.

Konrád and Szelényi identified the corrupting virus of the

Nomenklatura, but they ignored a budding rebellion by a small, influential group of "liberal" intellectuals. The first cracks in intellectual support for communism came from the Yugoslav Milovan Djilas. Originally, Djilas was an ardent admirer of Soviet models. After Yugoslavia's break with Stalin in 1948, however, he began to revaluate his early enthusiasm. He remained a convinced socialist. What bothered him was the role of the Leninist-style "vanguard" Party. As it amassed dictatorial powers, he argued that it was turning into a brake on progress towards socialism. The Party should be dissolved, he advised, to make way for spontaneity of the masses and the withering away of the state. In January 1954 Djilas was expelled from the Central Committee, then subsequently deprived of all state offices before he resigned from the Party after more than two decades of leadership.

From this time on, Djilas was harassed and jailed. But his heresy could not be undone. By 1956 Krushchev had gained firm control in Moscow and given his dramatic speech condemning Stalin. Eastern European intellectuals themselves perceived and denounced the Stalinist crimes in their own countries. Their rallying cry remained "revision" not "revolution." Like Djilas, they spoke at first in the name of socialist values and ideals, of reforming the system. They wanted to create a new democratic socialism, faithful to the ideas of Marx, purified of Stalin's distortions and tyranny. Philosophers and historians, such as Hungarian György Lukács, Pole Leszek Kołakowski, and Czech Karel Kosík, argued that socialism must find a new morality, that principle must justify the means, and ethics take priority over power politics.

Such men, many of whom had embraced their new post-war communist faith so enthusiastically, spearheaded the upheavals of 1956 in Poland and Hungary. In Hungary, writers – all members of the Petöfi Circle, named after the revolutionary poet – first voiced demands for the relaxation of Party control and the return of Imre Nagy to power. The "Polish October" restored Church and press freedoms. New Catholic groups critical of the regime emerged, including the monthly *Więz* edited by Tadeusz Mazowiecki. Western films, plays and books flooded into Poland and the jamming of Western radio stations ceased. Polish art jumped to the center of European attention. Warsaw, normally the drabbest of cities, was suddenly compared to Paris as one of the liveliest capitals in Europe, teeming with excellent jazz clubs, modern-dance performances, avant-garde films, and plain good fun.

The freedom was shortlived. After Soviet tanks put down the 1956 uprising in Budapest, Polish party leader Władysław Gomułka gradually tightened his grip. In 1957 the groundbreaking magazine *Po Prostu* was shut down. In 1965 Karol Modzelewski and Jacek Kuroń, another former Party member, published a famous "Open Letter to the Party." It used Marxist techniques to condemn the bureaucracy for exploiting workers. More interesting than the diagnosis of the problem, however, was Modzelewski and Kuroń's prescription. They rejected the notion of gradual change in favor of overthrowing the whole communist system. "Revolution," they wrote, "is a necessity of development." Instead of seeing this fundamental change coming from a battle by technocrats and ideologists within the ruling bureaucracy, they argued that it would come from a battle between workers and the bureaucracy. "The revolution that will overthrow the bureaucratic system will be a proletarian revolution." Soon after publication of their ideas, Modzelewski and Kuroń were in prison.

Revisionism still enjoyed one last great fling: the 1968 Prague Spring. Many mark the Congress of the Czech Writers' Union in June 1967 as the starting-point for the entire reform effort. "Called to life by the intelligentsia," wrote Vladimir Kusin in *The Intellectual Origins of the Prague Spring*, "the Czechoslovak reform movement was led by a coalition between the intelligentsia and some change-oriented groups in the Party." The goal of this reform effort, it must be remembered, was to reform, not destroy, communism. This new non-Stalinist, democratic socialism would be installed without violence and would avoid non-constitutional forms of struggle or the overthrow of government. It was formulated by the Party and implemented by the Party.

The Soviet invasion of Czechoslovakia in 1968 ended these illusions. At a time when Western students were finding their inspiration opposing American troops in Vietnam, Eastern European students found their own Vietnam at home. Once and for all, the region's best and brightest turned against the system. The class of 1968 made up the front lines in the fight against communism. Their numbers read today like a *Who's Who?* of the Eastern European opposition: Miklós Haraszti, János Kis and László Rajk in Hungary; Adam Michnik and Jacek Kuroń in Poland; Petr Uhl and Jan Kavan in Czechoslovakia. These radicals were all raised in solid communist families and rose up through the ranks of the Party youth organizations. The Soviet invasion shocked them. They organized student demonstrations in support of the Czechs. "We were children of the system, good loyal communists," Haraszti recalled. "Then the police crushed us."

These once-loyal communist students were forced to rethink their entire positions. "We saw that students in the West were allowed to protest," Haraszti explained. "That turned our heads upside down." Two decades later in Budapest, I watched a video film about the student rebels of the 1960s. On the screen, yippie-turned-yuppie Jerry Rubin flashed his American Express card. The audience was stunned. "How could he?" stammered an angry Jan Kavan, an exiled Czech who runs the London-based Palach Press publishing house. "We Eastern Europeans are the only true radicals left from the 1960s. We're the ones who didn't sell out."

Before 1968, as communists, many Eastern European intellectuals saw themselves in the "vanguard," leading the liberation of oppressed millions throughout the world. Afterwards, they adopted a new humility. Instead of dictating to workers, they would work alongside them; instead of carrying the banner, they would follow and assist. It wasn't just the young who adopted this attitude; the older generation, personified by Professor Geremek, was also affected.

The grandson of a Kraków rabbi, Geremek was spirited out of the Warsaw Ghetto as a child of eleven, just before its destruction in 1943. Hidden in a village, he eluded the Nazis under conditions of terror. When the war ended, he returned to Warsaw and studied history. Like thousands of others, he joined the Communist Party. "I let myself be seduced by the socialist ideal," he now says. The Party treated him well. He worked for years in Paris, directing the Polish Cultural Institute there. He was also a fellow at the Woodrow Wilson International Center in Washington. Back in Warsaw, he became director of the medieval history section of the Polish Academy of Sciences.

A pinch of skepticism always intruded on Geremek's socialism. As a historian, he turned to the Middle Ages to avoid the "passions surrounding contemporary history." His socialist fervor, diminished under Stalinism, revived during the 1956 Polish October, vanished once and for all in 1968 with the invasion of Czechoslovakia. In that year, as in Budapest, police thugs broke up a student protest meeting at Warsaw University. More than 1,200 people were arrested, and the authorities proceeded to blame the unrest on "Zionist" agitators. Geremek, a non-practicing Jew, broke his remaining ties with the Party.

Turning a socialist scholar into a dissident and trade-union activist still took some time. During the 1968 student protests, workers reacted with indifference. During the worker unrest in the 1970s, the intellectuals remained silent. "The breakthrough could only come when we were together," Geremek recalled. Even after Adam Michnik and a few of his intellectual friends formed the Workers' Defense Committee (KOR) to help workers in Radom and Ursus, who were on trial for organizing a strike. Geremek still didn't see himself as a hands-on activist. His introduction to dissident politics came later as a lecturer in the new Flying University, modeled on the nineteenth-century precedent. Clandestine classes were held in different private apartments to escape detection.

When Geremek traveled to Gdańsk in 1980, his first intention was to warn the workers of the impending danger to the nation. On his arrival, events overtook him. The strikers took his presence as a show of unequivocal support for the strike. Wałeşa informed him that the intellectuals would ensure that the strikers would not be "sold down the river." Geremek answered that the intellectuals were experts in various fields. Before he could say any more, Wałeşa disappeared. He returned with a written mandate from the Presidium of the Inter-Factory Strike Committee for Geremek and Mazowiecki to set up a team of "experts." Geremek soon realized that Wałeşa and the workers' leaders were "able to think in political terms." What they lacked was an ability to express themselves.

Gradually, the worker–intellectual alliance grew stronger. Both sides realized that they shared a common cause. The day after the signing ceremony that created Solidarity, the experts held a meeting in the shipyard where they answered questions not only about setting up the independent and self-governing trade union, but also about civil rights and related problems. Over the next few weeks, the original group of experts expanded to include whole teams of union advisers in various related fields. Geremek and these other intellectuals exerted a moderating influence on Wałeşa and the workers. They always tried to find a deal acceptable to the communist government, one which it in turn could sell to Moscow. The moderate proposals often proved controversial. Many of the young workers who provided the backbone of August's strike wave wanted much more. They were wary of intellectuals like Geremek who had never worked in factories. "Geremek – he's not one of us," complained Gdańsk shipyard activist Maçiej

Plaziński. "He just uses the workers to get a good position for himself."

Like most Solidarity advisers, Geremek was interned on December 13, 1981. He spent the next year in prison camp. Following his release, he returned to his history books, completing a series of scholarly papers including the one on witchcraft. But in 1985 he was dismissed from the Polish Academy of Sciences, where he had worked for three decades. In reporting the dismissal, Polish newspapers denounced Geremek as "an adventurer," an extremist, one of the intellectuals who misled the good Polish workers. Warsaw Radio identified him as the son of a rabbi: a familiar use of official anti-Semitism. In addition to these professional troubles, he endured countless days of police interrogations. His passport was confiscated. Once when I visited him at his apartment he told me that he was being prevented from giving a series of lectures at Oxford.

Despite these pressures during Solidarity's long years underground, Geremek continued to help Wałęsa in drafting statements and speeches, always calling for dialogue and peaceful change. When a new strike wave erupted in 1988, he was once again in the front ranks. At the Manifest Lipcowy coal mine in southern Poland, management ridiculed the strikers for grammatical faults in phrasing their demands. The miners sent out a call to Warsaw; Geremek despatched a group of lawyers. "The miners are simple people who use simple language," recalled Father Bernard Czernecki, vicar of the Holy Virgin Mary Church in Jastrzębie. "They needed the advisers to rewrite their postulates."

A few months later, Solidarity entered into roundtable negotiations with the communists. Geremek created the formula which broke the deadlock. The trade union would become a political movement and would participate in semi-democratic elections. Many union activists, including his fellow "expert" Tadeusz Mazowiecki, criticized him. But Geremek's vision paid off. He became the head of Solidarity's Citizens' Committee and directed the movement's parliamentary campaign. He himself ran for office in the rural northern district of Suwalki. He won with more than 80 per cent of the vote, and proceeded to become Solidarity's floor leader in Parliament. By this time he had exchanged his tattered corduroy suits for snappy Parisian sports jackets. It became impossible to visit him at his apartment or share a long, leisurely dinner conversation as in the past. Once again, he was no longer writing history: he was making it. Speculation centered on his becoming Solidarity's first Prime

Minister. In the end, Wałęsa chose Mazowiecki. Geremek's previous adherence to the Party counted against him. His Jewish background also proved a handicap. His greatest drawback, however, was his very strength. As chairman of Solidarity's Citizens' Committee, Geremek had begun developing a considerable political base independent of Wałęsa. Mazowiecki was an ardent Christian, acceptable to the Church hierarchy, and more controllable.

When he was not named Prime Minister, Geremek was disappointed. He felt abused. But he refused to criticize Wałęsa either in public or in private. That is not his style. He is too painfully polite, too gentle and generous in spirit. I last saw him after Solidarity's election victory. He rushed up to me and shook my hand with a hearty "Bonjour." He had to dash off right away to give a press conference. "You know," he said, "I really regret not being able to sit down and have a serious talk like before."

In contrast to Geremek, the Polish intellectual who never quite achieved ultimate power, Czechoslovakia's revolution was led by a playwright, Václav Havel. A slight, soft-spoken fifty-three-year-old, Havel did not look the part of a charismatic working-class leader or politician. He did not have years of experience organizing street demonstrations or other forms of protest. Over the past two decades he had spent most of his time writing plays, poetry or essays which were translated and performed throughout the world but were read only in samizdat in his homeland.

Yet in that crucial moment when communism faltered, Havel vaulted into the front line and propelled his country to democracy. One simple, courageous quality made him such a powerful figure: his ferocious insistence about his homeland's gray, unrelenting totalitarianism. His writings earned him the title of "Keeper of the Czech Conscience." He is often compared to Karel Havlíček Borovský, the great nineteenth-century nationalist author who also saw his writings banned, or to Tomáš Garrigue Masaryk, the philosophy professor turned father of a country. "Havel has the status of a saint," explained an admiring Jiří Žižka, the director who mounted his latest play at New York's Public Theater. "People perceive him as a pure person, a strong man who never compromised his ideals."

A modest man, Havel rejects such comparisons. In my meetings with him in his Prague apartment overlooking the Vltava river, he often seemed impatient, tired by his fame and responsibilities. Inevitably he would light one of his chain of strong, unfiltered cigarettes. His English varied depending on his mood. If he was relaxed, it would be excellent – accented, but fluent and precise, revealing a charming and witty man. If he was nervous, he would be taciturn, and his words would come out staccato, difficult to understand. He is a formal, polite man. At home he dresses casually in corduroys and a T-shirt, but at diplomatic receptions he appears in a spotless three-piece gray suit.

By speaking out, Havel had a lot to lose. If he had just played by the rules he could have lived comfortably, enjoying luxuries bought with the royalties from his plays and books published in the West. His stunning apartment is furnished in modern Scandinavian style. Handsome bookshelves are lined with volumes, everything from Stefan Zweig and Kurt Vonnegut to a dictionary of American slang. Vivid modern paintings, by Czech artists, are hung on the walls. On one lower shelf sits a fancy Japanese stereo. On another is a Japanese video recorder with cassettes of *Amadeus, Hair* and *The Big Chill* lying beside it.

For years the communist press criticized this luxurious lifestyle. But Havel often reminded me that the authorities could have evicted him at any moment. Once, the police took his personal computer, saying it was needed for "state research." He lost valuable texts and wrote a letter to the courts in protest. The judge decreed that the police action was legal. "I always feared they would let me finish the renovation and then confiscate the apartment," he said. "I must be sure not to let this fear affect me."

In a world of grinding daily totalitarianism, Havel's home always seemed like a precious island of freedom. Before the revolution, you didn't call ordinary Czechs on the telephone to set up an appointment. You had to visit their apartments and leave a message. The telephone is tapped, they explained, and they must not be overheard talking with a foreigner. In striking contrast, Havel always answered his own telephone. Once I saw four plainclothes policemen standing watch outside his building. Upstairs, Havel seemed oblivious, working with friends on the latest issue of the underground newspaper *Lidoviý Noviny*. Havel assumed his apartment was bugged and he didn't care. Across the meadow from his country cottage in northern Bohemia, the secret police built a two-storey chalet. The woods which separated watcher and watched were cut to afford a better view. On a clear day, from Havel's cottage it was easy to see the officer on duty peering through his binoculars.

The point, Havel explained, was not to hide anything. It was to make the surveillance as blatant and frightening as possible.

In one of his best essays, Havel describes how a person finds this peculiar private freedom in a totalitarian world, how as playwright becomes a political activist, a simple honest citizen turns into a national hero. During the 1970s he worked briefly at a brewery. His boss loved beer and he didn't hesitate to write down his advice about improving the brewery. Management didn't appreciate the suggestions. It viewed them as a threat and denounced their author, the dedicated beer enthusiast, as a "political saboteur." The expert brewer lost his job. He became, in Havel's words, the "dissident" of the Eastern Bohemian Brewery. "You do not become a 'dissident' just because you decide one day to take up this most unusual career; you are thrown into it by your personal sense of responsibility," he argued. "It begins with an attempt to do your work well, and ends with your being branded an enemy of socialism."

Havel was born in Prague on October 5, 1936. His grandfather was a successful real-estate developer, his father a noted restaurateur and his uncle the owner of the powerful Barrandov film studio. Havel remembers himself as an unhappy, plump youngster, "a well-fed piglet who had difficulty not only climbing, but even jumping across a creek or turning a somersault." His rich family background and poor physical condition combined to give "the other children a welcome opportunity to tease me endlessly, and sometimes to engage in various forms of persecution."

When the communists took over in 1948, his family's properties were seized and, as a member of the bourgeoisie, twelve-year-old Václav found himself ineligible for any formal education beyond grammar school. While working at a chemical company scrubbing vials, he studied at night. His decision to enter the theater came by chance, after he became a stagehand. Seven years later, in 1963, his first play, *The Garden Party*, was produced. It is a powerful story of a student whose consuming interest is playing chess. On the strength of its critical success, he became artistic director of Prague's most important avant-garde theater, the Ballustrade.

In 1964, Havel married Olga Spichalová, a coat-girl at the Ballustrade. It is a marriage of opposites – the cultured, sometimes flighty intellectual and the sober, unsentimental working-class girl. But the unlikely mix worked. "In Olga, I found exactly what I needed: someone who could offer sober criticism of my wilder ideas, provide private support for my adventures," Havel said. "She's usually the first to read whatever I write, and she's certainly my main authority when it comes to judging it."

His second play, *Memorandum*, was performed at the Ballustrade in 1965. It revealed a mature writer, full of acerbic wit, probing irony and masterly satire. *Memorandum* explores what happens when a bureaucratic organization imposes an artificial, "scientific" language called *ptydepe*, which presumes that verbal ambiguity can be eliminated by making words longer. The result, of course, is total incomprehension, one word ending up being 319 letters long!

Havel's plays became one of the highlights of the Prague Spring. Sell-out crowds flocked to the Ballustrade to see his latest theatrical adventures. In May 1968, *Memorandum* was produced at New York's Public Theater. Critics such as Edith Oliver of the *New Yorker* hailed it as "one of the funniest and most exhilarating evenings in the history of the Public." It won the Obie as Best Foreign Play of the year. Havel traveled to New York to attend the opening. It would be his last trip abroad for more than two decades.

Three months later, when Soviet tanks invaded, Havel condemned the invasion in a courageous, clandestine shortwave broadcast from Liberec, a provincial town in northern Bohemia. During the grim "normalization" process which cut off the most prominent Prague Spring participants from their jobs and futures, Havel's books were removed from all libraries and his plays were banned. In 1969 he was charged with subversion for signing a petition against the Soviet invasion. But his trial was adjourned and the case never resumed. For a while, it looked as though he had reached a certain negative accommodation with the authorities. "There even appeared to be a tacit understanding that writers like Havel who already had a reputation outside Czechoslovakia could continue to publish and have their plays produced abroad – provided, of course, they declared their income and paid the taxes," recalled Paul Wilson, Havel's translator and close friend, who lived in Prague during the mid-1970s.

After the conviction in 1976 of a ragged group of long-haired musicians from a rock group called the Plastic People of the Universe, Havel wrote another essay repudiating "the world of rear exits," by which he meant the privilege of being left alone while others less well known were persecuted. Determined to act, he and 241 other writers and intellectuals founded the Charter 77 movement. Havel became one of the three original

Charter spokesmen. He helped draft the group's "Declaration," released on January 1, 1977. It called for "the right to freedom of expression," "freedom of religious belief," and an end to "tapping telephones, bugging homes, opening mail, carrying out house-searches, setting up networks of neighborhood informers." Within twenty-four hours he and four other organizers were arrested and their homes ransacked. Havel was held in detention for five months before being sentenced to a fourteen-month suspended term.

On his release, he told me that he never left home without carrying razor blades, toothpaste and a toothbrush – his emergency kit for prison in case police seized him. His next arrest came in 1979. Charged with "subversion," he received a four-and-a-half year sentence in a maximum-security prison. If he wanted to avoid the punishment, the authorities said, he must leave for the West. Renowned authors such as Milan Kundera and Josef Škvorecký and film directors such as Miloš Forman and Ivan Passer had already left for exile. Havel refused. "The solution to the situation does not exist in leaving it," he declared. "Fourteen million people can't just go and leave Czechoslovakia."

Prison conditions were bad. Havel's days were filled with hard labor as a steel-welder. He had trouble making the daily quotas. Even worse was the restriction on his writing. Except for one letter a week to his wife – maximum four sides – he was not allowed to write at all. The letters, according to prison regulations, had to be about "personal matters." For almost four years they were his only opportunity to express himself as a writer. If any part of the letter was unacceptable, the whole letter would be confiscated. The warden took a special sadistic delight in enforcing these instructions.

Havel began writing a cycle of letters to Olga about his philosophical views. "What's all this crap about 'the order of the Spirit' and the 'order of Being'?" the warden roared. "The only order you have to worry about is the rules of prison order!" So Havel started writing another series of letters on the subject of his moods, fifteen in all. But after the eighth, the warden forbade him to number them. So the last seven moods are unnumbered, but they are there none the less. "His very decent and polite manner may at first have persuaded the warden and some of the guards that he was soft and easily broken," remembered Jiří Dienstbier, who was imprisoned at the same time as Havel. "It was a wrong impression. Havel was visibly ill at ease in the presence of crude and threatening behavior, but instead of the expected submission, this was usually followed by a quiet and persistent refusal to back down."

Havel's strength as a writer lies in his ability to express in intimate terms the abstract concept of individual responsibility. In one of his most famous parables, he tells the story of a manager of a fruit-and-vegetable shop who places in his window, among the onions and carrots, the slogan "Workers of the World Unite." Nobody believes in the slogan, but if the manager refused to display it he would be demoted, he would lose the chance of spending his holidays in Black Sea resorts and his children would not be able to go to university. Out of fear, he continues to wave the slogan. If positive change is to come to communism, Havel reasoned that the owner must take down the false sign and begin "living in truth."

Mikhail Gorbachev is no savior, Havel believes. The savior is every one of us. Although this idea of "living in truth" was often patronized in the West as intellectual posturing, Havel explained that Westerners understood little of what it meant to live under a government founded on hypocrisy; one which signed human-rights declarations and then jailed its critics; one which destroyed public life while claiming to base its rule in popular support. In such an atmosphere, Havel kept reminding me, "the significance of truth is bigger than in the West. If the main pillar of the system is living a lie, then it is not surprising that the fundamental threat to it is living the truth." He added, "A single, seemingly powerless person, who dares to cry out the word of truth, has greater power, though formally disenfranchised, than do thousands of anonymous voters."

Havel was right. The demonstrations which overthrew the communist regime in November 1989 became possible only when hundreds of thousands of Czechs and Slovaks overcame their fear and discovered the power of the truth – when Czechoslovakia's greengrocers told the truth. Recalling the armed suppression of the 1968 Prague Spring, Havel realized that the communist state held the weapons, if it had the will to use them. He also knew that violence corrupts, that violence and hatred and, above all, lies were the methods of oppressors. Adopting them would mean losing the battle for truth. As the crowds in Wenceslas Square kept growing larger, he insisted on a dialogue with the Czechoslovak Communist Party, not on its destruction. Havel urged the angry masses to avoid revenge. In response, they screamed back, "We won't be like them!"

The lonely writer, who spent so many years pondering the deep, existential questions of existence, found himself a man of action who could provide quick answers. In this time of immense stress, he displayed iron nerves and a fine sense of timing. Overcome with fatigue, he maintained his wry sense of humor. When journalists kept clamoring for interviews, he told a press conference, "I have received hundreds of such requests. If I grant only a small fraction, I will have no time at all for the revolution. After the revolution, I promise I will hold a press conference if need be a day or two days long to satisfy all demands."

Within the diverse Civic Forum, which encompassed all ideological strains, everything from Trotskyites to Thatcherites, from young students to aging parents, he enjoyed a unique authority. "Everybody in school is talking about Havel," said Martin Mějstřik, a leader of the student strike. "He is our hero because he's a great, courageous man who stands up to the communists." Among older intellectuals he inspired similar respect. "Whenever there's a debate about what to do, Havel listens and reflects," explained Václav Malý, his fellow Civic Forum leader. "He'll say something and it's invariably wise."

Havel's influence throughout Eastern Europe is immense. As they gained their freedom, Havel knew that the Eastern Europeans could not afford to slide back into their pre-war quarrels. In 1987 he planted the seeds for new cooperation among the region's opposition movements by leading a group of Charter 77 chiefs to a secret meeting with their Solidarity counterparts on the Polish–Czechoslovak border. Poles talk with deep appreciation about Havel; his essays planted much of Solidarity's philosophical roots. "We can't forget Václav Havel," Lech Wałęsa once told me. "He has paid a high price for telling the truth, but reason is on his side."

In December 1989, pictures of Havel began to appear all over Prague. People wore red-white-and-blue buttons blaring: "Havel for President." The story of the greengrocer became the revolution's official text: throughout the country, I heard actors read it aloud. The audiences reacted with rapture. But Havel did not embrace power with pleasure. During our last conversation, in 1989, he said his greatest dream was to return to writing plays, living a quiet, peaceful life in his Bohemian cottage. That was now impossible – his beliefs forced him to take responsibility for his nation – but he vowed to be no conventional President. After his election, he refused to move into the palace on Castle Hill, preferring to remain in his own apartment. He even continued to wear jeans on many occasions.

Most remarkable was his refusal to hide behind a cloud of

politically prudent words. In his first address to the nation, a New Year's Eve speech on December 31, 1989, he warned against substituting a new totalitarianism for the old one. "We live in a spoiled moral environment," he said. "We have become morally ill because we are used to saying one thing and thinking another. We have learned not to believe in anything, not to care about each other, to worry only about ourselves. The concepts of love, friendship, mercy, humility or forgiveness have lost their depths and dimension, and for many of us they represent only some sort of psychological curiosity or they appear as long-lost wanderers from a faraway time."

A few months after taking office, Havel visited Washington and gave another moving, philosophical speech before Congress; the response was full of enthusiasm. Once again, he spoke of morality, of truth and lies, right and wrong. The reaction was euphoric. Many Americans who seemed to be searching for a new sense of substance in public life found it in Havel. But amidst all the praise, I sensed a vague reservation among American commentators and politicians. "Havel's a writer," they insisted. "It's natural that he writes a wonderful speech. But he's too intellectual. Such a literary figure won't be able to survive the rough-and-tumble of politics."

This attitude seemed misplaced to me. A politician must not just run things. He must reflect. He must stand for certain ideas. From this perspective, Havel is the ultimate politician, a true leader, because having lived through repression, he has reflected more than most American politicians ever will. His words described difficult dilemmas about a world which contains no absolutes, no easy rights and wrongs, a universe of shadows, shades of gray rather than black and white. Havel's was a voice of experience describing how to sort out the horrors of the past and construct a new future where lies would be treated as lies, and honesty as honesty. Any country would be fortunate to have him as President.

Chapter Seven

The Students:

An Explosive Generation Gap

My parents pleaded with me, "Don't go, don't go, it's dangerous, you'll jeopardize your career." I told them, "The Party's backbone isn't strong enough to stand up to us."

Kati Fábián, twenty-two-year-old student at Budapest University

Dariusz Radiak was twelve years old when the Solidarity trade union was born in August 1980. Eight years later, the baby-faced coalminer helped lead thousands of other young miners on a three-week strike at the huge Manifest Lipcowy coal mine in Jastrzębie in southern Poland. The strike spearheaded three weeks of labor unrest which brought the Polish economy close to collapse and forced the communist regime to open talks with Lech Wałęşa. The odd thing was that most of the Solidarity veterans stayed on the job. "The older miners feared for their flats and families," Dariusz said, sitting in his one-room apartment in a cramped workers' hostel, his eyelashes still blackened from coal dust. "We had nothing to lose."

In March 1988, more than 600 university students crammed into the Jurta Theater in Budapest. Although the occasion resembled a rock concert, with jeans-clad youth drinking beer and smoking cigarettes, it was a landmark advance for Hungary's growing youth opposition movement. The students voted to establish FIDESZ, the Federation for Young Democrats, the first independent alternative to the Communist Youth League. Immediately afterwards, the authorities declared the group illegal, threatening to expel its leaders from university and imprison them. The youthful activists refused. Within a few short months, the Federation had won more than 2,000 members.

The offices of the magazine *Mladina* in Ljubljana looked like the headquarters of any typical student newspaper. A few long-haired editors banged away at their battered typewriters. Unframed posters adorned the walls, well-worn wooden desks and crumbling chairs served as furniture. *Mladina,* which means "youth" in Slovene, represents Yugoslavia's most daring publication. In 1988 the magazine attacked Defense Minister Branko Mamula as "the Merchant of Death" for selling arms to impoverished Ethiopia, and forced him to take early retirement by revealing that he had used conscripts to build a villa on the Adriatic coast. "For us, *glasnost* is just cosmetics," said Robert Botteri, *Mladina's* defiant twenty-four-year-old editor-in-chief. "We have no taboos."

In Czechoslovakia, students organized a mass meeting on November 17, 1989, in memory of eight youths killed during a student uprising against the Nazis in 1939. About 500 strong, they made their way in the bitter cold down Národní Třida, a main thoroughfare in Prague, waving national flags and calling for the release of political prisoners and for the right of free speech. Suddenly, a squad of riot police attacked the peaceful marchers with tear gas, wooden clubs and attack dogs. More than 100 marchers were injured. The students declared a strike. Within days, they were joined by the entire nation and the communist stranglehold on power collapsed. "What a pleasant surprise," said Jiří Hájek, the seventy-five-year-old former Foreign Minister turned Charter 77 leader. "We older people thought it best to avoid provocations. Then these younger people come along and say, 'We must act.' "

From Poland to Yugoslavia, a defiant generation of youngsters led the challenge against Eastern Europe's communist regimes. When veteran dissidents limited their protests to signing petitions, their children fought on the streets. "The crisis involves – above all – the young people," said Alexander Dubček. Andrzej Stelmachowski, the respected president of the Polish Senate, agreed. "Everyone thought Solidarity was finished, that no workers cared about it any longer – until the young generation came along. They gave the movement a new dynamism and force."

Communism long aimed to attract the young to its ranks. Upon entering nursery school, toddlers were warned about capitalism's evils and instructed in socialism's virtues. Students were expected to participate in the Party's youth movements. Zealous high-school teachers assembled the parents of students who refused to join, mostly from Catholic families, and gave them a strict sermon. Those students who still refused to join found themselves ostracized, excluded from school outings and penalized on their university applications. Party youth groups organized impressive military marches, complete with candles, banners and pro-communist slogans. The organizations themselves resembled armies, counting more than a million members in each Soviet Bloc country.

By 1989 this strict Party discipline had collapsed. Membership of communist youth organizations had hit an all-time low. In an eerie echo of the West in the 1960s, long hair, heavy-metal rock, teenage sex and other forms of adolescent rebellion rolled across the region. Youngsters coming of age in Eastern Europe did almost anything to try to wriggle free of the constraints imposed upon them by communism for so long. They have channeled their energies into opposition politics. Fighting first for a series of previously neglected anti-establishment causes – a cleaner environment, the right to conscientious objection to military service, the withdrawal of Soviet troops from Eastern Europe – they soon demanded radical solutions. "Democracy works in Western Europe and in the United States," said Péter Molnár, a founder of Hungary's FIDESZ. "Why shouldn't it work here?"

Meeting Péter and other young Eastern Europeans represented a highlight of my travels. When I visited the *Mladina* headquarters in Ljubljana, the managing editor Franci Zavril greeted me with awe. "Oh, the *Christian Science Monitor*," he said. "You must be important." I shook my head in disbelief, thinking, "You're the one doing the really important work." Just a few days later, Franci was arrested because of his hard-headed investigative reporting and charged with divulging state secrets. How different these youngsters seemed from my own peers in the West. Where we dreamed of "making" it within the narrow guidelines of professional success, the young Eastern Europeans were taking on the world. We concentrated on making $100,000 by the age of thirty. They concentrated on winning freedom. We risked living in a cramped studio apartment. They risked going to jail.

Anger, despair and frustration, as well as courage, brought the students to the barricades. The most pressing preoccupation concerned housing. More than four decades after World War II, most young Eastern Europeans could still not hope to get their own apartment – even after they were married. In 1990 the queue for housing in Budapest stretched to 40,000 couples. Péter Molnár, twenty-six years old, still lived with his mother.

So did his brother and his wife, married four years before. They delayed having children until they could find a place of their own. When I met Péter, he described to me the daily drudgery and difficulties of living with this awkward arrangement. "My brother and his wife are uncomfortable, my mother's uncomfortable. They fight all the time," he said. "I just get stuck in between."

When Ryszard Szarflaski became engaged in 1983, he thought his worries were over. He and his fiancée Krystyna were young, talented and well-educated, graduates of Kraków's renowned Jagiellonian University, a mustached twenty-five-year-old English translator and a pretty brunette artist. He hoped for a decent job with a good salary, either teaching English at school or translating for the official government agency. There would be no more long nights outside, looking for a spot to embrace because they had no car and couldn't go home to one of their parents' tiny apartments. Marriage would make these frustrations vanish. Ryszard loved Krystyna and she loved him. To prove it, when I met them the couple turned and planted a big kiss on each other's lips.

Almost as soon as the engagement was announced, Ryszard and Krystyna's dreams collapsed. The waiting list for public housing in Kraków stretched to twenty-five years, and the couple was not wealthy enough to rent a privately owned apartment. The only solution was to squeeze in with Krystyna's parents. The newly-weds tore up Krystyna's girlhood posters and mementos. Instead of a new life, Krystyna felt she was living out her old life in an even worse situation. Everyone shared the same kitchen and the single bathroom. They lived in fear of an unwanted pregnancy. Their only privacy came in Krystyna's cramped six by ten foot room. Where would they squeeze a child? After months of searching, the couple finally rented an abandoned apartment in a block with no elevator. At their own expense, they installed heating, plumbing and electricity. Their landlord liked the results so much that he evicted them and moved in himself. They moved back in with Krystyna's parents. Months passed. Finally they found one small room to rent in a cottage on the outskirts of town. The landlord offered it for one year. "Four apartments in four years," Ryszard sighed. "If the search continued, I feared the pressure would lead to divorce."

They decided to build their own apartment. Construction costs could reach millions of zlotys or, as Ryszard said, "Two hundred years' annual salary for a normal Pole." To earn the money, Ryszard obtained a contract with a Polish construction firm in Iraq. Emigration from Poland soared in the 1980s. From 1985 onwards, more than 250,000 Poles left each year to work at least part time in the West. The longest lines in Warsaw were no longer in front of meat or bread shops. They formed outside Western consulates. Polls of high-school students conducted by Poland's official research center showed that close to 85 per cent of students believed they would end up living abroad.

Ryszard toiled in the desert for more than eighteen months, separated from his wife. He pocketed $16,600, at the time enough cash for his dream house. He found an empty attic large enough to turn into a four-room apartment. It was owned by a Roman Catholic convent and the nuns gave him permission to use the empty space.

Getting permission from the various state authorities took another year and a half. State firms said they would do the work – in twenty years' time. So Ryszard hired private contractors, only to run out of concrete bricks before long. As is frequently the case in Poland, no further supplies could be found. "The workers said we would have to wait," he said. They waited, ten weeks in all. Tiles for the floor, fixings for the shower, even a sink, were not available in regular stores. Ryszard was forced to buy them in the special state Pewex stores which sell a full array of Western imports – for dollars, not zlotys. By the time they moved into the apartment, they were broke. Instead of enjoying his new-found luxury, he felt obliged to go abroad again and earn some more dollars. He spent the following year teaching English to Polish emigrants in Chicago. Krysztyna was not able to come with him. "My marriage has been one big battle for an apartment," Ryczard lamented.

Ryszard was lucky. Other youngsters without his drive and determination were destined to much bleaker lives. Marian Karakuła left his home on a poor farm in southern Poland at the age of eighteen to work at the Manifest Lipcowy coal mine in Jastrzębie. With four other young miners, he shared two rooms in a grim hostel, with a peeling façade, broken windows and bare lightbulbs. From the living room, only smoke and smog were visible. Jastrzębie's main street was a pot-holed four-lane road framed by massive rows of tenements. For its 100,000 residents, there were only two restaurants, no cafés and no cinema. Because weekend bonuses made up more than half of their monthly pay, miners worked six days a week and two Sundays each month. "We're treated like slaves," Marian complained. "Down in the mine, the boss stands over our shoulder and yells, 'Dig harder, dig harder!' If we don't comply, he yells, 'Don't forget, you're a nigger.' "

Many of the "no-future" generation channeled their anger into destructive activities once normally reserved for the West. Skinheads proclaiming vague Nazi ideas smashed phone booths, damaged trolleys and buses and even beat up their teachers. The violence was often directed at foreigners. In 1988 in Budapest a punk gang started a much-publicized brawl with some Cubans, sending several of them to hospital with broken legs and concussion. East Berlin suffered from similar disturbances, provoking a crisis atmosphere among the former communist leadership which saw the country's *raison d'être* as a bastion against fascism. "We can forgive almost everything," said Frieder Bubl of the Free German Youth League "But given our history, we cannot forgive youngsters prancing around in support of Nazism."

Alcoholism and drug use were more common routes of escape. In every Eastern European hamlet and city there were bars and restaurants where each Saturday and Sunday groups of young men gathered to get drunk as fast as possible. Trying to grab a bite of lunch often proved hazardous to my health. I would enter one of these grimy bars and find it impossible to order over the din of drunken men, most of them in their twenties. It was not a joyful atmosphere. Even in the early afternoon, few women were present. Nobody was singing. Nobody was bantering. Shots went down at a fearful rate with the sole aim of producing senselessness. The drinking seemed most destructive in vodka-loving Poland, but it also was visible in the beer and wine-drinking countries of Czechoslovakia and Hungary.

Drug addiction, long considered a "capitalist" disease, also became a major problem. "I found that drugs in Czechoslovakia were the cheapest in the world, cheaper than our cheap beer," said Czech journalist Radek John after studying the problem. "People are going to their corner drugstore, loading up on amphetamines and getting high." In addition to pills, there was a flourishing trade in hashish, heroin, cocaine, LSD and, most dangerous of all, home-made concoctions called *kompot* in Poland and *pernik* in Czechoslovakia. These consisted of poppies or cough medicine boiled up with a mix of chemicals and then injected. After years of silence on the subject, in the 1980s every country in the Bloc except Romania admitted to a narcotics problem – from the Poles with 40,000 addicts and 200 overdose deaths per year, followed closely by Hungary and Czecho- slovakia, to Bulgaria, which has admitted to having about 750 addicts in recent years.

Rock 'n' roll provided another outlet. When the first under- ground Czechoslovak rock groups, called DG-305 and the Plas- tic People of the Universe, formed in the 1970s, they sang about people exasperated by shortages of food and household goods, and people despairing of the notion that hard work pays. Police proceeded to ban them and jailed twenty-two rockers on charges of writing lyrics which "contained extreme vulgarity with an anti-socialist and an anti-social impact." New bands – KGB, Death Clinic and Deserter – replaced them. They too dealt with tough themes – hatred of the state militia and army and the rejection of government propaganda.

All across the Bloc, rock caused havoc. In Bulgaria, state-run television and radio tried to excise Western music from broad- casts, only to discover that youth tuned into the rock-music broadcasts of the British Broadcasting Corporation, the Voice of America, and Radio Free Europe. In Hungary, members of the Coitus Punk Group were arrested in February 1984 and put on trial for alleged attacks on public order. Their repertoire of songs included one denouncing the Hungarian leadership as a "rotten, stinking communist gang," and asking "why had nobody hanged them yet?" The musicians were given two years in prison.

At the Remont Club in Warsaw, where I spent several eve- nings researching a story, the music was loud, the rhythm insistent, the tone bitter and the imagery apocalyptic. "War, war is coming," ran a typical lyric. "Love, love, it's like blood." Backstage, twenty-three-year-old lead singer Tomasz Adamski said Western heavy-metal music influenced him, especially groups such as Deep Purple and Aerosmith. For him, music "must be aggressive." That's why he named his group Siekera, which means Axe. Outside, the crowd, more than 1,000 strong, cheered. Many sported tattoos, shaven scalps and safety pins in their ears. Two seventeen-year-olds whom I interviewed went by the nicknames of "Pershing" and "Broom." Broom had cut her shaggy, dirty-brown hair to resemble a broom, while Pershing looked ready to blast off. A black-haired girl, she was dressed in a black leather outfit and danced in such a wild fashion that her friends told her she resembled an Amer- ican nuclear missile ready to explode. "We want to feel the music," they told me. American music, they said, is too "sweet." Eastern Bloc rock must be tougher. "Our lives here are tougher," they explained.

For years, communist officials claimed these young rockers would turn out to be apathetic and apolitical. If they wouldn't end up as loyal Marxists, at least they wouldn't turn into opposition activists. When I went to see Michal Szymańczak at the Polish Institute of Youth Problems in 1987, he had just completed a study which divided Polish youth into three categories: pro-Party, anti-Party and undecided. "The pro-Party group was bigger than the anti-Party group," he reported. "But the vast majority of youth considered themselves undecided." At the Remont, Pershing and Broom seemed to confirm these results. When asked to list their heroes, they named rock singer Buddy Holly. What about Lech Wałeşa? "Politics are nonsense," they answered in chorus. "All politicians want to do is declare war and make people stupid."

But rock proved much more subversive than was originally believed. The music provided a window to Western freedoms, often packing a powerful political punch. Instead of listening to the liturgy of Marx and Lenin, generations of would-be socialists tuned into the Rolling Stones and the Beatles. John Lennon's assassination on December 8, 1980, touched off tributes throughout the Bloc. The appeal centered on his lyrics professing belief in world peace. In Bulgaria, Lennon worshipers hung black-edged unofficial *necrolosi* – public death announcements generally reserved for deceased Communist Party members – throughout Sofia, while in East Germany the official Party paper *Neues Deutschland* gave banner headlines to the event, praising the song "Give Peace a Chance" as a monument to the peace movement.

The largest, most lasting outpouring of "Lennonism" surfaced in Czechoslovakia. Mourners first erected a monument on Prague's Velkopřevorské Square, adorning it with flowers until city officials removed it in 1981. Young fans then turned a wall near the French Embassy into a kind of Wailing Wall – a monument covered with drawings and lyrics honoring the dead star with calls for peace, love and revolution. Police came and erased the fans' graffiti, only to find the youngsters sneaking back to repaint them. The "Lennon Wall" soon became a sacred place of pilgrimage for young Czechs.

The Lennonists' message gradually became less escapist and more trenchant. On each anniversary of Lennon's death, hundreds of youth gathered at the shrine and marched through central Prague chanting "Freedom" and "Democracy." In 1988 march organizers went a step further and announced the formal creation of the John Lennon Peace Club. The agenda: withdrawal of Soviet troops from Czechoslovak soil and a civilian alternative to military service. "The Lennon activists started with music," explained Karel Srp, a leader of the Jazz Section, an independent artists' movement. "Then they turned to peace, to anti-war activities, and finally to anti-communist demonstrations."

Even punks were transformed from nihilist youngsters into courageous activists. Growing up in Budapest, Péter Veress was turned off by the Komsomol youth meetings. "They were so boring," he recalled. In his teens, he took to wearing a spike haircut and hanging out in seedy nightclubs. "I was a degenerate," he admitted. "I didn't care about anything to do with politics, I didn't read the papers, I went to rock concerts." When I met him, he was a nervous young man, his talent hidden by aggressive anti-conformist behavior. All my regular translators were busy and Péter spoke fluent English. Desperate, I hired him. He proved to be hardworking and curious. The only problem came when we had an interview scheduled for the Central Committee. Péter didn't own a tie. I loaned him one and off we went to the Hungarian Communist Party headquarters, the so-called "White House." "My God, my God," Péter kept muttering in the taxi *en route*. "I can't do this, I can't do this." He did it, though, keeping his composure.

We lost touch afterwards. Péter lived with his mother out in one of Budapest's nameless housing blocks and the apartment didn't have a telephone. It was impossible to contact him. But when I attended the inaugural meeting of FIDESZ at the Jurta Theater, who should be there but Péter! He told me that his earlier alienation was a type of political statement. "We were saying to the Party, 'Your society is boring; let us be free,' " he said. His moment of truth came at the age of twenty-seven when he saw some friends who shared his alienation form FIDESZ. He cut his hair and turned into a full-time activist. "It was my destiny to join FIDESZ," he said. "I found people like me, people who said what they thought, who wanted something honest, something true."

Amidst communism's spiritual emptiness, religion represented another powerful outlet for youthful disillusion. In the mid-1970s, the Polish Roman Catholic Church started a clandestine "Light and Life" movement that held spiritual summer retreats for teenagers. At first it attracted few adherents, but after martial law was declared in 1981 Light and Life's popularity mushroomed. Disillusioned supporters of the destroyed Solidarity found a refuge from their daily life. More than 600,000 teenagers now participate in the seminars, filling their summer days with Masses, singing and discussions on the various aspects of the liturgy.

Elsewhere in Eastern Europe, young people also returned to religion. In Catholic parts of Yugoslavia, a poll showed that the most popular personalities were Mother Theresa and the Pope. Lenin was ranked the least popular. A Zagreb newspaper headlined its article about the survey, "Pupils Study Marx But Think of God." In Czechoslovakia, students were particularly active in the underground Church, where priests stripped of state licenses said Mass in private homes. The alternative to official Roman Catholic services sprang up because of state restrictions on religious activity. "When young people don't find answers in the official ideology any more," explained Václav Malý, the dissident Czechoslovak priest, "they make room for God."

This search for spirituality catapulted young believers to the front lines of the battle for freedom. Jan Svoboda, a twenty-six-year-old theology graduate in Prague, helped form the new Czechoslovak Independent Pacifist Association. He wrote a letter to the authorities demanding the right to perform civil service in place of his military obligations. "My faith gave me the courage to say things out loud," he said. "Other people thought the same but were afraid to say it publicly."

Eastern European communists hoped that Mikhail Gorbachev's new openness would rekindle enthusiasm for communism in the frustrated and rebellious younger generation. When Czech journalist Radek John first tried to write about drugs, his articles were censored. In 1985 he was finally allowed to write a book on the subject. It became a bestseller. "I just told the authorities that *Pravda* and *Izvestia* were publishing articles on the same subject," he remembered. "I know a lot of people in the government don't like what I write, but they keep their criticisms to themselves." "Before Gorbachev, drugs and other youth issues were taboo," added Támás Urban, a Hungarian journalist for a youth magazine. "Everything is out in the open now."

In the 1980s, hitherto staid communist cultural organizations began sponsoring rock concerts. In East Germany, where former communist leader Walter Ulbricht once labeled rock music "ape culture," the authorities organized an official breakdance contest and even permitted American rocker Bruce Springsteen to play in the summer of 1988. Some 160,000 people showed up at the bicycle racetrack in East Berlin – the largest concert ever staged in Eastern Europe. They flew American flags and held up banners reading: "Berlin Greets the Boss." As Springsteen played "Born in the U.S.A.," tens of thousands of young people, many wearing the blue shirts of the Communist Youth League, raised clenched fists and thundered, "Born in the U.S.A.! I was born in the U.S.A.!" They knew every word. "Young people like rock music, so we say why not let them have it?" said Frieder Bubl of the Free German Youth League.

These efforts to win hearts and minds failed. During the 1980s the Hungarian Communist Youth League lost more than 200,000 members. In Poland, among the 12,000 students at Warsaw University, communist organizers could claim only 100 Party members in 1989. Nationwide, the proportion of Party members under the age of twenty-five had declined by 90 per cent since the 1970s, totaling fewer than 25,000 in 1990. "Young people mistrust everybody in positions of authority, especially the communists," said Andrzej Sosnowski, the twenty-seven-year-old leader of the Gdańsk Independent Students' Association. Even in Bulgaria, a country with little tradition of dissent, the young began to question the authority of their aging leader Todor Zhivkov. Students at the University of Sofia challenged France's President François Mitterrand for having decorated Zhivkov with the Legion of Honor. "Why?" one of them asked a startled Mitterrand during the French President's visit in January 1989. "What makes him deserve it?"

Youthful anger was first transformed into political power in the Yugoslav Republic of Slovenia. When police arrested some punks in 1980 for "disturbing the peace" with their haircuts and loud music, students fought back. Soon they were championing a long list of controversial "youth" issues: conscientious objection, gay rights, a ban on nuclear power and an end to celebrations of former President Tito's birthday. Under the umbrella of the Socialist Youth Alliance, they created independent associations of ecologists, pacifists and homosexuals. "We decided to fight for the punks, and everything just blossomed from there," recalled Ingrid Baksa, the movement's leader. "Now, you name it, we have a group for it."

The brash activism proved contagious. When *Mladina* magazine started criticizing the cult surrounding Tito, journalists at the official Slovene daily, *Delo*, plucked up courage to join the attacks. "They taught us all a lesson," said an admiring Mitja Meršol, a *Delo* editor. "When I saw what *Mladina* was doing, I became bolder and bolder." In 1988 *Mladina* reported that the Yugoslav army was planning a *coup* against the republic, and three of the magazine's journalists were arrested on charges of disclosing state secrets. Their trial sparked widespread unrest. Youth Alliance leaders organized a protest rock concert attended by 30,000 people. A crowd of 10,000 stood outside the courtroom, hailing the journalists as heroes when they were sentenced to prison terms ranging from five months to four years. *Mladina* continued to publish. "Those youngsters are naïve, they are slanderous," said *Delo*'s Meršol. "But they break all the old taboos."

The youthful urge to protest produced some strange manifestations. A group called Orange Alternative was founded in the 1980s in Wrocław, a grimy industrial city in south-west Poland. On Stalin's birthday, the group gathered 5,000 youngsters at the local zoo's chimpanzee cage, dressed in red, waving flags with Bolshevik slogans and singing Stalinist hymns. One Christmas, Orange Alternative wore Santa Claus suits and carried signs claiming "Only Santa can save you from poverty" – a gibe at the claims of both Solidarity and the communists. When the local Solidarity chapter called for the boycott of an election, Orange Alternative responded with a demonstration calling for Wrocław to become "the city where more than 100 per cent vote."

For Waldemar Frydrych, the leader of these so-called "Happenings," both official culture and earnest Solidarity protests were intolerable. The Happenings were designed to bring out the inherent absurdity of Polish politics. Orange Alternative groups soon spread to Poznań, Gdańsk, Kraków and Warsaw. To a generation tired of talking about economic and political reforms, which had little chance of working, anarchism seemed the most rational response. And to a generation which was too young to have been part of Solidarity and considered its leaders old and its methods ossified, anarchism was the best way to gain attention.

The fear was that youthful radicals would try to push their elders too far. In the late 1980s, when students in Poland began championing conscientious objection from military service, Solidarity leaders were scared that the issue would raise Soviet hackles. Poland had no pacifist tradition, and to Lech Wałęsa, proud of his own service as a corporal, the army remained a sacred national institution. Don't go too far, the legendary union leader warned the young pacifists. Don't question the army and alliance system with the Soviet Union. "The young are always more simple and direct in their way of expressing themselves," Wałeşa told me. "Today they say, 'Oh, that old man speaks too much.' "

The youngsters refused to listen, and formed a group named Freedom and Peace, calling on draftees to refuse to recite the military oath because of its reference to "brotherhood with the Soviet army." Unlike Solidarity, which at the time was engaged in passive resistance, Freedom and Peace insisted on acting out in the open. It attracted attention with hunger strikes, petitions and sit-ins. By 1988, more than two dozen youngsters were in prison for sending back their draft notices to the authorities. They demanded a new oath and alternative service for conscientious objectors – demands to which the government acceded. "This army serves Soviet, not Polish goals," complained twenty-three-year-old Jarosław Nakielski, who was imprisoned in 1986 for burning his conscript notice. "I would rather go to prison than serve in an army which supports the Reds."

Even after the Polish government offered to begin negotiations with Solidarity, young strikers demanded the immediate recognition of their union. Lech Wałeşa traveled to Jastrzębie, where the young workers, many of whom had spent three weeks holed up in a coal mine, shouted him down. It took him twelve hours to persuade them to leave. "Why should we give up just because Wałeşa tells us to?" one young miner asked. Solidarity ministers now fear that these angry youngsters could sabotage Poland's first non-communist government by launching unwanted boycotts and strikes. "Our youth is radicalizing," worried Bronisław Geremek, the parliamentary leader. "Young people who think Solidarity has failed may turn to violence."

History taught prudence to their parents' generation. Older Polish workers cannot forget the brutal martial law which destroyed their independent union in 1981; Czechoslovaks remember the 1968 Soviet invasion; Hungarians the bloody 1956 revolution. Instead of being traumatized by these dangerous precedents, their children have been inspired by them. "My parents are always telling me how we lost this war and that war, how 1956 was so bloody," explained József Szájer, a leader of the Hungarian FIDESZ. "I tell them, 'That's your problem, not mine.' " In April 1990, at the tender age of twenty-six,

Szájer was elected to the Hungarian Parliament – crushing the celebrated communist reformer Imre Pozsgay.

In Czechoslovakia, parents reacted with skepticism when students declared an "occupation" of all universities in November 1989. "My mother and father threatened to throw me out of the house," student Pavel Chaloupa told me. "All of us thought that we were alone, that the police would come and throw us in jail." But the police never came and the student action sparked a national mobilization. Posters were printed showing teachers muttering to each other, "We learned something from our students."

I met twenty-six-year-old Pavel at DAMU, the Drama University in Prague's Old Town, where, as one of the strike leaders, he sat in the administration room, wearing ragged brown corduroys and a battered woolen sweater. On a table in front of him, envelopes full of donations from around the country were piled up. "Look at all the money we've received to help us buy food and print banners," he said. "It's incredible, all this support." He told me how he had traveled to factories and farms around the country talking to workers and peasants. "I was afraid the workers would turn us away," he admitted. "Instead, they went on strike in support of us." And what about his parents? "They understand now," he reported. "They're even proud of me."

<u>Passions</u>

Chapter Eight

The Opposition: Change From Below

Do not think that this is socialism with a human face.
It is communism with a few teeth knocked out. He
has not been even more repressive because society
has not let him be more repressive.

*Adam Michnik, Polish opposition leader, on General
Wojciech Jaruzelski*

It was an inconspicuous gathering, far removed from the
throngs of striking workers or the masses in the streets that
would soon topple communism. A few dozen journalists met
in a small apartment in one of the nameless housing blocks that
make up the Polish capital. After the declaration of martial law
in 1981 and the banning of Solidarity, all had either resigned or
been fired from official communist newspapers. In the summer
of 1988 they were writing for the underground samizdat press.
Over shots of vodka, they drafted a declaration, announcing
the formation of a new independent association of Polish
journalists. Within two months it numbered 8,000 members.
"The regime can do whatever it wants," union leader Stefan
Bratkowski said afterwards. "We declared, 'We were, we are,
we will be.' "

A year later, Solidarity was governing Poland, and Bratkowski and his fellow journalists were running the major organs of
the Polish press. This amazing success did not come overnight
as a gift from Mikhail Gorbachev. It came after long years of
struggle, building up hundreds of independent organizations,
everything from the self-proclaimed journalists' union to a
private boy-scout group to a gay-rights movement. Slowly,
surely, these grassroots groups chiseled away at communist
power, exposing its immoral and unjust foundations until it
collapsed like a fragile house of cards.

Eastern Europeans call the chiseling process "Civil Society."
Civil Society was the opposition's central idea during the 1970s
and 1980s. It hypothesized a methodical, step-by-step process,

and fed off communism's failures. Problems from pollution to prostitution, which communists claimed existed only under capitalism, turned out to be just as bad, or worse, under communism, and somebody had to respond. Jiří Mueller, a Czechoslovak opposition activist, compared the process to what happens when a fire breaks out. People wait for a government fire engine. It doesn't arrive. One man begins taking buckets of water to try to extinguish the fire. "The authorities later jail him, saying he should have waited for orders," Mueller said. "Today, the fire was extinguished outside official control. Tomorrow, people ask what else must be done by themselves outside the official power?"

Civil Society enjoys a rich history in Western political thought, in the writings of Thomas Paine, John Locke, Alexis de Tocqueville and John Stuart Mill. It holds that society is distinct from government, and that government is but one of multiple institutions which form a strong democratic fabric. Paine, the French and American Revolutionary thinker, argued that a strong Civil Society was the only way to check a despotic paternalistic state. "Society is produced by our wants and government by our wickedness," he wrote in *Common Sense*. "The former promotes our happiness positively by uniting our affections, the latter negatively by restraining our vices."

Americans often find the concept of Civil Society difficult to grasp. My editors at the *Christian Science Monitor* refused to let me use the term. "No one understands what 'Civil Society' means," they insisted. On reflection, I realized that the problem was that Americans took Civil Society for granted. A multitude of voluntary organizations flourish in the United States. A century and a half ago, de Tocqueville wrote about how American Civil Society was always well developed while the American state remained weak:

> Americans of all ages, all conditions, and all dispositions constantly form associations. They have not only commercial and manufacturing companies, in which all take part, but associations of a thousand other kinds, religious, moral, serious, futile, general or restricted, enormous or diminutive. The Americans make associations to give entertainments, to found seminaries, to build inns, to construct churches, to diffuse books, to send missionaries to the antipodes.

In Eastern Europe the opposite was true. Communism aimed to control all social and cultural activities. The Party's leading role entitled it, in theory, to guide an individual's life from birth to death. One was born in a state-run hospital and buried in a state-run cemetery. In between, one attended a state-run nursery school, grammar school, high school, worked in a state-run factory or office, and socialized in a state-run club or café. Without the state's approval, one couldn't do anything. Independent action was scorned, considered unnecessary and dangerous.

While communists emphasized the collective will, oppositionists concentrated on the power of the individual. An independent journalists' union holds no special political significance in the American context. But in the Eastern European context, it became a dagger pointed at the communist heart. Bratkowski's journalists' union did not bother to ask for official approval. It just set up shop, began publishing a newsletter, paying benefits to banned writers, and daring the police to crack down. "Even if they put us all in jail," Bratkowski warned, "there would soon be replacements and we'd start again as soon as we were freed."

Eastern Europeans turned to Civil Society after realizing that traditional political activity was doomed to failure. In 1956 the Hungarians unleashed a violent popular revolution. Soviet tanks crushed it. In 1968 the Czechoslovaks unveiled a peaceful revolution from above. Soviet tanks again crushed it. In both cases, the West offered nice words, but no concrete aid. The lesson seemed clear: one could not count on foreign help, on meaningful change initiated from within a ruling Communist Party, or on change from a popular uprising. Violence was ruled out, for both pragmatic and ethical reasons. It offered little hope of emancipation and corrupted those who used it, leading to hatred, lies, torture, murder – the methods of the communists. A democratic society could be constructed only on the principle of non-violence. While the Czechs and Poles followed this prescription, Romanian revolutionaries did not and soon found themselves unable to control angry crowds.

If one person can be identified as the spiritual father of the strategy of social self-organization, it was Adam Michnik. Michnik is a curious, charismatic figure. He was born in 1946 in Warsaw to parents whom he describes as "Polish Communists of Jewish origin." His father spent time in prison for political activities in pre-war Poland. From his youth Michnik displayed an adversarial spirit. At fifteen he founded a political club which he called "Seekers of Contradictions." At eighteen he was arrested for the first time, for involvement in the writing and dissemination of a critical letter called "An Open Letter to the Party." From that day, his life turned into rounds of political activities alternating with prison terms.

Perhaps it is no coincidence that Michnik, a man of action who wields a powerful pen, suffers from a bad stammer. To speak, he concentrates all the muscles in his face until the words explode in rapid machine-gun-fire bursts. His words are bullets always full of biting, grating irony. He has a tremendous feel for the powerful phrase and the pungent image – like his unforgettable description of communist attempts at reform: "Do not think that this is socialism with a human face. It is communism with a few teeth knocked out."

In 1976, four years before Solidarity came into existence, Michnik wrote a seminal essay called "A New Evolutionism." The Polish political opposition was small and weak at the time. Michnik's genius was to recognize in the cracks the possibility of change. Had not Moscow and Warsaw already accepted such deviations from the Stalinist model as private farmers and an independent Church in order to produce some stability in Poland? Soviet troops could not be forced to leave Poland, but Soviet troops wouldn't stop a dozen Poles from meeting in an apartment to listen to an uncensored lecture on Polish history. The Polish Communist Party would not give up its leading role, but it might permit some workers to publish an independent newsletter. What if thousands of independent meetings were held, thousands of independent newsletters published? Moscow and Warsaw might find it better to accept such inconveniences than to try to crush them.

The conventional view held that the interests of the Soviet Union and those of Polish society were opposed. In his essay, Michnik came to the startling, different conclusion that "the interests of the Soviet political leadership, the Polish political leadership, and the Polish democratic opposition [are] basically concurrent." All wanted to avoid Soviet military intervention. For the Kremlin, intervention would mean a huge loss in political prestige around the world. For Warsaw's communists, it would mean the loss of its limited sovereignty. And, of course, the Polish opposition did not want to see its country occupied. The task ahead was to walk a fine balance. Do just enough to expand the limits of freedom. Don't do too much, which would provoke a crackdown. Society had to pressure the state to accept independent institutions. But it had to limit its demands and leave the state in communist hands. The opposition's ultimate

goal was no longer a "revolution," the overthrow of the government. It became "a new evolution."

The last question Michnik answered was how to organize a
force which would lead society along this delicate path. The
small Polish opposition was split between two major schools,
the lay left and the Catholic right. The lay left was composed
of people like Michnik himself, communists turned Social
Democrats, inspired by a vision of humane socialism. The
Catholic right had never succumbed to the lure of the socialist
Utopia. Deep mistrust marked the two groups. One was religious, one was secular. Here again, however, Michnik perceived a surprising congruence of interests. The old divisions
of left and right had already become irrelevant. Instead of
concentrating its fire against socialist atheists, instead of conducting "Jeremiads against 'Godless ones,' " Michnik observed
that the Church spent more time "quoting the Declaration of
Human Rights." His conclusion was simple and straightforward: because the two groups shared so much, they must
cooperate.

Michnik was soon acting on his own advice. He organized
and participated in an array of independent groups. Of them,
one stood out: the Workers' Defense Committee, KOR. In 1976,
price increases on basic food products sparked strikes in Radom
and Ursus. The government canceled the increases, but police
began detaining strike leaders and having others dismissed
from their jobs. KOR was formed to help those fired. The new
organization offered financial, legal and medical assistance to
workers and their families who had suffered in one way or
another. By Western standards, this represented social, not
political work. But in communist Poland, the police designated
KOR a subversive organization. Its members soon suffered the
repression against which they sought to defend the workers.
They lost their jobs. They were arrested. They were beaten. A
few even lost their lives.

At its inception in 1976, KOR consisted of only fifty-nine
members. It operated, for the most part, out of the Warsaw apartment of Jacek Kuroń, a longtime friend of Michnik and a
fellow activist. Located in the Żoliborz district of the Polish
capital, Kuroń's first-floor apartment door was always left open
and, like Václav Havel in Czechoslovakia, he did most of his
work over the telephone, assuming that the line was tapped.
KOR's operating philosophy was to act out in the open and tell
the truth. In a society swamped with lies, an organization
which told the truth held a special strength. An underground

conspiracy went against the organization's *raison d'être*. It spawned distrust. KOR instead aimed to nurture trust. It refused all state power, but hoped that its example of freedom would spread. "The long-range goal of KOR was to stimulate new centers of autonomous activity in a variety of areas and among a variety of social groups independent of KOR," observed Jan Józef Lipski in his history of the movement. "Not only did KOR agree to their independence, but it also wanted them to be independent."

In 1977, as a signal of its broader goal, KOR changed its name from Workers' Defense Committee to the Social Self-Defense Committee. It became involved in underground publishing. It offered support to private farmers, and it helped found the first Free Trade Union committees. KOR helped construct a bond between the isolated intellectuals and the isolated workers. It inspired Solidarity with its ideas of an "evolutionary reform" and "self-limiting revolution." In 1970 Lech Wałęsa and other striking workers burned down Communist Party buildings. KOR founder Jacek Kuroń now told them, "Don't burn down committees; found your own."

During Solidarity's first legal period in 1980–81, KOR veterans made up the intellectual heart of the worker movement. In September 1981, the members decided that KOR's role was being filled by Solidarity and voted the organization out of existence. Previous revolutions had tried to seize state power and use that power to accomplish certain goals. The Polish revolution of 1980 was "self-limiting": it did not aspire to state power, and rejected violence. Once again, Adam Michnik's personal contribution and example were crucial. In his book, Jan Józef Lipski records how Michnik helped save several policemen from being lynched by an angry crowd in the town of Otwock in May 1981. He won the crowd's confidence by declaring, "My name is Adam Michnik. I am an anti-socialist force."

The declaration of martial law in December 1981 did not mean the end of Solidarity or its parallel society. Although Wałęsa, Michnik and other leaders of the movement were arrested and jailed, the authorities could not arrest all Poles. They could not decree that people stop believing in Solidarity, that people stop acting as if Solidarity still existed. Solidarity's spiritual revolution continued. Poles ignored the communist state. They didn't believe its lies. Instead, they listened to Radio Free Europe and Voice of America, and among themselves they told the truth.

Underground, new leaders emerged to replace the jailed

ones. Actors produced skits in apartments, professors gave lectures on taboo subjects, and the country's best writers – people like Tadeusz Konwicki and Czesław Miłosz – shunned official publishers to offer their works to samizdat publishing houses. The underground Solidarity newspaper *Tygodnik Mazowsze* had print runs of about 50,000 copies and did not miss a single issue. In addition to these cultural projects, the underground sponsored KOR-like social activities. It organized election boycotts. It collected money for the families of those who were in jail or who had been fired for union activities. Even an underground insurance fund was created to replace automobiles confiscated from people accused of transporting unsanctioned publications.

Adam Michnik best described the paradoxical situation. After the declaration of martial law, he was imprisoned and held for more than two and a half years. Six months after his release, he was re-arrested, tried, convicted and given a sentence of three years. When he was freed again, I went to see him in his Warsaw apartment. He was in high spirits. While police with guns had been able to drive Solidarity off the streets, he believed they had failed to win the public support necessary to govern. "If martial law was a setback for the independent society," Michnik told me, "it was a disaster for the totalitarian state."

Inspired by Adam Michnik's and KOR's example Czechoslovaks founded Charter 77. Like KOR, Charter had no rules, statutes, permanent bodies or formal membership. It offered no program for political reform. In its inaugural declaration, dated January 1, 1977, the Charter described itself as "a free, informal and open community of people of different convictions, different faiths and different professions."

The Chartists came from a wider variety of ideological backgrounds than their Polish counterparts. At one end of the spectrum stood a colorful self-styled Trotskyite revolutionary Petr Uhl, along with former communists such as Jiří Hájek, Rudolf Slánský and Zdeněk Mlynář. Whereas left-leaning Poles such as Michnik had already made a decisive break with communism, their Czech counterparts had still not lost their belief in a socialist utopia. Often having wielded power – Hájek was Foreign Minister in 1968 – they were tempted by power again. Many were nicknamed "Tuesdayites" because they held their meetings on Tuesdays, or the "E-Club" because of their sympathies for Eurocommunism. The group disintegrated after Mlynář's forced emigration early in 1977, but resurfaced in 1988

161

under the name *Obroda* – Renewal. To this day, Petr Uhl, the self-proclaimed Trotskyite, continues to launch into enthusiastic speeches about the virtues of "class struggle" and fulminate against the danger of the "return of capitalism."

At the other end of the spectrum stood religious activists, both Protestants and Catholics, men such as priest Václav Malý and layman Václav Benda. These people were more interested in the Kingdom of God than the Kingdom of Man. Their influence was felt in Charter's stress on morality, ethics, and freedom of thought and action. Many of the religious Chartists were involved in the "underground Church." They scorned secular politics, considering it somehow unworthy and unimportant. After the revolution, Václav Malý turned down numerous offers to become an ambassador or a minister. Instead he chose to become a parish priest once again, taking up a new position in a small church in the Smíchov neighborhood of Prague. "My place is in the parish, not in politics," he told me.

One overriding goal united this diverse group: "respect for civic and human rights." Charter urged the involvement of citizens in guarding the rights outlined in the United Nations Universal Declaration of Human Rights and the Helsinki Final Act. After its founding, Charter expanded and diversified. Abroad, contacts were established with KOR. At home, informal working groups were established to investigate such issues as ecology and free labor unionism. Chartists were active in the underground classes, private concerts, exhibitions, theatrical performances and samizdat publications. Most important, a Committee for the Unjustly Persecuted, VONS, was formed to monitor and document specific cases of political persecution and imprisonment.

Repression was stiff. After VONS's creation, police arrested ten of the group's leaders, including Václav Havel, Petr Uhl, Václav Benda and Jiří Dienstbier, all of whom received long prison terms. Other Chartists were subjected to numerous police raids at home, detentions, loss of jobs and incessant pressure either to cease their Charter work or to emigrate. Through all the persecution, Charter continued to function. Although the number of its active supporters remained small, never totaling more than a few thousand individuals, the movement provided indispensable moral leadership.

When the number of unofficial groups began to swell in the late 1980s, Charter veterans gave advice and support. Martin Mějstřik and other student leaders entered politics when they helped organize the petition in March 1989 demanding Václav

Havel's freedom. Petr Uhl's cluttered, book-lined study always seemed packed with young firebrands. I met Hana Marvanová there. She had just been released from prison after leading the courageous demonstrations on the twentieth anniversary of the Soviet invasion in 1968. In her mid-twenties, she looked much younger. So courageous on the streets, she seemed timid and unsure of how to explain her actions to a foreigner. Uhl served as a father-figure. He translated her comments and then offered an analysis of the importance of her actions.

In November 1989, the nucleus of experienced Chartists guided the Civic Forum to power. They won genuine authority and respect. Students, artists, workers – all elements of society – looked to them for leadership. "While we were sleeping," one demonstrator told me, "they were fighting."

Elsewhere in Eastern Europe, the flame of Civil Society struggled to stay alight. Courageous individuals existed. The problem was that they remained isolated, failing to find a practical way of building up a parallel society, or even a secure island of freedom like KOR or Charter 77.

In the Balkans, much of the problem was rooted in the historical legacy of the Ottoman occupation. The Turks had trampled over the local élites, so, in contrast to the sophisticated Polish and Czech leaders, Romania and Bulgaria emerged from captivity as atomized societies. When I first visited Bucharest in 1986, only two dissidents dared speak with me. One was a tall, gaunt Peasant Party activist named Ion Puiu. Before World War II, Puiu was the party's youth leader. In 1946 he won a parliamentary seat. The next spring the authorities arrested the leaders and banned the party. Taken into custody and tried for treason, Puiu spent fifteen years in prison, and after his release he lived under constant police surveillance.

The other dissident was Mihai Botez, a bearded computer scientist and human-rights activist. Botez criticized the emigration of many of his fellow dissidents. "When we face persecution and leave for the West, the government can say we only wanted better living conditions on the other side," he said. "If a thousand of us would stay and stick together, it would have an impact." This goal proved impossible. Unlike the Polish and Czechoslovak opposition activists who overcame ideological splits, Botez denounced Puiu and the Peasant Party veterans as dangerous nationalists. He himself was a Western liberal. In 1966, at the age of twenty-seven, he earned a doctorate in mathematics. A computer specialist, he introduced himself as "an IBM man." Under persistent police repression, he cracked. At the beginning of 1987, plainclothes police beat him while he was walking in the street; he ended up in hospital. After that he decided to take a fellowship at the Smithsonian Institution in Washington. He now lives in California, where he holds a professorship at Stanford University.

Puiu remained in Bucharest. On the second day of the revolution in December 1989, his police guards vanished into the night and he was able to leave his apartment. He refused membership of the new National Salvation Front, disgusted that its leadership was dominated by former communists. Instead he began reviving the old Peasant Party. "For Ceausescu, two plus two equaled seven; for the communists in the Front, two plus two equals five," he said. "I will only accept two plus two equaling four."

His battle for truth represented an uphill struggle. After Ceausescu's downfall, a dozen or so new parties sprouted up. All had weak foundations. The new Green Party, operating out of the apartment of one of its founders, counted fewer than 100 members. Puiu's Peasant Party could at least draw on roots extending back to pre-war Romania. During the long communist nightmare, he had managed to keep the party's ideas alive by sending an occasional paper to be broadcast by Radio Free Europe. "I heard about Mr. Puiu from the radio and was impressed by his courage," said twenty-seven-year-old Radu Auer, leader of the party's youth branch. "But when I tried to visit him at his apartment, the police stopped me."

Of all the opposition parties, the Peasants were the first to acquire office space and telephones. A nineteenth-century baroque building, which the deposed communists had used for receptions, served as headquarters. When I visited in January 1990, the offices were bare, without typewriters, copiers, or any of the other materials associated with running a campaign. To make copies, party officials went around the block to the Ministry of Agriculture. They still had no access to state-run radio or television. And though the Peasants planned to start their own paper, they had not determined how they would find the necessary newsprint, hire the reporters and provide for distribution.

Puiu himself was named party vice chairman in January 1990. Aged seventy, he remained a vigorous man, with a sharply angled face and a shock of white hair. For him the most important issue was no longer democracy. It was the return to Romanian control of the Soviet province of Moldavia, detached during

World War II. "Moldavia is an open wound," he said. "It comes before democracy, before economic prosperity; it comes before everything." The cries of Romanian nationalism were drowning out the demands of democracy.

In Bulgaria, overt opposition emerged only towards the end of Todor Zhivkov's long reign when a group of restless communist intellectuals, inspired by the Soviet Union, gathered together in 1988 to form the Glasnost Club. Before, opposition activities had been localized in the northern border region of Ruse, where residents protested against pollution coming from nearby Romanian factories. The Glasnost Club represented a more general challenge. Unlike KOR or Charter 77, however, it did not base itself on independence from the state authorities; rather, it hoped to influence fellow communists to follow the Soviet lead. "Mikhail Gorbachev and Andrei Sakharov, they are our heroes," Alexei Sheludko, one of the group's leaders explained. "They inspired us."

Sheludko is a genial, white-haired, sixty-nine-year-old. A chemist of international repute, he heads Sofia University's Chemistry Department and lives in a beautiful, book-lined apartment, decorated with photographs of Einstein and scientific diplomas and full of beautiful, well-preserved pre-war furniture. He speaks fluent French. Over a cup of tea, he told his personal history. He joined the Party in 1941 and was active in the resistance during the war. After the communist takeover he kept silent despite his misgivings about the course of events. "I was frightened," he admitted, pointing to his comfortable apartment. "I had a family to feed; I didn't want to lose all this."

Gorbachev's arrival gave him new-found courage. Although police harassed leaders of the Glasnost Club after its founding, the group soon gained an international following. Chaloudakov and others met with the French President François Mitterrand. At home they gained less support, by the beginning of 1990 counting only a few hundred members. They preached a policy of slow, steady steps and supported the "reformist" line of the new Bulgarian communist leader Petar Mladenov. Their goal was a type of "socialism with a human face." Chaloudakov himself was considering running for Parliament as a communist. "Why shouldn't I run as a Communist Party candidate if I want to?" he asked. "Communists can be liberal too."

A young, more radical democratic opposition pushed for a more dramatic break. Unlike in Poland or Czechoslovakia, the fundamental ideological split between the younger Bulgarian radical opposition activists and the older communist reformers could not be bridged. Men such as Konstantin Trenchev, the thirty-five-year-old head of the Union of Democratic Forces, feared that "deals with the communists would sap the opposition's credibility." Of all the Bulgarian opposition leaders, Trenchev was the most impressive. Educated at a French *lycée* in Algiers, trained as a medical doctor, he became frustrated with the bureaucracy and backwardness of his hospital working conditions. "I realized that my personal problems came from the general problems of a totalitarian society," he said. The realization led him to found the Association for Human Rights at the end of 1988. He received telephone and letter threats. In the summer of 1989, police arrested him. After Zhivkov's fall, the communists asked him to negotiate a transition to democracy. Whereas in Poland and Czechoslovakia, Michnik and Havel entered into similar negotiations with supreme self-confidence, Trenchev hesitated. "The communists want us to join them to reform the economy right away," he says. "But there is no reason to give them free legitimacy."

Like the weak, incoherent Bulgarian opposition, the East German opposition experienced difficulties in building a strong, solid identity. Here again, perhaps success came too suddenly. Only a few months before the Wall came down, a few dozen artists and scientists gathered in a second-floor apartment of a once-fine pre-war building on Fehrbellinerstrasse in East Berlin. In February 1989, I first visited the place where East Germany's revolution began. The cobblestone street was shared by crumbling buildings, a dying park and vacant lots of rubble. Outside number 91, much of the ornate stone façade had fallen away. Inside, the floors sagged and paint flaked. Art posters and slick fasion advertisements were pasted on the stairwell walls. This was the home of sculptress-turned-political dissident Bäebel Böhley, the forty-four-year-old founder of the opposition group New Forum.

Böhley showed me into her large book-lined living room, decorated with abstract paintings, and then offered a cup of tea in her spartan kitchen. Her short, sandy hair was uncombed and she was dressed like the typical bohemian artist – all in black: black jeans and a black turtleneck. She smoked cigarette after cigarette. "People here are angrier than you think," she said. "They want to travel. They want freedom."

Along with many of her fellow New Forum leaders, Böhley

was drawn into dissidence by the deployment of American Pershing and Soviet SS-20 missiles in Germany at the beginning of the 1980s. She said she wasn't interested in politics; she was interested in "peace." From this perspective, she sounded much like Michnik or Havel; instead of battling for a concrete conventional political program, she was fighting for a moral cause. Like her Polish and Czech counterparts, she focused her energies on a concrete issue: missiles. The Americans and Russians should not point missiles at defenseless Germans. Becoming a spokeswoman for the East German Peace Movement, she appeared in churches, distributed petitions and sent them to Communist Party chief Erich Honecker. The regime didn't listen. It went ahead and deployed the SS-20s.

In January 1988 Böhley and six others helped find legal aid for some protesters who had been arrested at a demonstration in memory of the communist martyr Rosa Luxemburg. Again she was arrested, charged with "treasonable relationships," and given a choice: either she left the country or she could stay in prison for ten years. She chose to leave.

All Eastern Bloc regimes resorted to emigration in an attempt to decapitate opposition movements. In East Germany, the offer held a special power because of West Germany. Both Adam Michnik and Václav Havel refused free passage to the West. Neither could travel to a prosperous country next door which spoke the same language and shared the same culture and immediate citizenship. East Germans could. Every time the East German opposition gained a critical mass, it was defused by defections to the West. In the mid-1970s many of East Germany's most promising artists – men such as the singer Wolfgang Biermann, writer Rainer Kunze and actor Manfred Krug – were deprived of their citizenship and forced to leave. In the late 1980s the regime once again moved to silence the peace activists by forcing them into exile in West Germany.

For six months Böhley lived in West Germany and England. Although many of her friends were doing anything possible to leave East Germany for good, she wanted to go home. Eventually the government conceded, and after her return New Forum organized momentous mass demonstrations which set in motion a remarkable revolution. In December 1989 I was surprised to find Böhley and other opposition leaders downhearted and demoralized. At the very moment when the opposition should have been cheering, it was fragmenting into a noisy clash of competing factions. Many of the best activists had already left for the West. The hard work of political organizing bedeviled those who remained. At Böhley's apartment, I left a message. She didn't respond. I began searching for New Forum's office. In Prague, Civic Forum had set up headquarters centrally, in Wenceslas Square. In Warsaw, Solidarity occupied an entire building right next to the official press agency. But in Berlin, New Forum seemed invisible. None of my fellow journalists had the group's address or telephone number. Only after two days of searching did I locate its headquarters, up on the second floor of a nondescript office building. There I found Böhley. She looked terrible, her high cheekbones drooping under the weight of visible fatigue, her supple artistic body sagging. At our first meeting she had impressed me as a large woman; suddenly she seemed so small. "No, no!" she screamed in horror when she spotted me. "No more journalists, no more journalists." With that, she rushed out of the door.

The opening of the Wall had deprived the opposition of its best issue. New Forum couldn't decide whether to turn itself into a political party, or how much to cooperate with the existing system. Böhley resisted all connection to the system. Political parties tied to rich West Germany – the Christian Democrats and Free Democrats among others – rushed to fill the vacuum. Böhley opposed reunification with West Germany. "Being swallowed by the West, that's selling out," she had told me. "We want a democratic socialism." Such a Third Way enjoyed limited appeal among average East Germans. Bäerbel Böhley, the woman who could have been the East German Adam Michnik or Václav Havel, became an unpopular figure. The mass of East Germans didn't understand what she meant by a Third Way between communism and capitalism. They wanted unification and that's what they would get. In March 1990, when New Forum did put up candidates in the East German elections, they won few votes. "Who wants to listen to all those artists?" a Leipzig marcher asked himself. "Not me."

Isolation and inexperience, so fatal for the East German opposition, also plagued Hungary's opposition. In the wake of the blood-soaked tragedy of 1956, Hungarian Civil Society was crushed. The Kádárist regime which emerged from the ruins co-opted intellectuals by offering relative freedom and dealt with dissidents through sackings rather than prison. Economic reform satisfied stomachs. Political reform meant that, unlike anywhere else in the Soviet Bloc, for a long time Hungarians were able to consider themselves members of the "opposition" and maintain strong links to the "official" world. When I went to interview Tamás Bauer, a dissident economist, we met in his office at the Academy of Sciences. Solidarity posters hung on the wall. "Oh, yes," Bauer explained when I looked amazed. "That's acceptable here."

Lulled by this tolerance, no Polish-style opposition strategy developed. Hungary's closest counterpart to Adam Michnik, I think, is the writer György Konrád, author of the acclaimed book *Antipolitics*. As with Michnik, Konrád's works were banned in his homeland for many years. But he was never imprisoned and was always free to visit the West. Where Michnik wrote in bursts of rage, Konrád pondered in quiet contemplation; where Michnik rasped, Konrád soothed. *Antipolitics* is a political description, not a political prescription. Reviewing Czechoslovakia's sad failure of 1968 and Poland's 1981 martial law, Konrád drew the lesson that gradual, step-by-step change from below could not liberate his country. "The best we can hope to achieve," he wrote," "is an enlightened, paternalistic authoritarianism, accompanied by a measured willingness to undertake gradual liberal reforms." *Antipolitics* was written during the immediate aftermath of martial law in Poland and contained a direct lesson for Adam Michnik, then in prison. " 'Be careful,' I said to Adam," Konrád recalled. " 'The third time around it has to work.' It didn't. Adam is awaiting trial."

Michnik, of course, never considered Solidarity a failure or martial law a fatal defeat. When Jaruzelski offered Poland a "Kádárist" bargain, he refused it with contempt. Some Hungarians showed similar spunk, refusing all compromises. Most prominent among these "refuseniks" was Miklós Haraszti. After writing *Worker in a Worker's State*, he penned a new book which described his country as "the Velvet Prison." He, for one, wouldn't accept living in any prison. Ironically, Konrád and Haraszti are good friends, even though their temperaments are different. A slim, boyish man, with dark eyes and black hair, even today in his mid-forties Haraszti resembles a student activist. His movements are quick, tense. "You might take him for a reckless driver," Konrád once commented. "But he isn't. His grimaces are masterly; not even his best sentences can convey what his facial expressions and rakish, conspiratorial side-glances can."

Haraszti worked hard to promote independent samizdat publications; he also built links with nascent religious, ecological and pacifist opposition movements. But unlike his Polish and Czechoslovak counterparts, he failed to bridge the ideological chasm dividing the oppositionists. In Hungary that divide was between "populists" and "urbanists." The populists were nationalists who celebrated the virtues of Hungarian village life and promoted a Hungarian Third Way between East and West. The urbanists concentrated on human rights; like Haraszti, they were often Jewish and looked to Vienna and the West for a model. For the populists, the key issue was the fate of the Hungarian minorities in Yugoslavia, Slovakia and, above all, Transylvania. For the urbanists, the great issue was democracy. For the populists, cooperation with reform communists was possible, even desirable, and contacts were opened with Imre Pozsgay. For the urbanists, such cooperation represented treason.

In the late 1980s, the twilight of the Kádár era, a small flowering of Civil Society took place. Debating clubs, lobbies of various interest groups, foundations, formed. Pacifists pressed for the right of conscientious objection. Ecologists urged the end to construction of a dam over the Danube. Feminists fought for their rights. So did homosexuals and lesbians. "Everybody's just getting together and saying they are a club," said Mihály Horvath, founder of a discussion group dubbed called the Rakpart Klub. A "Network of Free Initiatives" was launched in 1988. I attended its inauguration and found a conscious attempt to emulate Solidarity.

Within a few months, however, the Network collapsed. Arguments between urbanists and populists proved too strong. Each group instead decided to fight for political power. The urbanists formed the Free Democrat Party. The populists coalesced into the Democratic Forum. An ugly dispute erupted between the two in November 1989 when they took opposing sides in a referendum on the method and timing of picking a President. The Free Democrats accused the Forum of anti-Semitism and ultra-nationalism. The Forum responded with charges of McCarthyism.

Besides the Free Democrats and the Democratic Forum, more than fifty parties emerged. On my most recent visit to Hungary, I went out on the campaign trail with Miklós Haraszti and found him, formerly an incorrigible optimist, pessimistic. For years he had campaigned for democracy. Now he was campaigning for power. Every weekend he toured a section of the countryside holding campaign meetings for local candidates. "Practical politics means becoming less idealistic," he said. "The first meeting is exciting, the second one less exciting. You must try not to lose your enthusiasm."

When Eastern Europe's communist rulers accepted the principle of a multi-party state, the need to create conventional standard political parties replaced the slow, step-by-step construction of Civil Society. The opposition assumed power. People who were conditioned to think only of what they didn't want now had to think in terms of what they wanted. They could no longer just be against. They had to be "for" something. Civil Society was a product of living in defeat. A new political structure and strategy were needed to manage victory.

The more developed its Civil Society, the better able a country was to manage the democratic transition. Squabbles between Hungary's numerous opposition parties reflected the immaturity of its independent community. Civil Society also remained weak in East Germany, Romania and Bulgaria, where the possibility for instability and violence was greatest. By contrast, the Polish and Czechoslovak oppositions, with years of grassroots experience, best managed to fill the power vacuum.

Appropriately, Civil Society's champions, Adam Michnik and Václav Havel, led the democratic transformation. After Solidarity swept the parliamentary elections, Michnik came up with the winning compromise formula: "Your President, our Prime Minister." Communist Wojciech Jaruzelski became President and Solidarity adviser Tadeusz Mazowiecki became Prime Minister. In Czechoslovakia, Havel announced at first that Civic Forum "does not aspire to any ministerial post." When the communists named a Party-dominated government, he changed his mind. The Forum forced a decent government on the communists and Havel himself acceded to popular demand by becoming President.

Both Solidarity and Civic Forum leaders expected their organizations to split and fall apart in the coming years. The range of opinions under the umbrella of their groups was too broad for more than a minimalist consensus. But these were men who had fought and suffered together for long years, and power is a potent glue. Once in office, it may be hard for them to give it up. Eight months into government, polls showed Solidarity still winning 80 per cent of the vote. Some twenty political parties had emerged in Poland, but none enjoyed more than one per cent of support. I talked to Jan Józef Lipski who had tried to rebuild the old Social Democrat Party. After he managed to recruit only a few dozen members, he gave up and returned to his old place within Solidarity. "The communists ruined all chances for new parties," he theorized. "People don't relate to ideology any more – any ideology."

The task ahead was to make sure that broad democratic movements such as Solidarity and Civic Forum, with their immense popular power, did not turn into new tyrannies and drown out infant democracy. In Czechoslovakia Civic Forum ruled almost uncontested for a while, making me reflect once again on Havel's famous story about the greengrocer. Today, that greengrocer's window probably displays a photograph of Václav Havel.

Despite all the dangers, I could not help feeling a surge of admiration for the budding Eastern European politicians. Western advisers flooded into Eastern Europe, teaching Western campaign techniques, polling techniques and advertising campaigns. To my mind, they could have learned much from the Eastern Europeans about the real meaning of politics. To Eastern Europeans, politics wasn't just about sound bites and statistics, about cutting up the pie, laying sewers and distributing social benefits. It was about the big questions, democracy or dictatorship, freedom or oppression. It was, above all, about morality.

Descriptions of left and right, conservative and liberal, didn't fit Solidarity or Civic Forum. "The question about socialism and capitalism gives me a sense of emerging from the depths of the last century," Václav Havel said. "These thoroughly ideological and many times mystified categories have long since been beside the point." In place of this outdated division of left and right, Havel and Michnik proposed a return to the more Judeo-Christian division between right and wrong, truth and lies. By expressing these moral imperatives through Civil Society, the Eastern Europeans constructed an ethical revolution, a "Revolution of Truth." Although no one could be sure that they would build effective democracies, they sent a clear signal of what they hoped to build by seizing power, without violence and without revenge.

After the Solidarity election victory in June 1989, I went to see Adam Michnik at the offices of *Gazeta Wyborcza*, the Solidarity newspaper which he edits. He was in high spirits. "It's a knockout," he said with a big smile. The eternal dissident was looking forward to entering Parliament as a deputy. He, the longtime prisoner, would soon be traveling around the world with a diplomatic passport. Michnik insisted that Eastern Europe's revolution must be different from all previous revolutions. No Bastilles would be stormed, because history teaches that those who start by storming Bastilles end up building their own. "Either we continue along an evolutionary path toward parliamentary democracy," he said, "or we will become a Romania in economics, a Romania in politics – and an Afghanistan on the streets."

When violence in Romania proved him right, I thought back to Michnik's prescient words. Fatalists had assumed that the communist stranglehold over Eastern Europe could never be broken. Now pessimists were saying that a rocky road to democracy lay ahead. But the new challenge did not scare Michnik. It excited him.

Chapter Nine

The Spirit: A Religious Revival

We want God, we want God, we want God in the
family circle, we want God in books, in schools, we
want God in government orders, we want God, we
want God . . .

Poles to Pope John Paul II

The pews in the baroque St. Nikolai Church were overflowing.
People stood in the aisles and outside the front door in the
church courtyard. For years, St. Nikolai in Leipzig, East Germany, had held "peace prayers" on Monday afternoons at 5
p.m. The services attracted all types of independent-minded
individuals. Some of the faithful weren't religious. "We come
to the church to get information," admitted a middle-aged
woman, a self-professed atheist. Throughout the turbulent year
of 1989, the crowds at St. Nikolai kept growing. On this cold
December day the congregation seemed formed of the entire
city. Everyone hushed as the pastor read from the Bible. With
understated emotion, he praised God and advised, "Go in
peace." The crowd streamed out on to Karl-Marx Platz to begin
another huge Monday night demonstration.

Across Eastern Europe, the Church played a front-line role
in the revolution. More than any other single activity of Civil
Society, it chiseled away at communist power. The battle for
religious freedom mobilized masses, and parishes such as St.
Nikolai provided the shelter, working space and moral authority
that protest groups needed to topple hardline communist
regimes. Priests and pastors offered invaluable leadership in
societies which had few other opportunities to nurture authentic leaders. Catholic lay leader Tadeusz Mazowiecki became
Poland's first non-communist Prime Minister, Lutheran Pastor
Rainer Eppelmann founded East Germany's Democratic Awakening Party and Czech priest Václav Malý became one of Civic
Forum's top leaders.

Sometimes, the region's patchwork of Roman Catholic, Protestant and Eastern Orthodox faiths blurred the Church's revolutionary role. The Polish and Slovak Churches had long served as the repository for Polish and Slovak patriotism, but the Bulgarian and Romanian Orthodox establishments followed the old Byzantine tradition of subservience to the state. The Czech and Hungarian Churches suffered from their historic identification with Austrian Hapsburg oppression. Post-war Poland was almost 100 per cent Roman Catholic, but Protestants represented a majority in East Germany and significant minorities in Czechoslovakia, Hungary, Romania and Bulgaria.

One common thread connected these different denominations: their people's need for a spiritual alternative to exhausted communism. In the 1950s Marxist state ideology was preached with the fervor of a religion. But by the 1980s it had turned into an empty shell, practiced only by cynical careerists. Wherever I traveled, Church officials emphasized that Marxism offered few answers to pressing personal questions, from mending a broken marriage to the meaning of death. Some Eastern Europeans found refuge in rock music or drugs. Others found religion. "Marxism is just a method," insisted Tamás Nyiri of the Hungarian Roman Catholic Episcopate. "The Church offers salvation."

Throughout the region, churches are crowded and pilgrimages attract thousands, even in the traditionally atheist, free-thinking Czech lands. Young believers have gravitated towards dynamic new spiritual forms, informal prayer groups called "base communities." Submissive Church hierarchies come under pressure from dissident churchmen. Fundamentalist Protestant sects such as Baptists, Pentecostalists, Adventists and Jehovah's Witnesses have became more active. "There are at least twenty sects trying to establish themselves in Budapest," reported Hungarian Pastor Gábor Iványi, who fought for more than a decade to legalize his Methodist congregation. "Many young people are joining."

Under communism, the religious were often forced underground to preserve their faith. I'll never forget going to a darkened Prague apartment, where a few spare candles flickered over a small wooden crucifix. The faithful, ranging in age from two to sixty, knelt. They prayed. They swayed. They chanted. The gathering was illegal because it was not sponsored by the state. Each member of the congregation faced up to two years in prison. Despite the risk, such clandestine churches flourished, ordaining priests, publishing independent newsletters and religious literature, and holding private Masses in apartments. "The state-sponsored churches simply don't satisfy many people," Jiří Kaplan, the meeting's leader, told me. "They want something more spontaneous, more informal, more free."

After the war, the new communist governments put the churches under their tutelage. Religious schools were closed, monastic orders dissolved, and Church leaders such as Hungarian Cardinal Jozsef Mindszenty and Polish Primate Stefan Wyszyński were imprisoned. The communists established Religious Affairs Offices to regulate Church affairs. The Religious Affairs Office had to give its approval before a bishop or priest could be named, or a denomination awarded legal permission to practice. Repression eased only after Stalin's death.

Over the years, many communists and churchmen reached a *modus vivendi*. As long as the churchmen accepted the validity of the communist regime, believers were allowed freedom to practice their faith. Approved churchmen even received generous financial support from the state.

The bargain achieved mixed results. While persecution persisted in hardline Czechoslovakia, religious tolerance flourished in Hungary. A Hungarian could receive catechism and follow religious correspondence courses without any fear of retaliation at his workplace. "You can go to church," said László Pai of the Hungarian Religous Affairs Office, "and be a good socialist."

Some communists even began to view religion as a useful weapon in their fight against social ills. In a plush Budapest hotel I watched communist officials from five Soviet Bloc countries meet with Catholic officials. The two sides found common ground on certain ethical values such as honesty, civic duty and the fight against alcoholism. "Religion is a moral substitute for many Hungarians," explained Mr. Pai.

This Church–communist cooperation always remained a fragile balancing act, with religious activists pushing the limits of the acceptable. In Hungary, György Bulányi, a silver-haired, charismatic priest at odds with the timorous Hungarian Church hierarchy, proclaimed military service to be incompatible with the message of Jesus. During the 1950s he had spent nine years in prison. In 1985 his own Church leaders had suspended him from celebrating Mass. "The atheist state wants to control what we teach," Bulányi told me. "My hierarchy should not cooperate."

In a Bucharest suburb in the winter of 1986, I stood with Baptist Pastor Buni Coca in the rubble of his bulldozed Church of Hope. After years of unsuccessful attempts to receive a building permit, Pastor Coca began building his church. The authorities warned him three times. His Baptist superiors disavowed him. "What Brother Buni did was illegal and not good sense," said Vasile Talpos, General Secretary of the Romanian Baptist Union. Coca kept on building regardless, supported by his congregation. "Soldiers blocked off the street, dragged us out of here and knocked it all down," he reported. "Is this religious freedom?"

Of all Eastern European churches, the Polish Roman Catholic Church was the most vigorous and active. Throughout Poland's many foreign occupations, the Church served as a sanctuary for nationhood, language and culture against the occupying Russian Orthodox and the Prussian Protestants. When Solidarity shriveled after the 1981 declaration of martial law, the Church stepped in. Weeks of Christian Culture were organized, featuring uncensored letters, plays, poetry readings and art exhibitions. Lectures by Catholic or dissident intellectuals ranged from ethics and history to independent reports on the economy and the political situation. "We now talk of the 'official' Poland and the 'real' Poland," noted Stanisław Stomma, director of a Warsaw-based Christian Democratic debating club. "The place where you find the 'real' Poland is inside the Church."

To get a feel for the Church's grassroots impact, I spent a weekend in 1988 with Father Stanisław Waszyński at his St. Wojciech Church in Konin, a small industrial town of 75,000 people in the center of Poland. When I arrived on Saturday morning, children in immaculate khaki uniforms were lining up in front of the church. They looked like Communist Young Pioneers – except for one crucial detail. Each wore a crucifix. They were assembled on this cloudy morning to pray for a martyred priest, hanged by Russian troops for smuggling arms to rebels during the 1863 popular uprising against the Tsarist occupation. Official Polish history books mentioned neither the martyred priest nor the rebellion, in order not to offend the Soviets. "We try to teach real history," Father Waszyński explained. "The Young Pioneers pledge 'to serve socialist Poland,' whereas Church scouts proudly declare that they 'honestly want to serve God and Poland.' "

Scouting represented just one small part of Father Stanisław's activities. Each day, he rose at 5.30 a.m. and retired after midnight. Besides running the parish and his clergy – six priests and eight nuns – he served as publisher for an independent newspaper, sponsored art exhibitions – including one for art created in prison under martial law – and ran a video movie theater. He even directed a summer camp for parish children. No financial support came from the state. Everything was paid for by parishioners, who made donations and volunteered their labor. Appreciative parishioners called their beloved priest "Stash." His voice was calm and comforting. At the age of forty-nine, wisps of gray ran through his hair. Steely gray eyes revealed a rare determination. "Father Stanisław has turned his church into the most powerful force in Konin," said Antonin Pominski, a Catholic journalist from nearby Włocławek. "He is the ideal parish priest."

Stanisław Waszyński was sixteen when he decided to enter the seminary. The year was 1954. Stalin had died the year before, but Stalinist Terror still reigned in Poland, with its atmosphere of fear, its show trials, its forced industrialization, its forced collectivization of farmers, its attacks against the Church and its persecution of priests. Stanisław's father ran a delicatessen in Sieradz, a village near Łódź, and both parents were religious and nationalistic. "There was no radio, no television," he said. "Friends would come over and tell us stories, about history, about the last war, about the uprising. I would sit under the table, listening."

When Stanisław declared he wanted to enter the priesthood, his parents and most of his schoolmates understood his decision. But his communist teachers warned him of dire consequences for the future. Even after he arrived at the seminary in Włocławek, one of 120 students, he was drafted into the army. For two long years he suffered through harsh training. "By drafting priests, the authorities wanted to draw people back from the ministry," he told me. "The effect was the opposite. More people came back to the seminary than they took into the army."

By the time he arrived in Konin in 1965, the rural community had been transformed by the exploitation of a coal mine and the construction of a steel mill in the 1950s. Peasants from the surrounding farms left the land and came to find work in the new industries. Rows of cement apartments rose to house them, yet there was no church. "This was supposed to be a socialist town, a new town, so churches weren't included in the plans," he recalled. "There were 20,000 people in the housing project when I arrived and no church."

Father Stanisław said Mass and held religious classes in a rented room in a pensioner's apartment. Crowds soon overwhelmed the restricted space, but when he demanded a building permit to construct a new church, the authorities refused. He applied the only pressure he could: on September 13, 1969, he began holding huge open-air Masses. Thousands attended. The authorities refused to budge, and when he and his parishioners constructed a temporary altar, police toughs destroyed it. The open-air Masses grew larger and larger. Finally, on September 5, 1970, the authorities gave permission to build a new church.

The battle was still far from won. Over the next three years, the young priest recruited volunteers to draw up architectural plans, to procure building materials and to organize construction shifts. Slowly but surely, the future church took shape. In contrast to the gray and grimy apartment blocks, it turned out to be a soaring structure, large enough to seat several thousand under its glittering, burnished copper roof. Its name: St. Maximilian's, after Maximilian Kolbe, the priest who sacrificed himself for a fellow prisoner at Auschwitz. St. Maximilian's opened in 1980. But before it was finished, Father Waszyński was transferred to the small village of Kalisz. "St. Paul says that one man plants, one waters and God makes things grow," he said. "My duty was to move on."

Konin remained close to his heart, and he was posted back there in July 1982. On his return, he found residents facing one of their toughest trials. The year before, martial law had been declared and Solidarity outlawed. Like other industrial towns, Konin had been a Solidarity stronghold. Many workers languished in jail, with their families hungry, desolate. Father Stanisław comforted the families and distributed contributions sent by Western Church organizations. Martial law had silenced millions of Poles, but Father Stanisław kept speaking out. The continued detention of his parishioners inspired him to create a monthly "Mass for the Homeland." The practice, begun by soon-to-be-martyred priest Father Jerzy Popiełuszko, proved as popular in Konin as in Popiełuzsko's Warsaw parish. To this day, on the last Sunday of the month parishioners flock to pray for all victims of the regime. I was in Konin on one such Sunday. From the pulpit, I heard Father Stanisław intone the milestones of Polish history: the 1830 and 1863 uprisings, the nation's recovery of independence in 1918, Solidarity's legal registration in 1980. "To love the Fatherland," he told me afterwards, "we must know its history properly."

After their release from prison, pro-Solidarity journalists, fired from the official Konin newspaper, asked Father Stanisław if he would let them start a parish periodical. The first edition of the bi-weekly *God Bless You* soon appeared. When the authorities tried to stop publication by refusing permission to print copies, Father Stanisław maneuvered around the ban by posting a single copy outside the church, where worshippers could look at the paper before or after Mass. "We still wanted to write the truth," said Krzysztof Dobrecki, the editor-in-chief. "The only place to do that was at the church."

Father Stanisław walked a tightrope between parishioners who wanted him to speak out and government which pressurized him to remain silent. When activists wanted to erect a memorial to Jerzy Popiełuszko, he agreed. But the activists approved an inscription proclaiming that Popiełuszko was "murdered by secret police." They also quoted Solidarity leader Lech Wałeşa and intended a shrine for the then banned union. Father Stanisław urged them instead to emphasize Popiełuzsko as "the martyr-priest" and insisted on an inscription with a reflective psalm, reading "The souls of the just rest in the hands of God." "I wanted something that would inspire love, not hatred," he explained. "Father Stanisław didn't come and order us, 'No,' " recalled Slawomir Czekowski, founder of the Fraternity for Father Popiełuszko. "He merely proposed a different text and told us to choose." In the end, Father Stanisław's version was chosen.

Pressures to stay quiet came not just from the communist authorities but also from the Church hierarchy led by the Primate of Poland, Józef, Cardinal Glemp. Glemp never warmed to the work by activist priests such as Father Stanisław. His priority was to preserve Church–state dialogue, not the spirit of Solidarity. In his opinion, an accommodating approach represented the only path to social peace. Cardinal Glemp ordered priests "not to deal in politics" and removed those he felt disobeyed him to remote parishes. The weekend I was in Konin, a Church official visited to check up. After reading the parish newspaper, meeting with leaders of the cultural club and talking to the scouts, he went away worried. "These social activities should not be primary," he warned Father Stanisław. "God should come first."

Against Glemp and the conservatives, Father Stanisław looked for support in the words and actions of the Polish Pope, John Paul II. On each of his three visits to his homeland, John Paul spoke out in support of God-given human rights of all Poles, believers and non-believers. "It is the clergy's duty," the Pope declared, "to defend the workers' interests against hasty and ill-considered government measures." To Father Stanisław, the Pope's words meant that the fate of the Church and its people could not be separated. As I left Konin, he told me, "I've had fights with the authorities, fights with my Church superiors, hard fights, long fights, about the new church, about the scouts, and I always tell them the same thing: 'I do what I do for the good of this country and its youth and the future of Polish freedom.' "

The election of Karol Wojtyła, Archbishop of Kraków, as the first Eastern European Pope galvanized many believers. His tumultuous visit to Poland in 1979 contributed to the emergence of Solidarity, and his subsequent visits increased the Church's already mighty power in the country. In his person, he nurtured hope and perseverance. I'll never forget watching a million pilgrims from all over Poland sway to the Pope's words in Warsaw, Gdańsk and Kraków. The crowds gathered hours in advance. Entire families came. Parents hoisted toddlers above their shoulders. Grandparents leaned on their children. Many cried. "I count on you, my Father," they chanted rhythmically. "I have confidence in you." For other Eastern European Roman Catholics – and a surprising number of Protestants too – the Pope conveyed the comfort and inspiration of a weighty ally in Rome. His emphasis on freedom inspired simple devout individuals to become heroes.

One such hero was Moravian peasant Augustin Navrátil, who organized a massive petition drive for religious freedom in 1988. Of all the stories I reported in Eastern Europe, Navrátil's moved me the most. His home village, Lutopečny, five hours by car east of Prague, ninety minutes east of Brno, consisted of one dirt road, 120 plain brick houses, and a single spare one-room railway station. I met Navrátil in the station, where he worked as a switchman. He told me that in his spare time he cultivated two acres of land and cared for two cows. A short, stocky figure with big, calloused hands, his intense gaze, mighty handshake and rapid-fire passionate speech suggested an iron will.

Alone, in 1987 this peasant Navrátil penned a thirty-one-point petition demanding greater religious freedom and mailed it to Roman Catholics around the country. He didn't expect much reaction – but four months later more than 500,000 people had signed. It was the most dramatic protest against the communist regime since the Soviet invasion two long decades before. "People in Prague told me that the petition wouldn't work, that it wasn't the proper time, that people wouldn't listen," Navrátil said. "I replied, 'No, we can't just talk, we must act.' "

At the time, the Church faced stiff persecution in Czecho-slovakia. Religious literature was in short supply. Only two seminaries were functioning. Outspoken priests lost their state license to practice their profession. Most of the remaining clerics were past retirement age, and ten out of the country's thirteen bishoprics were vacant. "It's catastrophic. We have twenty priests older than seventy-eight, eighteen older than seventy-six," Bishop Jan Sokol said. "I proposed three priests for a village; none was accepted. The authorities gave no reason – there never are any reasons."

Sokol and many other long-suffering Czechoslovak Catholics looked to Mikhail Gorbachev for salvation. "The atmosphere is different now with *perestroika* and *glasnost*," Sokol said. "Every-thing depends on how the situation develops in the Soviet Union." Meanwhile the peasant Navrátil was acting. With passion, he plunged into the details of his long struggle. Like many other Moravian hamlets, Lutopečny had no priest and he watched with dismay as atheistic propaganda was drummed into his children at school. He followed the progress of East–West negotiations on human rights on the Voice of America, BBC and Radio Free Europe. In 1976, two years after Czecho-slovakia signed the Helsinki Accords, he wrote his first petition for religious freedom, calling for increased access to religious literature, the right to organize lay religious groups and repeal of the state's power to license priests and assign parishes. The authorities responded by arresting him and, claiming he suffered from "paranoia," confined him to the Kroměříž Psychi-atric Hospital.

Released seven months later, Navrátil bought all the mental-health books he could find and collected statutes relevant to his case. He wrote an analysis demonstrating that he had been incarcerated illegally and sent it to the President, Prime Minis-ter, the police and several ministries. They did not answer. He also wrote letters to officials asking if he was allowed to initiate a petition. Article 29 of the Czechoslovak Constitution guaran-teed the right to petition the government. None of the bureau-crats dared give him a straight answer: they referred him from one office to the next and then back to the first. A simple citizen had managed to embarrass the authorities just by taking them at their word.

Navrátil continued to write open letters about issues of re-ligious freedom. In one, he protested the murder of a friend,

Přemysl Coufal, a secretly ordained priest. Police raided his apartment and arrested him for "incitement against the state." He was detained in the psychiatric hospital and shoved into an eight by fifteen foot cell with only a bucket for a toilet, no running water, no soap, no towels. Nightly, other inmates threatened to kill him. When he was brought to trial the judge cited the diagnosis "paranoia" to claim that his remaining at liberty would be a danger to society. After almost a year in detention, he was released – only to be beaten up by six unknown assailants. When I met him, he opened his mouth to reveal missing upper front teeth and showed me a nasty scar above his right cheekbone which he said still gave him headaches.

Undeterred, he drafted yet another petition and set off to Prague. Intellectuals dismissed him and his petition as the fantasy of a peasant who had never finished high school. "We really thought there would be no popular support," recalled Josef Zvěřina, a leading Catholic layman. "Navrátil just wouldn't listen." The country bumpkin took his case straight to the aging Cardinal František Tomášek, who wrote him a supporting letter reading, "I remind you with all strength that cowardice and fear are not worthy of a real Christian." Back in Moravia, Navrátil used his home-made copier to make 1,000 copies of the Cardinal's letter, and mailed it with his petition to friends around the country.

The petition movement swelled. Activists stood outside church, urging believers to "support the Cardinal." Some priests spoke up at Mass for the petition. Within three months more than 500,000 people had signed. In the spring of 1988, representatives from parishes across the country brought the lists to Cardinal Tomášek in Prague. Navrátil was not with them. A month before, he had been arrested and charged with disturbing the peace and slandering a public organization. "This Navrátil, he thinks he is the spokesman of the Catholic Church," said a scornful František Jelinek, Director of Religious Affairs. "The petition means nothing. We will negotiate only with the official representatives of the Church."

In June 1988, however, two months after receiving the petition, the Prague government agreed with the Vatican to appoint three bishops for the first time since 1973. It also opened some new female orders and accepted the use of lay deacons to hold religious services. For Church activists, these concessions represented a direct result of the petition's pressure. "The authorities are scared. They know this petition represents the voice of the people," an astonished Zvěřina said. "If it had just come from us intellectuals, it could have been ignored."

Navrátil's personal trials were not over. In October 1988, only a few weeks after we met, he was arrested again and confined once more in the mental hospital. He himself admitted to me that he may be "paranoiac," but insisted that he could function normally and that there was no reason to confine him full-time in an institution. To me, he didn't sound crazy, just stubborn. Or then again, I thought, to be so courageous perhaps you had to be a bit mad.

In Czechoslovakia, Navrátil's petition helped galvanize the democratic opposition, which was soon launching its own petitions about freedom for political prisoners. In Romania, a charismatic pastor sparked the entire revolution. His name was László Tökés. When police took him from the pulpit of his Inner City Reform Church on Sunday, December 17, 1989, a peaceful vigil outside his church erupted into an anti-regime riot. Crowds of students and workers joined his followers in the streets. The demonstrations spread throughout the country, toppling dictator Nicolae Ceausescu. Parishioners told me that Pastor Tökés was a special person. While the leaders of his Hungarian Reformed Church collaborated with the tyrannical communist regime, he stood up almost alone and spoke out against persecution of his fellow 1.7 million ethnic Hungarians. "They shut down our schools, our universities, our cultural institute," said Istvan Tolnay, one of his church supporters. "Pastor Tökés was the only one who stood up and said 'no' and spoke the truth."

A few days after Ceausescu was executed, I visited Tökés. He was living in the isolated village of Mineu in the north-west corner of Romania. The path was tortuous, a river of frozen mud, rutted and littered with gravel. Outside the village, soldiers searched our car. They were "protecting" the Father of the Revolution from revenge by the feared Securitate.

When I arrived, it was Sunday morning and Tökés was preaching in the village church. Bells pealed from the wooden tower. Inside the church, peasant women sat separate from the men. White cloths with a typical Hungarian motif of red lilies were draped over the hard wooden pews. A crown of wheat was suspended from the rafters. There was no heat, even though the temperature was below freezing. Light fell in shafts through the windows. Tökés walked up to the raised pulpit and began the service with a hymn. He spoke in a deep, full baritone. He had just returned from Bucharest, where he had met with Romania's new leaders. They impressed him, but he warned that the battle was far from over. It was up to each individual to participate and make sure the regime kept its democratic promises. "We have a chance for freedom," he said. "We must grab it."

Afterwards, the worshipers filed past him. He kissed the women's hands and the men on both cheeks. He kissed a soldier who stood guard at the churchyard fence. Then we went back into his house, right next to the wooden bell-tower. Speaking in English, a bit rusty but eloquent all the same, he told his story. For months he had complained about the closing of Hungarian-language schools, the seizure of Hungarian historical archives and the forcible migration of Hungarians from their Transylvanian homelands. Particularly menacing to Tökés was a "systematization" plan to raze up to 8,000 mostly Hungarian villages and replace them with housing blocks. "In the autumn of last year, I raised my voice together with my colleagues from Timisoara against the systematization of the villages," Tökés said. "This was my heaviest sin in their view, and this began the more brutal oppression of me."

He was denied a ration card to buy food, and parishioners who tried to bring him provisions were stopped by police. His telephone was cut: it came on only late at night, permitting menacing calls. The harassment escalated further. Four masked thugs broke into his apartment and stabbed him. "I was lucky to escape," he said. "If two friends had not been visiting and helped me fight back, I think they would have killed me."

One of the more remarkable results of Tökés's struggle was how it united Romanians and Hungarians, at least temporarily, against a hated despot. Members of both groups stood firm in the vigil outside his church in Timisoara. "Here is the last possibility to catch the reconciliation between Romanians and minorities," he said. "All the Romanian people can see clearly that Ceausescu was a monster-man." But as a Hungarian, Tökés's personal political future was limited. "As a Hungarian minority representative, I don't think he has much role to play in Romanian politics," his brother Istvan said. "He has only a unique position as representative of a minority." Tökés accepted this role with grace. He said he was happy in Mineu. His wife was pregnant with their second child. When the situation calmed, he said, he would return to his church in Timisoara. For now, it was enough to spend some quiet days with his family and his parishioners.

Some Church leaders relished their political power. When I arrived at East German Pastor Rainer Eppelmann's unpretentious second-floor flat in the working-class East Berlin district of Prenzlauer Berg, he was excited. "I'm so sorry," he excused himself. "I can't see you right now." Before I could ask why, the doorbell rang and West German Foreign Minister Hans-Dietrich Genscher entered. "*Guten Tag!*" the Minister said, grabbing his host like an old friend. "We've got a lot to talk about."

Later, the goatee-bearded, balding, forty-six-year-old Eppelmann told me that he often saw Genscher. The corridors of power were a long way from his origins in a working-class Berlin family and his first job as a bricklayer. Realizing that bricklaying represented "no lifetime vocation," at the age of twenty-six he began to study theology. Like Latin American priests who embraced liberation theology, he always saw his religious responsibilities as encompassing politics. "As a Christian you had to get involved, to oppose injustice, and there was a lot of that here," he argued. "This made me a political pastor from the beginning."

After entering the ministry in 1974, he opened his simple red-brick Samaritan Church to nonconformists and independent thinkers, believers and non-believers, pacifists and ecologists as well as punks and rockers. Like St. Nikolai in Leipzig, his Samaritan Church sponsored regular Peace Masses opposed to the installation of Soviet SS-20 missiles. "Pastor Eppelmann was crucial for the opposition," recalled Werner Wiemann, a leader of the Democracy Now movement. "His church was the only place where we could express ourselves."

Although the former communist government of Erich Honecker cultivated a cooperative relationship with the churches, its tolerance had definite limits. Uniformed police officers often surrounded the Samaritan Church during services, ostensibly to provide "protection." They checked the identity papers of those who wanted to enter. Inside, plainclothes officers posed as participants and tried to sabotage the meetings by asking provocative questions. Pastor Eppelmann's telephone was also bugged. "Once they arrested several people from the congregation," said Edeltraut Pohl, the church's secretary. "One was expelled from the country."

Among the inexperienced artists directing the East German opposition, Pastor Eppelmann provided a rare mature voice. He founded the Democratic Awakening Party. "At a time when parties and politicians hardly exist," he explained, "I feel an obligation to step into the void," He no longer managed to keep up with his pastoral duties. He spent all his time on the campaign trail. After elections in March 1990 he was named Minister for Disarmament and Defence in the first (and probably last) East German government. For the longtime peace activists it was the perfect position, combining his political and spiritual aims. "I'm a divided man," he concluded. "I love my ministry work. But I cannot turn my back on society."

Despite Pastor Eppelmann's prominence, the Church's political role after the revolution looked likely to diminish. In East Germany, parties opened offices outside Church premises and most demonstrations were organized without any Church help. Attendance at services fell off. "The Church's importance will decline," predicted Pastor Christian Führer of St. Nikolai in Leipzig. "People now have other places in which to follow their ideas."

In Poland, I visited Gdańsk after Solidarity's legalization and was surprised to find Father Henryk Jankowski sounding sad. For years Jankowski had sheltered Lech Wałęsa in his St. Brygida Church. Wałęsa would speak at Sunday Masses before thousands of the faithful, and used the priest's sitting room to meet foreign journalists and diplomats. But now Wałęsa had moved his headquarters from St. Brygida's into a six-floor office building in the city center. "I feel like a father when his child goes out into the world," said Father Jankowski, sitting in his ornate sitting room, full of dark, baroque, Gdańsk-style furnishings. "Solidarity will still depend on me for moral support, but it has become self-sufficient."

During the Polish election campaign, parish priests challenged Communist Party propaganda on state-controlled televison. Church billboards were plastered with Solidarity banners. At Masses, priests often told their parishioners that God could never vote for the godless communists. But ideological differences between the Church and Solidarity appeared. The night before the vote, Primate Józef Glemp received two Christian Democratic candidates who were running against secular Solidarity leaders, Jacek Kuroń and Adam Michnik. Kuroń and Michnik won anyway – each carrying more than 70 per cent of the vote. "The Church's interference in the electoral campaign was poorly perceived by the people," Michnik told me afterwards. When the ecclesiastical hierarchy backed a move to ban abortion, protesters picketed Parliament, carrying placards reading "Down With Both the Red and Black Dictatorship." "I've fought all these years for freedom from the communists," my friend Krystyna Wróblewska said. "Now I want freedom from the Church."

Having led the revolution to success, the wisest members of Eastern Europe's churches voluntarily decided to step back from power. No one expressed this sentiment more eloquently than Czech priest Václav Malý. During Czechoslovakia's revolution, Father Malý became Civic Forum's first spokesman. Before cheering crowds of hundreds of thousands, he stood on a balcony in Wenceslas Square and proclaimed in a clear, melodious bell of a voice, "There can be no confidence in the leadership of a state that refuses to tell the people the truth and give them the rights and freedoms that are common even in Third World countries." The crowd cheered, "Long live Malý," and overnight, Father Malý became a household name.

It was the culmination of a decade-long struggle. In 1979, Father Malý had lost his state license to preach. If he celebrated Mass or just put on a clerical collar, he risked a two-year prison term. After his license was revoked, he cleaned toilets in the Prague subways and worked as a stoker in a hotel, pouring lumps of dirty brown coal into a red-hot furnace. Eventually he received a small stipend from a religious foundation in the West which enabled him to study theology. He turned his cramped apartment, which he shared with his widowed father, into a sort of monk's cell. The kitchen consisted of a cot and a spare table which doubled as a desk. His face was ruby red with enthusiasm. This was no thin, timid clergyman. Michelangelo could have sculpted his stocky, broad shoulders and his thick, large, hands. In his home, Father Malý always offered visitors a cup of sweet Chinese tea and began to speak with compassion and hope. His English was halting, measured, but with a strangely powerful eloquence. When he searched for a word, he looked down at the table and concentrated. An interview with him inevitably became an invaluable lesson in personal courage.

Father Malý lost his license for talking to young people in a church outside the parish where he had been assigned. His politics also marked him as a troublemaker. Of the nine priests who signed the Charter 77 documents, all lost their licenses. Cautious figures within the Czechoslovak Roman Catholic Church criticized the banned priests as too provocative. Malý rejected this timidity. "They practice some philosophy of little steps," he said. "They believe that if you collaborate and make small compromises, you will gain some small advantages."

In the new democratic Czechoslovakia, he said the Church had won much goodwill for its stronger stands in favor of national independence and human rights. Old restrictions against religious freedom had vanished. Pacem in Terris, the communist-supported group of priests condemned by the Pope, was disbanded. An unlimited number of youngsters could enter seminaries. Malý feared this new-found public esteem could be jeopardized if the Church became embroiled in partisan politics. So he turned down offers to join the government as a minister or become an ambassador. Instead he decided to become a parish priest once again. At the beginning of 1990, he took over a small church in the Smíchov neighborhood of Prague.

I attended Father Malý's first public Mass. It was not an ordinary Sunday church service. Czechoslovakia's best and brightest, the artists, actors, scientists, those who made the miraculous November revolution, packed the large St. Margaret's Cathedral, an eighteenth-century baroque master-piece. A huge Czech tricolor framed the altar. The congregation sang the Czech National Anthem. They raised their hands in the V-for-Victory sign. Many of the faithful predicted that Malý would become a national hero, at the least enjoying a prominent career within the Church hierarchy, perhaps as successor to the aging primate Cardinal František Tomášek. "He's Tomášek's right-hand man," said Jiří Knot, a Church activist. "I see him as the future Cardinal." Such suggestions made Malý blush. When we talked after the Mass, he said the simple joy of saying God's blessing in public was compensation for his long years of political struggle. "It was a strange, beautiful feeling giving Mass," he said. "I'm not a professional politician. I'm only an imperfect servant of God."

Chapter Ten

The Society:

Public and Private Worlds

> It would be very unreasonable to understand the sad
> legacy of the last forty years as something alien, which
> some distant relative bequeathed us. On the contrary,
> we have to accept this legacy as something we com-
> mitted against ourselves. If we accept it as such, we
> will understand that it is up to us all, and up to us
> only, to do something about it.

> *Václav Havel, inauguration speech, January 1, 1990*

Under communism, Eastern Europeans lived in two separate
worlds, the public and the private. Their public lives were
bankrupt, frauds, devoid of meaning. Their private lives were
rich, warm and fulfilling. In public, people were rude and
hostile. Clerks in hotels, waiters in restaurants, secretaries in
offices could be counted on to produce a scowl instead of a
smile. Sit the same people down for a beer or a coffee in the
local café, and suddenly they became understanding and warm.

The dichotomy compensated for frustrated ambitions. On the
job, an individual enjoyed few responsibilities, few opportunities to achieve true satisfaction. Instead of being tied to
performance, wages and promotions were linked to connections
and political loyalty. Off the job, the same individual could
finally open up and express his true emotions. Often I was
invited to people's homes for eating, drinking and baring one's
soul. These were not just private dinner parties. They were
outpourings of genuine emotion. Outside the family, hypocrisy
ruled. Within the family, honesty reigned.

The revolution's great achievement – perhaps its greatest
achievement – was to signal the end of this double life. People
no longer have to endure inner emigration, offering outward
conformity in the university or workplace. They no longer have

to say and do things in public which they wouldn't honor in private. They can say out loud what they always believed.

This new freedom comes at a cost. Democracy demands that individuals become responsible for themselves. Capitalism forces them to stand up for themselves. They will no longer be able to slough off at work without fear of unemployment. As in the West, where career ambitions can eat away at family ties, Eastern Europe's new freedom may dilute the warm private ties which helped people overcome the public frustrations of life. But there is no choice. Communism humiliated the individual, reducing man to a force of production and nature to a tool of production. It produced its own terrible type of stress. Because one was truthful only within the family and felt free to lie in public, people developed a talent for manipulation and confrontation. A healthy society means an honest society.

Nowhere did the tension between the public and private worlds result in so many personal tragedies as in Romania. When I went to cover the country's blood-soaked revolution in December 1989, the saddest and most shocking sight I saw was in Bucharest's Municipal Hospital. Abandoned babies wailed; sick, pregnant young women moaned; and doctors worked twenty-four-hour shifts doing abortions. In an effort to increase Romania's population, Nicolae Ceausescu had banned contraceptives and made abortion punishable by up to five years in prison. The result was Europe's highest infant-mortality rate, overflowing orphanages, and the deaths of many pregnant women.

Although the outline of such problems had been known for a long time, only the revolution revealed the true extent of the disaster. One of the first actions of Romania's new regime was to legalize abortion. "We can finally change this madness," said a relieved Dr. Traian Rebebea, head of the gynecology department at Bucharest's Municipal Hospital. "You can hardly imagine what these draconian policies did to people – it's beyond belief. Only the most evil, sick and stupid mind could have proposed such a program."

Thousands of desperate pregnant women flooded to hospitals across the country for treatment. One was Marcica Negru. She had been married for four years and already had two daughters. The family lived in a one-room apartment, sharing the kitchen and toilet with sixteen other families. When Marcica became pregnant for the third time in August 1989, she decided to abort. But since abortion was illegal, she resorted to self-abortion, pushing a rubber tube into the uterus. The procedure caused bad bleeding. "The revolution saved me," Marcica said. "I was very, very sick. I could hardly move, but I was so frightened I couldn't tell anyone. As soon as I heard that Ceausescu was finished, I had enough courage to come to the hospital."

The rationale behind all this suffering was a grandiose scheme to boost Romania's population from 22 million to 30 million by the end of the century. Ceausescu defended the policy as essential for economic and national survival. A great nation, he liked to say, needed a great number of people. In his belief, he was not alone. All Eastern European Communist regimes considered baby-making an issue of national survival. Surrounded by Slavs, Romanians feared for their Latin culture and Hungarians for their unique Magyar identity. The Bulgarians, on the other hand, wanted to promote the Slavic majority in the face of the fast-growing Turkish minority.

Economics provided another reason for the preoccupation with birthrates. Except for in Poland, Eastern European populations are aging. Hungary, for example, counts some 2.3 million pensioners out of a total population of around 11 million. In the 1980s, many countries faced labor shortages; East Germany and Czechoslovakia even imported "guest-workers" from as far away as Vietnam. "A healthy economy means a healthy population structure," argued Dr. András Klinger of the Hungarian Statistics Board. "To plan an economy, you must be able to plan the number of workers."

Western governments shy away from population policies. Much as they might worry about declining birthrates, they consider the decision of whether or not to have children a private matter. The main exception is nationalistic France. Believing that power lies in numbers, former President Charles de Gaulle proposed the doubling of France's population to 100 million. His successors pursued a policy of giving generous amounts of financial aid to large families. At Paris's prestigious National Institute of Demographic Studies, Director Gérard Callou has held several conferences uniting French and Eastern European researchers. "Alone in the West," he explained, "we share the Eastern European fear for the nation's future."

Eastern Europe's communists offered French-style financial incentives to have babies. Women received a monthly family allowance for each child. Since most women still do have at least one child, only a small sum is given for what demographers have dubbed this "child of love." The sum was doubled for a second child and tripled for a third. Throughout the region, three children became the official goal for families.

Enticing as these payments were, they remained insufficient. Demographers estimated that benefits made up only about 20 per cent of the cost of bringing up a child, and the number of babies born did not rise. The Hungarians began offering additional inducements. For six months after giving birth women received full salaries, and for up to three years mothers were allowed to stay away from their job while receiving three-quarters of their salaries. After this period they were assured of having back their old jobs. Couples with three children received priority for kindergarten places and vacation tickets. Perhaps the most important perk concerned housing: fertile Hungarian couples were given priority on apartment waiting lists.

In Romania, Ceausescu increased coercion. In addition to the ban on abortion and contraceptives, all women received gynecological check-ups in their workplace. Once a pregnancy was spotted, so-called "Demographic Command Bodies" were called in to monitor the woman. Any miscarriage was investigated and the Securitate was serious about catching offenders. Doctors at Bucharest's Municipal Hospital know of several of their colleagues who served time. "The police were everywhere," said Dr. Alexandru Anca. "Whenever we made a diagnosis, they would come and interrogate us. If we performed an abortion on a woman we said was in danger of dying, they would be all over us."

Most women didn't dare see a doctor about the complications of illegal abortions for fear of being reported to the security police. Their desperation was extreme. While births were promoted, possibilities for providing them with proper conditions became more and more difficult as Ceausescu instituted a crash program to pay off the country's debts by, among other things, exporting food and rationing energy.

A so-called "scientific nourishment" program failed to provide even the most elementary diet. "It wasn't just that you couldn't find Pampers in the store," Marcica Negru told me. "Your apartment was too small, it was unheated, and you didn't have enough to eat; you didn't even have milk for the baby."

In 1987 the Romanians broke with international medical protocol by imposing a thirty-day delay in registering births, presumably to avoid recognizing deaths in the first month of life. The true infant-mortality rate was even higher than the (already alarming) rate officially reported. Doctors admitted that passive infanticide was practiced on a wide scale. Unable to provide for their babies, mothers let them die from treatable illness and malnutrition.

The ultimate tragedy was that, despite all the suffering, Romania's birthrate never rose much over the rate in countries where abortion is common. By 1990 the population still stood at only a little more than 22 million – its level when Ceausescu launched his ambitious natality scheme soon after coming to power in 1967.

Amidst the general decline in Eastern European populations, one exception stood out: Poland. After martial law was declared in 1981, Poland's birthrate soared to a post-war high. Night curfews provided one incentive for baby-making. Beyond this, demographers also believe that Poland's political *impasse* produced a deep emotional shift in attitudes. By 1983 one-fifth of all births in Europe outside the Soviet Union occurred in Poland. "People retreated into their families," explained Gérard Callou, director of France's National Institute of Demographic Studies. "They no longer found any outlet for public expression."

Mikołaj Kozakiewicz, president of the Polish Family Development Association, told me that the baby boom started right after World War II. More than 6 million Poles lost their lives and "a psychological, nationalistic feeling overcame the country," he said. "People replaced the losses." Many other countries, including the United States, experienced a similar boom, but the phenomenon was more pronounced and lasting in Poland. A strong Roman Catholic heritage and the communist government's pro-natality policies added to the population pressure. The Church promoted large families and opposed birth control, while the Communist Party believed that more births represented a sign of national virility. Under these circumstances, the country's population grew through the 1980s by an average of a percentage point each year until it neared 38 million. "We have Europe's youngest population," Kozakiewicz said. "Children are this society's holy cows."

Somehow, I didn't think this was the whole story. When farm populations immigrated to the city, birthrates traditionally fell. But Polish peasants-turned-workers continued to have many babies. Lech Wałeşa and his wife Danuta, for example, have eight children. Even more, in this stoutly Catholic country, single mothers are considered socially acceptable. One out of ten mothers is single. I once met a girl, Eva, who had just decided to have a child out of wedlock. She experienced no shame. "On the contrary," she said. "People admire me. They understand that you have to have a family – at all costs."

As in Romania, it was not easy to start a family in a destitute country such as Poland. State-provided services, everything from maternity wards to bib manufacturing, did not keep up. The few apartments available were usually small. Michal and Jolanta, a couple in their early thirties, consider themselves fortunate. They live with their five-year-old daughter in a small one-room apartment. "We know other families who have five children in a two-room apartment," the young couple explained. Jolanta worked in a children's-rights protection committee which tried to help couples find apartments and to ease the social difficulties of unmarried mothers. It was an impossible task. Schools are so overcrowded that they run in two shifts, one in the morning, one in the afternoon. "What you in the West would consider common problems, getting children clothes and toys," she said, "become pathological problems here in Poland."

The authorities struggled to adapt to these difficulties. When the crisis first became apparent in the mid-1970s, Kozakiewicz of the Family Planning Association tried to convince government leaders to change their pro-natalist policies. They refused, afraid of offending the Church. By the end of the 1980s, the problem could be ignored no longer, and the Family Planning Association was allowed to open more centers and distribute more birth-control devices. The Ministry of Defense started a birth-control program for young draftees. But the results were not promising. Contraceptives remained in short supply. Condoms were unavailable, and only 2 per cent of Polish women used the Pill.

Solidarity's rise to power worsened the tensions over social policy, creating a conflict between the movement's more religious and less religious elements. In the spring of 1989, when some parliamentary deputies introduced legislation to ban abortion and sentence women convicted of aborting their fetuses to three-year prison terms, the Church hierarchy supported them. Solidarity was divided. Its Christian right wing supported the ban and prison term. Left-wing Social Democrats such as Jacek Kuroń ended up equivocating. While he is against abortions, Kuroń declared during his parliamentary campaign that he does not want to see people put in prison for having them. "We need the Church," he said, "but the Church should not rule us."

A deep contradiction persisted in Polish attitudes. While Poles appreciated the Church for its independence, they were selective in their adherence to its teaching. People looked to the Church for spiritual renewal, but ignored its policies regarding sex, abortion and divorce. Polls showed that a majority supported the present liberal abortion law, enacted in 1956. The reasons were easy to understand. In a country in which most other forms of contraception were difficult to obtain, abortion became the main means of birth control. An estimated 300,000 abortions took place each year. Stung by public criticism, the Church finally withdrew its support for the proposed ban on abortion.

I came away convinced that almost no artificial methods could stimulate or depress the birthrate. The only sure method looked like a political crisis. Unless they suffered from a debilitating let-down similar to Poland's martial law or Czechoslovakia's Soviet invasion, causing the birthrate to soar, Eastern Europeans would retain control over this most personal, private of decisions. Freedom and democracy were bound to result in a decrease of the birthrate – even in Poland. Sure enough, after Solidarity won power, Polish demographers began reporting the first signs of a downturn in the number of new babies. The trend would be reversed, I suspected, only if the revolution were reversed.

Some Western researchers noted how a high and growing percentage of Eastern European marriages ended in divorce, and concluded that family ties must be weakening. However, divorce rates stayed below Western levels. In Hungary and Czechoslovakia, for example, about a third of all marriages break up. In the United States almost half of marriages end in a split. Considering the greater difficulties facing young Eastern European couples, that points to the surprising strength of the marriage institution, as well as strong barriers against divorce. Partners couldn't just go out and rent separate apartments. After separations family structures didn't crumble, leaving lots of lonely singles. Instead they often emerged reinforced. Anthropologist Janine Wedel studied the question in her book *The Private Poland* and found that "after divorce, children usually live with their mothers, sometimes together with the mother's parents."

Parent–child relationships survived political as well as emotional strains. I often encountered parents and children on different sides of the ideological barricades who nevertheless remained close at home. Janine Wedel told one poignant story of how a Communist Party member invited her to march in the government-sponsored May Day parade. "When I met him several weeks later, he told me proudly that his daughter participated in the Solidarity May Day demonstration," she recalled. "I learned that he secured the release of several of her friends, arrested on suspicion of having engaged in planning the illegal May Day demonstration."

Family was not just defined by blood ties. It often included distant relatives and good friends, and in difficult living situations people depended on their friends to provide texture to their all-too-often dull and dreary professional lives. Unlike young American professionals, Eastern Europeans displayed little professional ambition. My Hungarian friend Magda had the talent to do much more than her simple editing job at a publishing house. With a little effort, she could have tried to open up her own publishing company, or even started a joint venture with a foreign publishing firm. We discussed the possibility a few times until it became clear that Magda Seleanu had little intention of following my advice. "I don't want to own my own publishing firm. I just want to have time for my friends," she said. "You in the West dream about making something of your lives. We don't dare have those dreams. We just want to enjoy our family and friends."

This reliance on family and friends was practical as well as emotional. In theory, the communist state should have provided everything. In practice, it provided next to nothing. Suppose somebody in Warsaw, Prague or Sofia decided to buy an iron or a refrigerator or a hair-dryer or a vacuum cleaner. He couldn't just go into a department store and buy it. There just weren't enough consumer goods to go round. The purchase had to be "arranged." An informal exchange network formed the backbone of the Eastern Bloc's economic and social system.

Here's an example of how it worked. My friend Dorota Kowalska and I decided to go on a reporting trip to the Polish provinces. We needed gasoline for her Polski Fiat. But Dorota had no more gas coupons left. So she called up a friend and offered him English lessons in return for some coupons. We got the gas and took our trip. After Solidarity's re-legalization, gas rationing was eliminated, but the perverse practice of "arranging" purchases persisted. Stations ran out of fuel. Huge lines of cars stretched around the stations. Instead of finding friends with lots of gas coupons, Dorota began trying to make friends among the local gas-station attendants.

Technically, all these transactions came under the heading of "black market." The term was always misleading, carrying connotations of shady and direct transactions. Exchanges on the Eastern European black market were considered respectable and depended on personal, long-term relationships. Since most city-dwellers in Eastern Europe are one generation from the land, they retained close ties with relatives living in the country-side. These connections proved invaluable in feeding their families. The first time I visited a Polish apartment, I remember being greeted with an immense platter of fresh cheese and vegetables.

"Isn't food in short supply?" I asked.

"It is," my host replied. "This comes from the countryside."

Next to his country cottage, local peasants sold him produce from their private plots.

Connections were needed to accomplish everything from buying fuel to overcoming bureaucratic *impasses*. The best example I remember came in Prague. It was impossible to find a hotel room. Every place I called, the receptionist snapped "No," and hung up the phone. She didn't know me and she gained nothing by giving me a reservation. I finally contacted my friend Michál Donath. "No problem," Michál said. A few hours later, I had a reservation in one of the best hotels in town. Michál never told me how he "arranged" the reservation. Perhaps some money changed hands, but perhaps not. I was afraid to bribe the clerk. One had to know him. In most of his dealings, Michál said, the key ingredient wasn't money. It was contacts. He knew hotel clerks personally, and they trusted him.

If one knew how to wiggle and finagle, one could obtain almost anything in Eastern Europe. There may have been nothing in the stores and the statistics may show that incomes and living standards were falling. But people still seemed to live better than the figures suggested. I spent some time in a fancy Villamosság Electronics store just off Váci Ut in Budapest. Shiny new Sharp stereos were priced at 12,500 forints – three times the official monthly salary. It didn't matter. Eager buyers snatched them up. Where did they get the money? Many said they worked at second jobs. Others had rich relatives in the West. Hungarians had simply developed a keen ability to adapt to the mounting strains in their society. They joked about the phenomenon. The average Hungarian worker earned 5,000 forints a month, somebody once explained. He spent 7,000 forints a month – and banked the rest.

*

Before the revolution the contradictions of daily life in Eastern Europe were so blatant and wild that they created immense social pressures. In pure economic terms, the use of informal barter arrangements was inefficient and impractical. Wherever regular money had lost value, some substitute had to be found. In Ceausescu's Romania, penalties for holding dollars were so stiff that the most valuable currency became Kent cigarettes. Not Marlboro. Not Pall Mall. Only Kent. I tried to find out why. No one offered a clear answer. The Kent currency was just a long tradition. Everybody accepted them. Nobody smoked them. They just exchanged them. When I wanted a train ticket from Bucharest to Brasov, the salesman said none were left. I slipped him a packet of Kents. Two first-class tickets slid under the counter.

Apart from Romania's bizarre example, Eastern Europe's substitute currency became the American dollar or West German mark. The reason was simple. Most items – from coffee to computers – were unobtainable with Polish zlotys or Czech crowns or East German marks in local stores. But these same goods could be obtained in state-run "dollar" stores. In Poland, these stores were called Pewex; in East Germany, Intershop; and in Czechoslovakia, Tuzex. For years in Poland almost all products and services were priced in dollars. An organization called Polmot sold Polish cars for dollars, another called Locum sold apartments for dollars. Private plumbers repaired pipes for dollars, doctors made house-calls for dollars, and taxi drivers refused rides until offered dollars. "We have a bi-currency system," said former Finance Minister Bazyli Samojlik. The situation had become so extreme that it spawned some wild humor.

"What do Poland and the United States have in common?" one joke went.

"In both countries," the answer came, "Polish zlotys buy nothing and US dollars buy everything."

The Polish government, like all Eastern European regimes, turned a benevolent eye on the thriving hard-currency market. It needed the dollars to pay back the country's debts, and from its point of view, better Poles spent their dollars at home than abroad. Citizens were permitted to hold dollar bank accounts – with no questions asked about where the money came from. By 1988, Finance Minister Samojlik said 3.5 million of the country's 37 million citizens held dollar accounts. Everywhere one went, people would ask to change money. Hotel bellboys, restaurant waiters and taxi drivers offered at least four times the official exchange rate. Well-dressed men waving wads of zlotys stood outside the hotels and harassed foreigners. I was sure they were secret-police agents. Still, no one seemed to be afraid. "Sure they're secret police," my friends joked. "They also give good rates."

At the headquarters of the Pewex dollar shop, located on the thirtieth floor of what was then Warsaw's tallest building, Marek Pietkiewicz greeted me. In his mid-thirties, he was the firm's vice president. He had a trim beard and wore a neat three-piece suit. With a little stretching of the imagination, he could have passed for a young banker on Wall Street. He told me that until the late 1970s Pewex was restricted mostly to VIPs and tourists. Then the Polish economy collapsed. Consumer shortages, once rare, became endemic. Pewex was opened up to the general public and professional managers like Pietkiewicz were brought in to run it. By 1988, the chain had 650 stores and was growing by 20 per cent annually. Sales totaled almost $400 million. "Everybody buys at Pewex," Pietkiewicz boasted to me, "including Wałeşa."

Solidarity leaders were troubled by Pewex. During 1980 and 1981, the union complained about the selling of many Polish goods in Pewex stores. Although the authorities forced Pewex to stop for a while, the practice resumed after the imposition of martial law. The system's inequality mushroomed. Any Pole receiving a mere $50 from a generous aunt in Chicago could change the sum for upwards of twice the average monthly wage. With dollars, life suddenly became cheap – and enjoyable. Lavish dinners – pheasant, duck, veal – could be bought for a dollar. I took to buying Russian caviar in the local private market. A tin cost $3–4, depending on the season. But without dollars, making ends meet became almost impossible. A small Fiat cost $1,500 – not much for a car by Western standards, but thirty-six months of the average Polish salary. While waiting lists to get an apartment for zlotys stretched beyond two decades, beautiful apartments could be had immediately for dollars. "Anyone with access to dollars lives fine," Solidarity leader Bronisław Geremek complained. "But those who can't get dollars are becoming poorer and poorer."

Even before Solidarity came to power, the communist authorities acted to curb the problem. Moves were made to bring supply and demand into line and to narrow the dollar–zloty gap. Dollar "auctions" were launched in which enterprises could buy dollars at the going rate to finance imports. State stores were allowed to buy the dollars in order to make Western goods available – for zlotys. Finally, the Black Market itself was legalized. The official state travel agency Orbis opened exchange booths around Warsaw selling zlotys at what it called "the free-market rate." When Solidarity gained power, it took dramatic actions to bring the currency situation under control. Prices were freed and the cost of many basics increased by 100, 200 and even 500 per cent. Strict controls were placed on the money supply. As fewer and fewer zlotys were printed, the dollar rate began falling and the zloty became convertible. Living standards fell at least 20 per cent. People turned in their license plates saying they could no longer afford gas for their cars. Less bread and less meat were sold. Elderly pensioners were seen in grocery stores buying just one carrot. But queues disappeared. Purchases no longer had to be "arranged." Money meant something. Competition between shops picked up. Poland received a necessary, if painful, injection of "truth."

The dramatic Polish financial program involved great risks, particularly concerning inequality. Under communism, the theory was that no one was supposed to be much richer, or much poorer, than anyone else. Salaries were set at about the same rate, regardless of how much individuals produced. The more qualified a worker became, the less he was actually paid, out of socialism's glorification of the muscular manual worker. Coalminers for a long time earned more than college-educated engineers and three times as much as Ph.D.s in the humanities or theoretical sciences. The prejudice against white-collar workers stemmed from their bourgeois tinge, and from their lack of political punch. Eastern Bloc regimes feared the grimy coalminer or shipyard worker. They didn't worry about the man in the tie and jacket.

Reformers realized that they needed to restore relations between qualification and reward. They called for more incentives to raise productivity. Hungary and Poland took the lead in encouraging entrepreneurs, even at the price of mounting differences in wages. Private businessmen plugged gaping holes left in the state sector, running restaurants, directing greenhouses and creating computer-software firms. A new class of *nouveau riche* appeared. In Warsaw and Budapest, it became possible to see people driving fancy West German cars and wearing the latest in Western fashions.

The most famous of these so-called "new rich" was a Polish entrepreneur named Ignacy Soszynski. He founded a cosmetics firm called Interfragrances-La Forêt in 1980. As soap and shampoo disappeared from Polish stores, Interfragrances stocked it. Customers were charmed by the firm's handsome packaging and efficient service. The company boomed. In four short years, sales increased fifteen times, and Interfragrance shops spread all around the country and even abroad. Soszynski became rich – very rich. According to the firm's reports, he made $5 million in 1985 alone. He bought a sumptuous villa outside Poznań. To the Polish newspaper *Polityka*, he described himself as "the richest person in Eastern Europe." His wealth aroused envy. After the article appeared, communist activists in Poznań began to complain about the "millionaire" in their midst. The provincial prosecutor charged him with fraud. Soszynski finally fled to West Germany, where he died in disgrace.

Another example was Hungarian Ernő Rubik, creator of the worldfamous Rubik's Cube. When I met him, he was running his own toy studio and living in a comfortable villa perched on the Buda hills. He said he encountered little jealousy over his wealth – from the state or the public. "The state encourages me," he said.

Most Eastern Bloc *nouveau riche* are not as rich as Rubik or Soszynski, or even rich at all by Western standards. In Poland, "millionaires" came to mean those who earned as little as $35,000 a year. On that salary they were able to buy large luxury apartments in the cities or elaborate villas in the country. They might be able to afford Western automobiles. In Budapest, wealth meant having a comfortable villa, a Soviet or Czech auotmobile, and a few Western products. "I felt so poor when I visited the West," complained one shopper buying a Sharp stereo at the Villamosság Electronics Store.

While polls showed that market-oriented reforms were popular if they produced more consumer goods, the same polls showed rising anger over the "new rich." "We advertised equality so much before, that the change creates tension," explained Iván Berend, president of the Hungarian Academy of Sciences. "Even if it often means creating an equalization of poverty, the idea of equality is deeply rooted, and it's popular." Economist Tamás Bauer recalled the "cherry-pit" scandal of the mid-1980s. A pharmaceuticals company needed cherry pits to produce a certain drug. It couldn't obtain a large enough supply. An enterprising individual located an agricultural cooperative which had a supply of cherry pits. He bought the pits and then resold them to the pharmaceutical company – at a large mark-up. He was jailed for speculation. "On the one hand, the Party leadership understands that true economic recovery

cannot be obtained without implementing good ideas and letting people succeed – like Rubik," Bauer said. "On the other
hand, it can't accept the full meaning of this concept. People
who just buy and sell aren't considered deserving."

Along with the problem of the "new rich," a related plague
appeared – poverty. Communism failed to rid its countries of
this ultimate symbol of capitalism. As the region's economies
began to stagnate and come apart, the signs of destitution
could no longer be denied. They were visible in the blocks
of state-owned apartments marred by crumbling façades and
broken doors and windows, and in the growing numbers of
bedraggled beggars and homeless. By 1989, studies of economists at Warsaw University showed that 30 per cent of all Polish
families earned less than the minimum amount defined by
government officials as covering necessities, and that their
numbers were increasing.

Worst off were pensioners. In Budapest I found scores of
white-haired grandfathers and grandmothers passing time on
park benches. Their stories were almost all tragic. Mrs. Istvan
Madarász was a petite wisp of a lady of nearly eighty. She had
been a pensioner since 1968. Her monthly income made it hard
for her to make ends meet. "I buy a chicken," she told me,
"and I make it last through three days of meals." During the
1980s pensions kept falling further behind the inflation rate.
"We have a terrible social-security crunch," lamented Lajos
Föcze of the National Council of the Aged. "Every 100 forints'
[about $1.75 at early 1990 exchange rates] increase per month
means adding 2.3 billion forints every year to a total pension
budget of 120 billion forints," he said. "It's so much for us –
and so little for them."

In desperation, the growing number of poor fell back on their
families. Mrs. Madarász said that her daughter and son-in-law
helped her get by, and that she was considering moving in with
them. "If I didn't have them," she said, "I don't know what I
would do." But this could not be a solution for everyone.
Economic reformers in Hungary and Poland expressed concern,
but they had few spare funds to provide relief. The burden
began to fall on private organizations.

In Warsaw the Church has begun sponsoring homeless shel-
ters and soup kitchens. The Polish capital's first free soup
kitchen, opened in 1982, was tucked away on the second floor
of a crumbling tenement in the center of the city. At lunchtime,
a couple of dozen haggard old people were sipping bowls of

gooey-looking potato soup. All were pensioners who couldn't make ends meet. Some were homeless. "I've become like a dog," one seventy-five-year-old woman named Marianna Kuran said. "I just get up and begin looking for scraps."

At the moment of its liberation, Eastern Europe's landscape was littered with the capitalist ills of inequality, as well as such social plagues as suicide, alcoholism, mental illness and crime. The transition from a coddled communist society to a more individualist capitalist one resulted in visible new stress. Western-style free markets promised potential prosperity – and hard work. In Hungary, where people were first given the most freedom for private initiative, this dark side of capitalism reared its ugly head with the greatest force. Following the introduction of the New Economic Mechanism in 1968, the number of deaths from cirrhosis increased by twelve times. Hungarians killed themselves more than any other nationality in the world – one-third more often than the runner-up Danes, and two-thirds more often than the neighboring Austrians. "We don't seem able to deal with pressure," said Béla Kolozsi, a sociologist at the University of Budapest. "Deviant behavior has reached alarming proportions."

Admittedly, alcoholism and suicide have deep roots in this part of the world. Drinking was a traditional form of socializing under the Austro-Hungarian Empire. Historians theorize that as members of a small beleaguered nation surrounded by enemies, Hungarians took to killing themselves because they felt oppressed and powerless, without prospects. Capitalist-minded reforms brought back these pressures. They created resentments, jealousies. An estimated 15 per cent of Hungarians take sedatives on the job. One survey concluded that half the public has trouble falling asleep at night because of job-related worries.

A soaring crime rate was another sign of *malaise*. Before the economic reforms, violent crime was almost unknown in the country. You could walk the streets of Budapest at midnight without fear. In the 1980s that changed. Court official Tibor Horváth told me that burglaries and robberies had increased by 20 per cent. "With the new second economy and all our social pressures we have many more burglaries," he said. In Romania the revolution unleashed a crime wave. The new Deputy Minister of the Interior, Jean Moldoveanu, said the number of assaults, which were almost unknown before, suddenly soared to more than 300 a month.

What was crime to some was not crime to others. Making ends meet in the communist world had always meant circumventing the system. You were expected to break the rules. In 1988 some Polish sociologists were sent into a factory to study the ravages of the informal second market. They disguised themselves as workers and each spent a month in five different factories. They published their study under the evocative title *When Crime Is Not Crime*. Workers supplemented their earnings by stealing materials from factories, substituting poorer-quality pieces for better ones, or just avoiding all work. The practice took various simple forms. A construction worker siphoned off some bags of cement for his own use. He took his own tools and exchanged them for new ones allotted to his factory. Or he took factory tools for his personal use. One common practice had workers at tractor factories repairing their managers' cars in return for their managers letting them use the factories' heavy tractors. "Our study," the researchers wrote, "only confirmed our most pessimistic predictions."

For a long time the communist authorities argued that these deficiencies were products of capitalism. Sociologist Béla Kolozsi remembers how in 1950 the main Budapest hospital specializing in treating the mentally ill was closed. "We believed that mental illness would disappear in a just society," he said. "Today, we are far behind in our treatment methods. We need Western advice." Both the World Health Organization and Western religious organizations have helped establish centers for psychological counseling in Hungary. *Glasnost* made a difference. Suicide statistics, long guarded as state secrets, were released, and a group of Hungarian professors, led by Kolozsi at the University of Budapest, launched an exhaustive research project on social ills. When it was published in 1986 it sparked much public debate. "We have a situation full of conflicts," Kolozsi admitted. "At least the public now knows about it."

As Kolozsi suggested, the first step in combating the problem is to recognize that it exists. Communism's greatest disservice was to force people to lie. The return of democracy must be accompanied by the end of such lies, the end of all the hypocrisy which pervaded public lives. For a society to function well, authority must win respect and confidence. In this respect, history has not been kind to Eastern Europe. Most of its nations have suffered through long occupations under which clandestine, illegal activities were considered courageous and admirable. As the communist grip on power crumbles, this attitude could change. Rules will be respected and enforced equally. A state of law will be enacted. People will want to be responsible for themselves.

Eastern Europeans themselves recognize this challenge. As soon as Václav Havel became Czechoslovakia's President, he lectured his countrymen on the need to "live in truth." Everywhere, people seemed to sense the possibilities. In the Bucharest Municipal Hospital I met a group of young doctors who were making the most of their new-found freedoms. All spoke fluent French and English. All cared about their patients. They rushed to tell me all the horrors they had endured under madman Ceausescu. "None of us could do our job," one explained. "The police were everywhere, questioning us about everything."

One young doctor, Danulu Boscu, particularly impressed me. She was twenty-seven years old, married with a two-year-old son, Alexander. The family of three lived in a one-room flat. During the long Ceausescu years, she fell back on her family for support. "You couldn't talk to anybody else," she said. "Whenever you said something out of the house, you kept your voice low out of fear." After the revolution, she and her fellow doctors had all begun working overtime without pay. They kept the hospital's one operating room going twenty-four hours a day, caring for all those wounded in the fighting. Danulu helped pregnant women in need of abortions. Until the revolution, she would have turned them away, scared of losing her job and prison. "I can't tell you how satisfying it is to do a good job," she told me, letting out an enormous sigh. "For the first time in my life, I can tell the truth."

Workers Against the Workers' State. The workers at Gdańsk's Lenin Shipyard first revolted in December 1970. It took four more uprisings over the next two decades to win their battle for a free Poland.

A dreary landscape. Poles consider themselves lucky to obtain an apartment *(above)* in one of these concrete blocks in Warsaw. Hungarians window shop on Budapest's Váci Street *(below)*, where economic reform never managed to produce more than a façade of prosperity.

lution in Prague. Foul air covered the statues on the magnificent medieval Charles Bridge with
ne. Many had to be removed to a museum for safekeeping.

Failed economies. Workers at the Ganz-Mavag locomotive plant in Budapest *(above)* faced unemployment as Hungary moved towards a market system. Hungarian "goulash communism" filled food markets but failed to cure the underlying problems of a bankrupt communist economy.

The new generation. Poland never managed to build enough day-care centers to deal with its baby boom *(above)*, but the strength of Eastern European families overcame much hardship. Polish Church scouts *(below)* defied the state monopoly on scouting.

Student protestors. Youngsters led the revolution everywhere in Eastern Europe. Here Polish high-school students in Warsaw celebrate the coming of summer in 1988 with an offbeat protest against the humorless communist authorities.

Spiritual and intellectual nourishment. The Polish Roman Catholic Church sustained the nation's faith through its long years of communist oppression. Worshipers *(above)* kneel at the grave of a militant priest Jerzy Popiełuszko at Warsaw's St. Stanisław Church. In Eastern Europe, writers are revered and enjoy an avid reading public. Large queues often form outside bookstores like this one *(below)* in Warsaw.

Lighting the Night. Prague demonstrators in November 1989 give the signal of the revolution – the V-for-Victory salute.

Chapter Eleven

The Economy:

Reviving the Dinosaurs

There is no unemployment, but no one works. No one works but the plan is always fulfilled. The plan is fulfilled but there is nothing to buy.

What is communism?
The longest road from capitalism to capitalism.

Eastern European economic sayings

The bureaucrats of Budapest called it "Reform" with a capital R. Under a bankruptcy law issued at the beginning of 1987, companies which didn't make ends meet would be forced to close. The axe fell first in the city of Kecskemét when the Kecskemét Bath Company became the first business in communist Europe to be declared insolvent.

An hour and a half by car south-east of the Hungarian capital, Kecskemét is a handsome provincial town, birthplace to the composer Zoltan Kodály and home to a prestigious music institute. Neighboring farms are renowned for their apricots. The Bath Company was another story. Located on the city outskirts, it looked like a relic from the early nineteenth-century Industrial Revolution – dusty, dark, decrepit. Outside the front gates, a statue of Lenin stood guard. The floors were covered with mud and grease, the air filled with grime and smoke. Workmen shoved red-hot bathtubs in and out of furnaces using long metal pincers. Dangerous sparks crackled from the molten pig-iron, but nobody wore hard hats or safety glasses.

The antiquated factory produced expensive, old-fashioned cast-iron tubs. In the West, modern tubs are made out of sleek plastic, which is cheaper and cleaner than iron. An iron tub weighs 200 pounds; a plastic one weighs only 50 pounds. Iron tubs, hard to color and mold, come only in basic white and in the traditional oblong form. Plastic tubs, easy to color and mold, come in a myriad of colors and shapes. The bathtub factory, I concluded, was a logical candidate for closure.

I was wrong. Even after being declared "bankrupt," the state bank had granted a ten-year moratorium on the company's debts, permitting it to stay in business. The Kecskemét factory was Hungary's only bathtub producer, and both workers and management emphasized to me how confident they were for the future. "I knew they'd never let it close," said Péter Toth, an assembly-line worker. "Where else would we get bathtubs?" No imports could substitute, because the Hungarian forint was not convertible. "If the steel industry closes in the United States, you can just import from South Korea," the economist Támás Bauer explained. "We wouldn't have any steel."

The bathtubs and bankruptcy saga taught me important lessons about reforming Eastern European economies: even the best-intentioned attempts at change would encounter unexpected problems. Step-by-step plans to inject market elements into decaying state-run economies just didn't work. No compromise between a market economy and a centrally planned economy existed. Instead of a "socialist market economy," Czechoslovak Finance Minister Václav Klaus said, "a market economy with no adjectives" was needed.

Economic failure played a key role in the Eastern European revolution. As an ideology, communism placed primacy on economics, and yet, ironically, it produced appalling economic results. It was like a terminally sick person. The illness was chronic and structural. Symptoms included stagnant growth, slipping innovation, accelerating inflation and foreign debt, and plummeting incomes and living standards. The operation to relieve the pain could no longer be gradual and partial. A swift and bloody procedure was needed. "You can't take a man suffering from an acute heart attack and just administer him a Band Aid," explained Harvard economist Jeffrey Sachs. "You have to take him to the Emergency Room and operate right away."

As Eastern Europe attempts to modernize, the best lesson comes from failed past efforts to reform. The countries which attempted the boldest market-oriented changes – Hungary, Poland and Yugoslavia – ended up with the worst economic crises. Poland and Yugoslavia suffered from hyperinflation, and, together with Hungary, from a crippling foreign debt. "Obviously," as Professor Sachs noted, the reform efforts went "seriously awry."

Of all the Soviet satellites, the Hungarians moved the furthest towards constructing a market economy. The Soviet invasion of Czechoslovakia scared off any other would-be reformers within the Bloc. Only Hungary eased central planning and encouraged private enterprise from the late 1960s. The process pressed forward in spurts, one step ahead, one step back, advancing as much as possible and then retrenching so as not to frighten the orthodox Soviet Big Brother. After Mikhail Gorbachev's ascension to power, more dramatic moves were made. Foreign investment was welcomed. Bond and stock markets were opened. Unemployment was authorized and, climactically, the pathbreaking bankruptcy legislation was put into practice.

Some successes were clear. As prices moved more into line with supply and demand, empty shelves and long lines disappeared for most commodities except apartments and cars. Budapest shop windows display everything from stylish eyeglass frames and fur coats to swimming rafts and potted cactus plants. Services improved. Before the reforms, visitors discovered that "express" dry cleaners' shops took four weeks to clean a shirt. "Express" now means same-day service. Elegant cafés offer tempting plates of pastries, restaurant menus list such exotic specialities as turtle soup, and the main market near Vaci Street smells of paprika and pigs' heads.

Agricultural advances are the greatest achievement. When farms were first collectivized in the 1950s, peasants resisted and centralized decision-making destroyed harvests. At the Balaton Nagybereki State Farm near Lake Balaton, manager Tibór Makai recounted how bureaucrats ordered him to grow carrots. "The quality was terrible," Makai recalled. "They were like mush." Then in the mid-1960s, the system was changed. Directors were allowed to decide what to grow and peasants gained private plots. The peasants were even encouraged to use the collective's equipment and facilities for their own purposes after they had done their share of work for the state. At the same time, the state invested large amounts in processing plants and small factories. The result was a type of Western-style agribusiness – with Western-style results. Overall, Hungary produces more pork, poultry, eggs and apples per capita than any other country in Europe and average yields of wheat and corn rank among the best in the world. Instead of cultivating mushy vegetables, the Balaton farm grows grains and raises pigs and cattle. "Our meat is just as good as in Texas," manager Makai insisted over lunch. Enjoying the juicy steak at the farm's restaurant, I could not disagree.

But such successes were partial and incomplete, and came at a heavy price. In the 1970s Hungary took out massive Western credits in an attempt to make an economic leap forward. The effort collapsed at the beginning of the 1980s when a recession shrank the appetite of Western markets for Hungarian exports. In 1982 the country almost went bankrupt. Although astute bankers managed to paper over the problem, the debt soared to an astounding $20 billion by 1990. That was the highest per capita rate in the East, higher than in Poland, and in the same range as Mexico and Brazil.

Hungarians ended up with the worst of both worlds: the constraints of communism without the benefits of capitalism. Enough market forces were unleashed to produce a capitalist income gap, while too few freedoms were granted to eliminate socialist inefficiency. Wages and pensions fell behind inflation and a frenzied race to keep up standards took place. Unskilled workers, young couples with large families and, above all, the large numbers of pensioners were crushed. The underclass sank into poverty. In the 1980s official figures showed that up to a quarter of the population lived below the poverty line. These people couldn't afford the food piled high in the markets.

Most people took two, even three jobs, an official one to ensure eligibility for state benefits and a private one to earn money. Moonlighting was institutionalized as factory workers were encouraged to use firms' equipment for themselves after hours. The shadow economy created a sort of schizophrenia – communism in the morning and capitalism in the afternoon. Carpenters and masons made much more than college-educated engineers or bankers, because housing was in such short supply and tremendous demand existed for private building services. One popular outlet was taxi driving. "I never stop working," one driver with a Ph.D. complained. "In the mornings I'm in the lab, in the evenings I drive the cab."

Private industry remained limited to small service sectors, restaurants and repair shops. Entrepreneurs were allowed to fill gaps left by the state but not to compete against it on equal terms. As late as 1990, the private sector accounted for less than 2 per cent of GNP. Complaints were legion. In the Budapest suburb of Szentendre, I met Marianna Császbok, who had opened up one of the first private boutiques in the country. Called Charlotte, it was a beautiful shop, with wood paneling, a shag rug, and fashions straight out of *Vogue*. Marianna designed the clothes herself and worked "seven days out of seven, from nine in the morning to nine at night." But she didn't aspire to become the next Coco Chanel, because if she tried to export she would have to work through a state company. Under regulations in force until 1989, it was even difficult for her to think of expanding beyond her one store. "I don't dream about being a millionaire," she said. "Remember, here everything is relative."

Reformers in Budapest explained away the restrictions by saying that state-run firms were asked to act like capitalist ones and respond to market forces. State managers were given much freedom to set prices and outputs. A similar formula, they insisted, worked in the West with such state companies as the French automobile-maker Renault. But Hungarian firms were not exposed to true competition, either from alternative domestic or foreign suppliers, because foreign trade was rationed by quotas and the lack of a convertible currency. A firm's financial position gave few indications of its true strength, and in any case the government could not shut down monopoly suppliers.

The system hinged on what Hungarian economist János Kornai described as "soft budget constraints." Profit-makers handed over their earnings to the central government, which turned the funds into cheap credit, subsidies or tax breaks to keep alive money losers such as the Kecskemét Bath Company. In 1990 the state budget still accounted for two-thirds of Hungary's GDP and profits were taxed at a 90 per cent rate.

Market reforms invited additional irresponsibility. As state enterprises received more decision-making powers, they took out bad foreign loans and granted pay increases to workers. Managers faced no risks. If the project worked, they would benefit; if it failed, the state would bail them out by taking over the loans. Workers acted with similar irresponsibility, demanding pay increases with impunity which managers regularly granted. Both sides knew that the state would pick up the cost. The results were the waste of billions of dollars of credits and soaring inflation.

Every time I returned to Hungary, officials promised that this time they were serious: money-losing firms in outdated industries would be closed down. Every time, I found that they were bluffing. For me, Kecskemét's bathtub bankruptcy provided the final proof. In the 1970s the company received a large loan to expand and produce more bathtubs. When the housing market contracted in the early 1980s, it found itself drowning in debts. After bankruptcy was declared, the Ministry of Industry took over the debts and hired a new manager, István Halász. He moved twenty-seven employees from one job to another, let sixty others leave voluntarily and pronounced the end to "restructuring." With the state writing off the firm's debts, he had no fears for the future. "Bankruptcy was quite a good thing for us," he told me. "It got us back in business."

Not long ago, the communist economic model, today seen as bankrupt, was considered the motor of remarkable industrialization. Except for the developed Czech lands and Silesia, Eastern Europe's economies were historically mired in backwardness and dependency. In the nineteenth and early twentieth centuries, they supplied foodstuffs and raw materials to the developed West, primarily Germany. After 1945, central planning achieved recovery from the devastation and a certain modernization of these impoverished, rural societies. Homes, roads and factories sprang up out of the rubble. Millions of people migrated from the depressed countryside into new industrial towns. New Lenin Steel Works, Lenin Mines and Lenin Shipyards were inaugurated.

Through the mid-1960s, officially reported Eastern European growth rates were among the highest in the world, and it was even possible to believe that communism was outperforming capitalism. A whole generation of workers, children of peasants, obtained apartments with running water and toilets. While the Nomenklatura enjoyed privileged status, everyone had jobs, housing, basic health care and schooling. For most Eastern Europeans, this represented a considerable improvement over their miserable standards before the war.

In economic terms, the gains were achieved by what economists call "extensive growth." Ever-increasing amounts of investment, labor and resources were mobilized. Once the industrial transformation was achieved, however, the system proved incapable of making the new factories work well. The command model could not promote "intensive growth." It could not upgrade outdated technology, improve labor productivity or use energy in an efficient fashion. The models of communist modernization, those Lenin Steel Works, Mines and Shipyards, were concentrated in outdated, declining industries, and could not keep up with world standards. "I still think the first period of communist development was necessary to industrialize," Jozsef Bognár, Director-General of the Institute for World Economics, said. "But it was too one-sided, concentrating on heavy industry."

Czechoslovakia, long an industrial powerhouse, enjoyed living standards before World War II which compared with those of Britain, France and Germany. During my first trip to Prague, diplomats urged me to visit the National Technical Museum. Housed in a Bauhaus building, the museum displayed a treasure trove of vintage products. The Škoda car from 1936 was a sleek beauty, as swift and shiny as the 1936 Mercedes and Audis displayed next to it. the 1928 Java motorcycle stood up well beside the BMW and Harley-Davidson models. There were Homolka telephones from 1895, motorized Laurin bicycles dating from 1899 and Nirodna record players from 1920.

Contemporary Czech products were much less impressive. A 1988 Škoda was a chunky rear-wheel-drive monster and the Java motorcycles looked ancient compared to a modern Harley. The museum's "electronics" room was closed for repairs. Only one computer, a Commodore knock-off called the Družba, was displayed in the entire three-floor museum. "Our factories are becoming the Industrial Museum of Europe," admitted Karel Dyba, of Prague's Economic Forecasting Institute. "We're using machines from the beginning of the century to produce the same old stuff."

The Czechoslovaks recognized the problem in the early 1960s, and the need for economic reform became one of the driving forces behind the Prague Spring. Under the urging of economist Ota Šik, a "New Economic Model" was instituted at the beginning of 1967. The methods and the goal, the construction of a "socialist market" economy, resembled the Hungarian reform which was being drawn up at the same time. Enterprises received more autonomy and merit-pay was instituted. Prices were to be freed, and in the long run the Czech crown would be made convertible. Šik's vision retained much Marxist language and thought. Communism's social gains – the elaborate welfare net – were not to be touched. Private enterprise would not be permitted, state ownership would dominate, and central planning would guide the market. Appropriately, Šik's book summing up his plans was called *Plan and Market Under Socialism*.

After the Soviet invasion, these plans were abandoned and chilling central planning reinstituted. Investment in infrastructure was neglected and modernization deferred in outdated plants. The gap with the West widened. By the end of the 1980s, Czechoslovakia was manufacturing 1,000 different types of machine tools, almost none of which was saleable on the world market. It produced a staggering 15 million tons of steel, as much as Great Britain, and the highest per capita figure in the world. For each ton of steel, twice as much energy and manpower was needed than in neighboring West Germany. Officially, growth sputtered along at an annual rate of 2 per cent. Unofficially, the growth figure was zero – or even negative.

The waste could not continue. Before the war, Czechoslovakia did 80 per cent of its trade with the West. It now does about 80 per cent with the East. Czechoslovakia used to export high-technology machine goods. Most of its exports to the West now are coal and other low-value-added products. Communism instituted an inefficient, autarchic form of foreign-trade re-lations. All the Soviet Bloc countries were united under the umbrella of Comecon, which was presented as the Eastern equivalent to the West's Common Market. Instead of promoting free trade, however, Comecon ran on a rigid bilateral barter. Exchanges were calculated in so-called "transferable" roubles, which in fact were not transferable. Czechoslovakia, for example, sold its machines to the Soviet Union and earned roubles. But it could not use these roubles to buy shoes or salami made in Hungary.

Eastern Europeans perceived this trade system as "exploi-tation." That judgment was too simple. In return for raw ma-terials such as oil and gas, which it could sell on the world market, the Soviet Union received substandard Eastern Bloc industrial products which could not be sold on the world market. As the quality of Eastern Bloc goods fell further behind the West, the subsidy kept growing until it totaled billions of dollars annually. *Glasnost* showed to Gorbachev and his fellow reformers just how expensive their empire had become.

Paradoxically, this Soviet largesse hurt its Eastern European clients by locking them into inefficient barter agreements. Subsi-dized energy provided no incentive for conservation, and shel-tered competition provided no reason to produce better quality goods. "If we had real competition in our Soviet trade, then we would be forced to produce better goods," Dr. Ivan Angelis of the Czechoslovak Foreign Trade Institute admitted. "It would be painful in the short run, but beneficial in the long run."

Under Mikhail Gorbachev, the Russians began refusing deliv-ery of low-quality and obsolescent Czechoslovak products. Un-wanted goods began piling up in warehouses. Prime Minister Lubomír Štrougal called them "uselessly dead production" and said that by 1988 they totaled an astounding $3.5 billion. In that same year, Štrougal and other slavish Prague communist officials admitted the need for their own version of *perestroika*. To great fanfare, they launched *pestravba*. Companies were given more powers to make their own decisions about what goods to produce and where to sell them, at home or abroad. Most dramatically, thousands of bureaucrats enjoying cushy positions in Prague ministries were shifted to do real work in companies.

The plan flopped. In economic terms, it failed to touch the nonsensical price structure, and for all its promises of decentralization, kept tough central control. In psychological terms, it did not inspire public confidence. The reforms were proposed by the same leadership which sabotaged 1968's market-oriented reform. Many snickered that the bureaucrats who did nothing in government offices would continue to do nothing once pushed out into industrial ones. A typical joke ran like this:

"In 1948, the workers staged the revolution which brought the communists to power, and the intellectuals stared.

"In 1968, the intellectuals staged the Prague Spring revolution, and the workers stared.

"In 1988, the communists staged a reform – and everybody stared."

Real economic reform meant pain, fewer subsidies and higher prices. It meant closing unprofitable factories. To make Czechoslovak industry competitive, economists estimated that up to a third of the country's smokestack factories should be shut. Communism promised that it would help the workers and the weak. Reform promised to hurt the workers and the weak. Communism called for the end of full employment and equality. Reform represented an end to the status quo forged after the Soviet invasion, which assured the population a stream of subsidized goods in return for keeping quiet about politics. People would work better only if they earned more money, so wage differentials would have to rise.

Communist reformers faced a yawning credibility gap. Unlike the first generation of workers, the young generation coming of age in the era of stagnation no longer enjoyed the prospect of obtaining an apartment, a secure job and significant social benefits. This post-war generation didn't trust the communists. In order to introduce economic reform, the most astute Party leaders recognized that they had to offer some guarantee to society that the sacrifices were worth it. That meant political reform. In Hungary, János Kádár's bargain was that you could have economic liberalization only by limiting political liberalization. His successors reversed the equation, declaring that political reform was essential for implementing true economic reform.

Poland's dire deadlock illustrated the crucial necessity of political reform. After declaring martial law in 1981, General Jaruzelski announced bold economic plans. Poland's GDP had fallen well below 1978 figures, when the debt crunch struck. Real wages were plunging, inflation was soaring and shops were empty. Their model, Polish officials suggested, was South Korea, where authoritarian rule ushered in an economic boom.

The reform never took hold. Almost as soon as it was legislated, branch ministries intent on establishing their own authority stripped enterprises of independence. Everyone remembered how price increases had set off worker unrest in 1956, 1970, 1976 and 1980. Fearful of another explosion, Jaruzelski didn't dare take the fundamental steps to end the enormous subsidies on basic consumer goods and to raise prices.

When Gorbachev came to power, Jaruzelski decided to try once again. He handed over control of economic policy to Zdzisław Sadowski. Sadowski was not a Party member. In a country with a strong tradition of producing brilliant reform economists, from Oskar Lange to Włodizmierz Brus, he enjoyed a reputaton as an able economist. When I interviewed him, he appeared the perfect professor, a balding, bespectacled man who talked in technical terms of "market-resource allocation" and "equal treatment of the public and private sectors." Put in plain language, his plan called for bringing supply into line with demand by increasing prices while holding wages steady. Planned price rises were dramatic – up to 200 per cent on basic goods, from food to gas.

The Sadowski program was announced in the fall of 1987. Its author understood all too well that success depended on politics as much as on economics. In 1982 stagnation had reigned in the Soviet Union. Now Gorbachev was in power. "When we first started reform we were not able to be consistent and comprehensive," Sadowski said, "Now there is a convergence among socialist countries in favor of such radical solutions." Sadowski also pointed to improved economic relations with the West. The United States had lifted its trade sanctions, imposed in 1982 in response to martial law, and Western creditors had agreed to reschedule the country's foreign debt. The International Monetary Fund had just admitted Poland. "The IMF is a signal to all parties that we are serious about this reform,"

Sadowski said. "It gives us a guarantee to potential investors, it can offer us standby credits and it can help convince the World Bank to make loans."

But if the external climate was improving, the internal climate remained bleak. For all his talk of promoting private enterprise, of giving the private sector equal treatment with the public sector, the details of Sadowski's program favored public ownership. I did a story on one frustrated young entrepreneur named Henryk Dutkiewicz. The local administration blocked his application to open a grocer's shop. "They decided the neighborhood didn't need another grocery," he recalled. "Perhaps it would have been different if we had bribed them." Undeterred, Henryk decided to open a carpentry firm. But there was no bank to lend him money for tools. Even if he went to West Germany and found a job on the black market to raise the necessary funds, he worried about taxes, which would eat up a whopping 85 per cent of earnings. Under Sadowski's plans, that figure was not supposed to change. Even worse, a central price board would continue to set fees on carpentry work for all state institutions. "They always set the fees lower than the cost of obtaining wood and other supplies," Henryk complained. "Unless I can charge what I want, there's no purpose."

Jaruzelski refused to let Sadowski curb the corrosive practice of appointing loyal communists as managers. This procedure not only ignored professional qualifications; it favored political reliability over profits by making managers dependent on the approval of their Party superiors. "For some of the largest enterprises," Sadowski admitted, "we will have to take into account the interests of the Party."

Worst of all, Sadowski was not allowed to talk with Solidarity. His plan depended on the acceptance by workers of a wage freeze. Solidarity's leaders praised Sadowski as a talented economist, and supported his plan – provided that their union was legalized. "This is our reform," Bronisław Geremek said. "But why should we give our support without getting anything in return?"

To win public support, Sadowski called a referendum. Poles were asked whether they would accept the price increases in return for freedom of expression and the freedom to form private associations. Although calling for a referendum showed how Sadowski realized that his reform depended on politics as much as economics, it still sidestepped Solidarity. The banned trade union declared a boycott. Large numbers of abstentions marred the vote, which took place on November 29, 1987. The reform package was rejected. Sadowski announced that the price rises would take place anyway, though in a more gradual fashion than planned. "If the patient answers no, it does not mean that the doctor gives up the operation," he explained. "It means the patient just isn't ready for a complex operation."

The denouement was predictable. When prices were increased at the beginning of 1988, workers responded with strikes and managers granted large inflationary wage increases. The Sadowski plan died. The dream of creating a Polish South Korea faded. Only one solution remained for General Jaruzelski, the solution which he had said he would never take, the solution which he had tried to avoid for seven full years – talking to Lech Wałeşa and Solidarity.

On the eve of the communist collapse, Eastern Europe was divided into two main groups. The first, Hungary and Poland, embraced economic change and its political consequences. The second, the so-called "Gang of Four" – Romania, Bulgaria, Czechoslovakia and East Germany – rejected reform. Their leaders saw the dangers of the Polish and Hungarian economic experiments. "Hungary and Poland are bankrupt," said Milan Jelinek, foreign editor of the Czechoslovak Communist Party paper *Rudé Pravo*. "That's no example for us to follow."

While Czechs and the Bulgarians paid lip-service to *perestroika* as a political gesture to Mikhail Gorbachev, Romania and East Germany rejected all attempts at even verbal reform. Both countries were somewhat special. In Romania the despot Ceausescu ran over all opposition and embarked on a crash program to repay the country's debts by starving and freezing his population. In East Germany the regime hid behind inflated statistics, a belief that Germanic thoroughness could make streamlined central planning work and, above all, annual transfers of hard currency from West Germany which covered the total interest burden on its hard-currency debt.

While Ceausescu relied on oppression, the East Germans, Czechs and Bulgarians counted on a steady if sloppy supply of consumer goods to stave off public discontent. Honest economists within the apparat knew that change was necessary. On every trip to Prague I would visit the Czechoslovak Institute of Economic Forecasting, where I met with bearded, bespectacled economist Dr. Valtr Komarek. In his gilded baroque office just behind Wenceslas Square, he delivered a scathing verdict on the state of Czechoslovakia's economy. The country was producing too much steel, too much coal, and too much outdated heavy machinery. A "mafia" of incompetent managers was responsible. Instead of inefficient central planning, enterprise autonomy and free prices were needed. "Communist industrialization is nonsense, it is bankrupt," he said. "Unless we move and move fast, we risk becoming an industrial museum."

During the Prague Spring, Komarek worked with economist Ota Šik developing an economic reform. After the Soviet invasion, he was stripped of his position and remained unemployed until 1971. Instead of joining a dissident group, he received permission from then Prime Minister Lubomír Štrougal to create the Economic Forecasting Institute. "We were protected by Štrougal," recalled Karel Dýba of the Institute. "Komarek managed to bring back a whole group of really competent economists who had been purged after 1968."

While ministry officials offered over-optimistic views, Komarek and fellow economists at the Forecasting Institute uncovered the true figures and preached their vision of a market economy. They produced papers and voiced their opinions. But they wielded little power. "There's no real commitment to reform – it's window-dressing," Karel Dýba told me after the announcement of the *pestravba* plan. "People in the government are deeply pessimistic about the future of the economy, but afraid to take real action." According to Dýba, it was little accident that Hungary and Poland, the two countries with the weakest, most vulnerable economies, were reforming while the strongest economies avoided change. "It's easier to reform in a situation of near total economic collapse than of mere stagnation," he explained. "I'm afraid that we could happily stagnate for a long, long time."

For years reform-minded Eastern Europeans aimed to create a "social market economy." They wanted to obtain the prosperity and efficiency of capitalism while retaining the social benefits of communism. This vision was shared by officials and opposition in both Hungary and Poland, by people as different as Solidarity leader Wałeşa, Communist Party leader Jaruzelski and reform economist Sadowski. But in the second half of the 1980s a new group of free-marketeers, disciples of Friedrich Hayek and Milton Friedman, emerged as a major force. For them, the social market economy was a mirage. Communism could not be reformed. It had to be junked.

The free-marketeers formed associations of entrepreneurs. In Hungary their main organ was *HVG*, an official journal published by the Chamber of Commerce. (*HVG* stands for *Heti*

Világgezdeság or *World Economy Weekly*.) Founded in 1979 as part of a government attempt to publicize economic reforms, it first made its name by publishing company profit figures and trade results. "When we began publishing facts and figures, it was unique," said editor-in-chief Iván Lipovecz. "Our newspapers tended just to reproduce vague press releases." During the mid-1980s *HVG* expanded its coverage to politics and adopted a tone which admirers said resembled the sharp British weekly, *The Economist*. Its initial print run of 14,000 copies grew to 170,000. In a country where government subsidies to the media were considered normal, *HVG* shunned them and made a profit. In 1989 it moved into a fancy new office in a plush Buda villa and became more outspoken in its support of dramatic, free-market reforms. "There's no Third Way between capitalism and communism," Lipovecz insisted. "There's only capital- ism."

Although furious debates took place over whether the goal was a raw American or Scandinavian Social Democratic system, these arguments seemed to me sterile and academic. Both the Social Democrats and the neo-conservatives wanted to privatize and marketize the economy in Western fashion. The relevant question was how to promote growth and prosperity to create the wealth which could then be divided in Swedish or American fashion. As Lipovecz insisted, "Sweden is capitalist, with a private economy, integrated into the West."

Once the passion of the political revolution passed, the rough stuff still lay ahead: economic revolution. All revolutions enjoy an initial phase of extraordinary euphoria. People pour out their personal grievances, exploding the symbols of tyranny and despotism, of all the things which they hated. A market econ- omy could be destroyed overnight through nationalization and fixed prices. But the world had no experience of exits from socialism to create a market economy. As French political scientist Jacques Rupnik suggested, it was easy to make chicken soup out of chicken. But could one make chicken out of soup?

Experts were needed to pick up the revolutionary rubble and construct new market economies. Most opposition leaders were intellectuals and workers who provided moral leadership. Somebody else was needed to provide practical leadership. East Germany's budding opposition found itself crippled by a lack of experts. Its artist leaders continued to talk in vague terms of a Third Way between communism and capitalism, while thousands fled across the border to enjoy the proven success of capitalist West Germany.

Poland's Solidarity, Hungary's Democratic Opposition and Czechoslovakia's Civic Forum found themselves in a much better situation. Many independent-minded experts had worked for years in obscure institutes doing research without real impact on policy. Solidarity's Finance Minister Leszek Balcerowicz refined his radical Friedmanite free-market ideas in an obscure department of the Academy of Sciences; Hungarians Marton Tardos and Tamás Bauer of the opposition Free Democrats had low-level jobs in the same economic institute as Communist Party leader Rezsö Nyers.

In Czechoslovakia, Komarek and his fellow economists at the Forecasting Institute sided with the opposition Civic Forum. With his theatrical speaking style and his dramatic appearance – his bushy gray mane and beard give him a strong resemblance to Trotsky – Komarek seized the nation's imagination with a televised address and a press conference detailing communist incompetence. Posters soon appeared in Prague reading, "Komarek into the Government." When the government was named, Komarek became Deputy Prime Minister responsible for the economy. Other Forecasting Institute economists were given key policy-making positions: Vladimir Dlouhý became Budget Minister and Václav Klaus Finance Minister. They came to office determined to break up state monopolies, to create capital markets, to overhaul the banking system, and to make the Czech crown convertible.

The open question was speed. In Poland, Solidarity put free-marketeers, led by Finance Minister Balcerowicz, in charge. They opted for a dramatic "shock program" which ended all price controls, balanced the budget and made the zloty convertible. When the program went into effect, it provided a rude awakening. Almost overnight, communism's empty shelves and endless queues vanished. Butchers' shops overflowed with sausages and hams, television stores with televisions, gasoline stations with gas. The catch was that nobody could afford to buy the available goods. Prices had soared. A nervous mixture of fear and exhilaration swept through the population. Lines formed outside banks as mobs flocked to exchange their dollar savings for the new hard zloty. After a few weeks prices began to fall a little and inflation cooled. The Solidarity government faced down early attempts by the miners and the post-office workers to crack the wage ceiling. Managers of state-run enterprises who came running to the Finance Ministry looking for subsidies were sent packing. As they stopped paying their workers, the workers stopped showing up for work. Companies faced imminent bankruptcy.

People stopped driving except in emergencies because they didn't have the money to fill up their cars. But when they needed gas, they were pleased that they could get it. I saw Leszlaw Kuzaj, the fervent free-market leader of the Kraków Manufacturing Association. A few months earlier, he had been skeptical about Solidarity's intentions, believing that it was committed to protecting workers, not promoting capitalism. Now he was planning a leveraged buy-out of the leading Kraków newspaper. "Solidarity has done everything right," he said. "It is so courageous." What amazed him and other Poles was the public trust which Solidarity enjoyed. A poll taken after the "shock" showed 80 per cent support for the government. The communists who opposed the plan received one per cent support. Admittedly, the true test of Poland's determination to reform still lay ahead. As lay-offs and plant closures mounted, many wondered whether Solidarity would stick to its policy of tight credit. "We could have a social explosion," worried Bronisław Geremek.

The Czechs and Hungarians looked less bold. They waited until their spring elections to introduce economic programs. The interim governments "didn't have a mandate for real reform," insisted economist Dýba. "They only had mandates to prepare for free democratic elections." Even after new governments were formed, officials in both countries suggested that they should spurn the Polish example and opt instead for a slower, "step-by-step" program. Unlike Poland, Komarek explained that Czechoslovakia had full shops and no huge foreign debt. His plan was to redistribute resources, not jolt the country back to capitalism. Free prices and a convertible crown would be introduced over a longer period, say ten years. Instead of investing more in inefficient coal mines and steel plants, light industry and services such as tourism would be emphasized. "Austria makes $10 billion a year in tourism. We make one-fiftieth of that," Komarek said, sweeping his hands upwards to show off his beautiful baroque office. "With treasures like this, we too should make $10 billion a year." Polls showed that nearly half the Czechoslovak public wanted the economy to remain state-controlled. Less than 5 per cent favored capitalism. As Komarek put it, "We believe in a liberal system, a market economy. We don't believe in capitalism."

This halfway program looked insufficient. Hungary had followed the Komarek recipe, emphasizing light industry and tourism, and after two decades of meager results concluded that the transition to the market needed stronger medicine. "The step-by-step approach doesn't work," Deputy Finance Minister Zsigmond Járai told me. "We need a 'shock.'" At Harvard, Professors Jeffrey Sachs and János Kornai also made convincing cases for shock programs. They were not disinterested observers. Sachs was advising the Polish government and Kornai the Hungarian opposition. Both agreed that the transformation to a market had to be swift because, as Sachs put it, "reform is a seamless web." Without a swift operation, the mammoth bureaucracy would sabotage reform, while a market shock would sidestep its influence. Another compelling reason was political: the necessary changes were so immense and so painful that affected interest groups would pick away at them unless they were implemented in one swoop.

Key to the shock plan were free prices and immediate currency convertibility. Since a market works on price signals, only free prices would signal which enterprises were profitable and which were bankrupt. Convertible currency would force the government to balance its budget and put an end to easy credits. It would present monopoly state producers with the immediate task of facing foreign competition. Privatization was necessary to discipline the state sector. But Kornai and Sachs agreed that dismantling public ownership would take years. In the meantime, market discipline must be imposed by allowing private firms and importers to compete.

Reform of trade with the Soviet Union could wait. I attended the first Comecon meeting after the revolution and found lots of talk about reform but little concrete action. A committee was named to study Comecon's problems and prepare a document for a new meeting in three months' time on the best way to achieve free trade. "We don't need to study the problem," complained Czech Finance Minister Klaus. "There is nothing to invent. We just have to return to the normal rules of international commerce." The problem, even for the radicals, was that free trade would cause pain at first – they would have to pay more for Soviet oil, while many of their manufactured goods would no longer have a market. Finland showed that some counter-trade can be incorporated into a strong market-oriented economy. So, while engaged in getting their own houses in order, the Eastern Europeans concluded that they would be able to live with inefficient Comecon.

The role of the West will be crucial. Instead of just offering nice words, the West must take concrete action to open its markets. Protectionist Western European farmers still block Polish hams and Hungarian salami from entering the Common Market. All remaining restrictions on exports of high-technology goods to Eastern Europe should be lifted. For a long time, Cold War Luddites delayed making it impossible for Poland to upgrade its terrible telephone system and for the Solidarity newspaper to buy the Apple computers it needs for typesetting.

The Eastern Europeans want to join in the Western European economic integration, and the Western Europeans must give them a chance to compete. This means debt-relief. Eastern Europe's emerging democracies are crippled by $100 billion in debt. Professor Sachs suggests that, provided Polish-style market plans are implemented, much of it should be canceled. "Any attempt to collect more than a small share of these or the lesser sums owed by other countries would subject Eastern Europe to financial serfdom for the next generation; a plight that would be particularly bitter since the debt is a legacy of communist mismanagement, over which the public had no control," he argued. West Germany, holders of the largest amount of this debt, "should champion the cause of debt-relief. After each world war the Germans had to grapple with a crushing debt burden. Relief came too late the first time – only after Hitler's rise to power had confirmed Keynes's prophetic warnings to the victors of World War I against trying to collect reparations. In 1953 West Germany's creditors showed far more vision, canceling much of its debt and thereby buttressing the financial basis for its spectacular economic recovery."

Debt-relief should not be confused with granting large amounts of unrestricted new credits. In the 1970s billions of dollars of Western loans were wasted on inefficient prestige projects. Most proposals for renewed Western aid threatened to make the same mistake, offering unwarranted, unjustified government-guaranteed export loans, propping up inefficient state enterprises. Instead of encouraging government-to-government ties, the goal of Western aid should be private-to-private ties – building links between businesses, churches, environmentalists, students. Loans should be focused on the new private sector, in particular on small and medium-sized firms.

A model for this type of investment is the private Soros Foundation, the first independent foundation to operate in Eastern Europe. Since its inception in 1983, the Foundation has funded everything from international art exchanges to independent student groups – all for an annual budget of $3 million. In Budapest, where it began, it was the moving force behind the launch of the new International Management Center, the first Western-style business school in a communist country, and the $100 million Soros Mutual Fund for the budding Hungarian Stock Exchange. George Soros's actions captured the Hungarian public, turning the American financier into a folk-hero. "I expected it to make a dent, but it's made much more than a dent," he explained.

Soros is a charming, mild-mannered, sixty-nine-year-old financier, an archetype of the American rags-to-riches dream. His family left Budapest in 1948, fearing that anti-Semitism would worsen under communist rule. In New York he created money-market funds. His fortune reaches an estimated $300 million, but he is no egotistical money-obsessed braggart. When I met him in Budapest he was dressed in simple slacks and an open-necked shirt, and he impressed me with his modesty and thoughtfulness. "After you've made a lot of money," he said, "you get more interested in finding ways of spending it."

Soros spent his money to obtain maximum impact. Because the Hungarian forint was not convertible, the Soros Foundation provided hard currency for Western imports such as medical equipment which the hard-pressed communist regime could not afford. The hospitals paid the foundation in forints, which were then channeled back into cultural projects: buying books for local libraries around the country, funding renovations of small-town churches, and sponsoring research projects ranging from gypsy culture in Transylvania to the study of the bloody 1956 uprising against Soviet domination. The Foundation sent hundreds of Hungarian academics, businessmen and students to the West to study. "If you spend efficiently, you can get a bigger impact for your money here," Soros explained. "Three million dollars goes a long, long way."

As Hungary moved towards free elections, his Foundation expanded its activities. It launched a competition for "New Democratic Organizations," financing new independent trade unions, the new independent students' union FIDESZ, and opposition political movements such as the Free Democrats and the Democratic Forum. The money was spent in such practical ways as buying computers and copying machines. New Soros Foundations were set up in Warsaw, Moscow and Beijing, though the Chinese one was closed, at least temporarily, after the Tiananmen Square massacre. Others began to copy Soros's ideas. The West German Free Democratic Party set up its own foundation in Budapest, and larger American foundations such as the Rockefeller Foundation expanded their work behind the crumbling Iron Curtain. The Soros effort showed that Western money could make an essential contribution to the reconstruction of democratic capitalism in Eastern Europe – if it was intelligently used.

Chapter Twelve

The Environment: A Polluted Utopia

Our environmental problems are not just simple environmental problems. They show the bankruptcy of the traditional socialist model of industrialization.

Valtr Komarek, Czechoslovak Deputy Prime Minister

Marcela Malíková often woke up with a dull headache. Outside her window, a black blanket of air lay suspended over her home town of Most, Czechoslovakia. Stepping outside, smelling the stench, her breath became short and her eyes burned. "I worry so much about Filip," she said, pointing to her seven-month-old son. "I can't even take him outside."

Her suffering testified to the environmental nightmare gripping Eastern Europe. In my travels I discovered a disaster zone of dying forests, contaminated rivers, poisoned farmlands and crumbling cities. By nature I am not an ecologist; I don't agonize over the Greenhouse effect. But in Eastern Europe I couldn't help but be bothered by pollution. As with Mrs. Malíková, the telltale smell of burning brown coal often turned my breath short, burned my eyes and caused stomachaches.

The physical damage is terrifying. In Kraków and Prague, poisoned air has eaten away at centuries-old baroque statues which had survived centuries of invasions and two world wars. Pieces of masonry often fall from church steeples, balconies crumble and the faces of graceful, sculpted saints are deformed. Jan Škoda, chief of Prague's Environmental Commission, admitted that 80 per cent of the city's 2,000 registered monuments need restoration.

Once-unspoiled countryside is under attack. In the lush Erzgebirge Forest on the East German–Czechoslovak border, tourists used to scale the Fichtelberg mountain to marvel at the view. When I went there, all I saw below me was a huge expanse of dead trees and broad brown patches. It looked as if the forests had been ravaged by fire; the real culprit turned out to be a deadly mix of sulfur dioxide, nitrogen oxides, heavy metals and other noxious gases pouring from power plants and factories. Data from the United Nations suggest that from a quarter to a third of all Eastern European forests show "irreversible" pollution-induced damage. Foresters have tried planting tougher trees, but they too are withering away.

The destruction is making people ill. Hospital clinics contain ward after ward of infants breathing through tubes, suffering birth defects and brain damage. Respiratory ailments and cancer are increasing at an exceptional rate. Life expectancy is falling. The Hungarian Environment Ministry says that one in seventeen deaths in the country is related to pollution. In Poland, villages in industrialized Silesia have been declared unfit for human habitation because of high levels of heavy metals in the soil. In Czechoslovakia Mrs. Malíková was not waiting for a formal decree. "We're moving to a cleaner town," she told me. "This place is not safe for families with children."

Communism's collapse opened new possibilities and problems in the battle against pollution. Evidence of poisoned air and water was no longer hidden and ecologists were freed to fight for a cleaner environment. But factories continued to belch out the pollutants, and new democratic governments trying to cut state spending and pay foreign debts resisted the huge outlays needed for anti-pollution equipment. Environmental groups, freed from restrictions, drifted towards broader political agendas or split into factions.

Ironically, communist officials had long dismissed pollution as a product of capitalism. Capitalists, they argued, were more interested in making money than in preventing pollution. Communism eliminated the profit motive, the main cause behind industrial pollution. As the owner of all factories, the state could impose uniform purity standards.

The truth turned out to be the exact opposite. Under central planning, a manager was judged on his factory's level of production, not on its level of waste. Fines levied against polluters ranged from low to non-existent, and in any case the government, as the owner of all property, ended up paying the penalties. Inspectors would go into factories, find pollution violations, collect fines and deposit the money in government coffers. The company would turn around and request money from the same coffers to pay the fines. It was a vicious circle. To meet their plans, managers dumped anything and everything into the rivers and air. "We thought we could eliminate pollution through central planning, only to find that central planning puts the plan above everything else," admitted Petér Reményi of the Hungarian Environmental Protection Office.

If their economies flourished, the Eastern Europeans might have overcome the damage and paid for expensive environmental controls, much as Western industries have done. Unfortunately, the economies stagnated. Dirty old plants continued in production. The transition from heavy manufacturing to a service economy was not made. No money was available to buy pollution-control equipment. Today, high-sulfur brown coal, obsolete in the West, continues as the primary energy source for the most heavily polluted countries – Czechoslovakia, East Germany, Poland and Hungary. Eastern Bloc agriculture relies on high-phosphate fertilizers, while cars are based on 1960s models, many of which use inefficient "two-stroke" engines and all of which lack anti-pollutant devices such as catalytic converters.

A cramped geography aggravates these unhealthy practices. Unlike the huge land masses of the United States or the Soviet Union, which can absorb much pollution, Eastern European countries are squeezed into a narrow, heavily populated corridor. Where pollution is concerned, the East–West divide has never held. Clouds heavy with acid rain drift across borders, while a complex river-system carries poisoned water from one country to the next. The worst polluted region is the heavily industrialized area where Czechoslovakia, East Germany and Poland meet. Residents dub it the "Bermuda Triangle of pollution." The Vistula, Poland's main artery flowing into the Bay of Gdańsk, alone accounts for two-thirds of the 131,000 metric tons of nitrogen flowing each year into the Baltic Sea. Along the coast, vacationers can no longer swim and children cannot even play in the wet sand of once-worldfamous resorts such as Sopot. "Pollution knows no boundaries," noted a Hungarian diplomat. "Against it, there are no effective fences, no Checkpoint Charlies."

Kraków, a magnificent medieval city, illustrates the perverted logic which turned the region into an ecological disaster zone. The city's Gothic spires and fine ramparts include some of Europe's most cherished architectural treasures, including the 1,000-year-old Wawel Castle. Alone among major Polish cities, it survived World War II without significant damage. Its rich Renaissance buildings housed wealthy merchants and university intellectuals. This is the home of Pope John Paul II, and the Church's influence is omnipresent. In 1939, some 250 churches served a population of 300,000. Almost every block of the Old Town has its own house of worship. "The communists took one look at the people here and said, 'We'll get back at you'," one resident told me. " 'We'll give you a proletariat.' "

They did. Europe's largest steel mill, the Lenin Steelworks, was built only nine miles from the Wawel Castle. It included a vast network of power plants and foundries, apartment complexes and public halls, and employed 33,000 workers. On a rare clear day, the smokestacks are so large they can be seen from the castle. Kraków's population has soared to 700,000. Nearly 250,000 workers and their families live in block upon block of dreary Stalinist-style apartments in the suburb of Nowa Huta.

The plant produces 80 per cent of the noxious gases which hang over Kraków, along with 50 per cent of the dust and 60 per cent of the solid wastes. It uses anachronistic open-hearth technology and includes none of the pollution-control equipment which rescued such American steel centers as Pittsburgh. Such equipment would cost millions, perhaps even billions. Plant managers say they cannot afford the price tag. Kraków meanwhile crumbles. In the Old Town, the Renaissance and baroque facades are black with grime. Entire blocks are falling into ruin. Paint is peeling on even the renovated buildings. "As soon as the painters finished, it started turning black," a tour guide told me, pointing to a dirty yellow façade. "That building was renovated only two years ago."

Kraków is no isolated case. Other cities are even more ravaged by industrial waste. One example is Most in Czechoslovakia, a city of 50,000 located in north Bohemia near the East German border. It is not far from the famed spa towns of Karlovy Vary and Mariánské Lazně. Kings and queens came to the region at the turn of the century, attracted by the pure air, verdant forests and sparkling mineral baths. The spas remain handsome resorts, if a bit run-down. Nearby Most, by contrast, is a disaster. Officials discovered a rich coal deposit under the Old Town. To obtain the coal, they took a logical, if extreme, decision. They leveled the entire city.

Only the old baroque church was saved. Its foundations were dug up, the building placed on a moving truck and transported to a new site at the edge of the mine, where now it stands alone. Next to the church, strip-mining left a giant, gaping dirty-brown hole spreading out over the horizon. Across the highway an entire new town of gray, soulless concrete apartment blocks were built to house the miners. When it was planned, officials said no one even thought about the potential pollution problem. "We were so involved in building the new town that we didn't pay much attention to the environment," admitted František Pátek, president of Most's District Committee. "When the snow started turning black in town, we knew we had to do something."

In the mid-1980s, Patek and other town authorities instituted wartime-like restrictions. Residents were advised to go every weekend to the countryside. Children were taken away for weeks to cleaner South Bohemia and, during the worst pollution times, schools were ordered to keep children inside and limit their physical exercise. Some improvement was reported. Thanks to a vigorous tree-planting program, the town's surrounding forests stopped dying. Desulfurization equipment and air-filters were bought for municipal heating plants and a program started to convert residential heating from coal to natural gas and to restore damaged buildings.

But the pollution problems continued to ravage the town. For every house restored, many more deteriorated. Production remained the priority. Authorities were unwilling either to shut the coal mine or to promote energy savings by raising prices. The area around Most held the dubious distinction of having the highest density of sulfur-dioxide emissions in Europe – an astounding 228 pounds per acre each year. More than 60 per cent of teenagers suffered from respiratory diseases, serious skin ailments or digestive problems. "Everything is being done too slowly," complained František Ruba, the twenty-seven-year-old founder of a youth ecological group called Brontosaurus. The group's name, taken from the extinct dinosaur, signalled the urgency of the problem. As Ruba told me, "we'd better do something quick or we too will be extinct."

With lives threatened, Eastern Europeans organized themselves to fight the pollution plague. Instead of pitting a few isolated intellectuals against the power of a totalitarian state, the fight for a clean environment brought together a broad range of society and helped dissidents break out of isolation. "Ecology and pacifism unite all sorts of people into independent movements," argued Hungarian Miklós Haraszti. "You can say, 'I want clean air and clean water' or 'I want peace' without saying 'I want human rights.' " While human rights represented an abstract concept, environment was concrete. "When trees are dying, when the water is dirty, when the air is dangerous for little children, that's worse than prison," said Czech activist

Lenka Marečková. "Everybody can see what's being done near their house or town. Everybody wants their children to have the right food, water and air."

Movements to clean the air, save forests and protect the environment marched arm-in-arm with drives for democracy. Under Marečková, Charter 77 started an Environmental Section, issuing a major report called "Let Our People Breathe." In East Germany, Evangelical churches held environmental services, started environmental libraries and began tree plantings. Bulgarians founded Eco Glasnost. In Poland, ecology emerged as a major force in the heyday of the Solidarity movement in 1980. A group of union shop stewards, journalists, doctors and academics founded the Polish Ecological Club. After a massive campaign of demonstrations and legal action, it succeeded in forcing the government to close the Skawina aluminum plant. The ecological group continued its work when martial law was declared, and it was joined by new opposition movements such as "Freedom and Peace."

The most interesting and influential Eastern European environmental group was Hungary's "Danube Circle." It was created in the early 1980s by a small group of scientists, economists and other "apolitical" professionals. These were not dissidents. Typical was Anna Perczel, an architect by training and a housewife by choice. "We really aren't against communism," Anna insisted. "We just felt this project was wrong."

The project was a mammoth dam and hydroelectric project across the Danube near its famous Bend, one of its most bucolic and historic spots. The plan involved rerouting a stretch of the mighty river and building two big dams, one at Nagymaros in Hungary and the other 120 miles upstream at Gabčikovo in Czechoslovakia. Hungarian officials argued that the dam would improve navigation on a shallow stretch of the Danube and provide both Czechoslovakia and Hungary with badly needed peak-time electricity. "If we don't build the dam, we will have to build another coal-burning electricity plant," argued Petér Reményi, of the Environmental Protection Authority. "That will pollute the river and cause much more environmental damage."

Danube Circle experts disagreed, saying that the damage to drinking-water supplies, to local agriculture and to the spectacular natural beauty of the tourist-attracting Danube Bend outweighed any potential benefits. "The dam's electricity will cost twice as much as that from a traditional power plant, while destroying the country's historic heart," said János Vargha, a biologist and Danube Circle founder. In pressing their case, the Danube Circle activists used techniques common in the West, but new to the communist world. They assembled scientific data to support their contentions, took out newspaper ads, collected a petition which gathered more than 10,000 signatures, printed leaflets and organized demonstrations. They even drummed up support abroad, from West German and Austrian Greens, and from American groups such as the Sierra Club and the Connecticut-based Foundation to Protect the Hungarian Environment. Danube Circle became, in the words of Judit Vásarhelyi, "a laboratory for mobilizing the opposition."

The liberal Kádár regime initially tolerated the Circle, regarding its criticism as apolitical and acceptable. Vargha gave public lectures and published his views in official newspapers. The Academy of Sciences created a commission to study the project. In 1986, the commission recommended continuing with the dam, but only after spending an additional $75 million on environmental safeguards.

When Danube Circle continued its protests, the police cracked down, banning a demonstration with Austrian and West German Greens and threatening to lodge criminal charges against protesters. Frightened Danube Circle leaders called off the march. Those who went ahead anyway were beaten with truncheons and hit with tear gas. A few months later, Vargha was fired from his position on the staff of the Hungarian version of *Scientific American*. The movement's application for legal recognition from the Academy of Sciences was turned down. "Give them whatever name you want," said Iván Berend, the Academy's President. "The Party is afraid that they will turn into a kind of political opposition."

The crackdown underlined the fundamental ambivalence of communist regimes towards independent ecology movements. As long as their activity was perceived to be motivated only by a concern for environment and health, the groups were tolerated. Once their attacks were perceived as an attack on the communist system, they were suppressed. In 1987 East German police raided the environmental library in Zion Church. The next year in Czechoslovakia, the regional Bohemian party reacted positively to an ecology petition. But Slovak officials in Bratislava responded to an independent report on pollution in the city by blasting its authors as anti-state agitators.

Danube Circle floundered, unsure how to respond to its problems with the police. Some members wanted to cooperate with the communists; others wanted to remain independent. Some wanted to form an ecology foundation; others saw no point in continuing. The movement revived only after Kádár was ousted in May 1988. A new demonstration was organized with Austrian and West German Greens. This time the police did not intervene, and some 10,000 people marched in front of the Parliament in Budapest. A new petition was launched, calling for a referendum on the dam. It gained more than 100,000 signatures. The country's reformist leaders backtracked. In 1989 they finally acknowledged the colossal economic and environmental mistake that the dam represented, and canceled it.

By the mid-1980s, most Eastern European regimes had begun to take anti-pollution measures. The problem was just too bad to ignore. Environmental protection agencies were established, environmental codes tightened and environmental spending increased. In 1985 the Czechoslovak government announced plans to spend $9 million over fifteen years to combat air pollution. It increased the allocation to $200 million the next year. Poland launched a major program to reduce pollution in the Vistula river, building large numbers of water-purification plants. New industrial plants were banned in Kraków and other high-pollution areas. The Hungarian Environmental Protection Agency's budget increased by six times between 1985 and 1990. Modest successes were visible. A decade ago, Hungary's Lake Balaton was so dirty owing to chemical waste from nearby farms that swimming was discouraged. Now Hungarian officials judge the vacation spot's water "first class."

Multilateral ecological agreements were developed in the communist world. Hungary began sharing environmental information with Czechoslovakia, Yugoslavia and the Soviet Union, while Comecon set common standards for water purity. In 1987 Poland, East Germany and Czechoslovakia even held an ecological summit. Deputy Premiers from the three countries agreed "to expand and deepen cooperation in environmental protection."

The picture remained bleak, despite these modest successes. Instead of moving faster and pushing conservation, most Eastern European countries promoted nuclear power as the "clean" solution to their pollution woes. All engaged in massive nuclear construction programs drawing on Soviet technology. Between 1978 and 1986, nuclear-power production in Eastern Europe doubled, according to a U.S Central Intelligence Agency report.

In 1986 fifty-one reactors were already in operation in the region and thirty-three more were being built. At last count, Poland had two nuclear plants under construction, Czechoslovakia eight under construction and eight in operation, and East Germany six under construction and five operating. Czechoslovakia, East Germany and Hungary each hoped to satisfy about half of their energy needs with "clean" nuclear fuel by the turn of the century.

When I visited the Hungarian nuclear complex in Paks in 1986, director Tibor Láczai Szabo told me that it already supplied 14 per cent of Hungary's electricity. Two more nuclear reactors went into operation in 1987, increasing the amount of the country's electricity provided by nuclear power to 25 per cent. Four additional reactors are still planned to be built in the 1990s, meaning that nuclear power will supply between 40 and 50 per cent of the nation's electricity by the turn of the century. Eastern Bloc economies mobilized to meet such ambitious targets. In Czechoslovakia, for example, a diplomat insisted that the entire population of the southern Moldavia region was "retrained to build nuclear power plants." At Paks in Hungary, director Szabo said that 2,000 apartments, a dozen new schools and stores – in short an entire new city – were constructed for nuclear-plant workers.

The Chernobyl disaster on April 29, 1986, did not deter this nuclear push. At the time, I was in Budapest. Official press reports limited coverage of the accident to a few paragraphs. Only after neighboring Austria said that its nuclear levels were above normal did the government admit that Hungary also suffered from "a slight increase" in nuclear levels. Even then, officials continued to play down the danger, refusing to reconsider their nuclear projects because of budgetary constraints. "The Austrians built a $300 million nuclear plant and then stopped it from operating," Szabo said. "We don't have that money to waste."

No additional safety precautions were taken. Officials said that the largest amounts of radiation traveled over northern Europe away from the country, and added that Hungary's own nuclear plant in Paks was of a later, safer design, which used pressurized water to slow down the neutrons. The Chernobyl reactor instead used volatile graphite. "We have taken many more security steps than in the Soviet Union and incorporated many Western design elements," assured Dr. Jozsef Bognár, director of the Institute for World Economics. When I visited Paks, Gabor Vámos, the plant's operation manager, insisted that no design changes were envisioned. "Not a single worker left his job," he added. "Everything is calm."

He was right. I did hear some cynical jokes about Chernobyl. ("How do you measure Soviet–Polish friendship?" Answer: "With a Geiger counter." Or "What is the highest stage of communism?" Answer: "A melt-down.") But behind the black humor, I found more fatalism than anger. Unlike Western Europe's enraged ecologists, Hungary's Danube Circle leaders refused to engage in a fight against nuclear power. "We need nuclear power to satisfy our energy needs," argued Iván Baba. "There's no public opinion against it here," added Judit Vásarhelyi. Eastern Bloc publics waiting in line to buy scarce meat or gasoline have more mundane worries than invisible radiation. "It was easy to mobilize opposition for the Danube dam because everyone could see how the dam would change the local landscape," Vásarhelyi explained. "A nuclear plant, by contrast, doesn't destroy the landscape." She even saw nuclear power as a necessary evil to ease a worsening energy crisis resulting from expensive Soviet oil imports and scarce domestic fuel resources. "Compared with the dam, which will produce little electricity, nuclear power looks like a rational way of supplying our needed energy."

Elsewhere, I found a similar reluctance among dissidents to attack nuclear power. Among their political priorities, opposition leaders put Chernobyl far down their list of pressing problems. "Unlike in the West, we have more important things than Chernobyl to get mad about – like martial law," said leading Solidarity activist Jacek Kuroń. At $22 a barrel, imported Soviet oil remained expensive. Domestic coal resources were dwindling. This coal was also dirty to burn, much dirtier than nuclear power. "With our air and water pollution already horrible," Jiří Dienstbier said, "nuclear power looks like the best way out."

Today, Eastern Europe faces a stark choice over its ecology crisis. Either the region's new governments change the way their economies are run and commit a larger share of their resources to environmental protection, or pollution will suffocate their countries. The trade-off will be difficult to accept, both politically and economically. It means nothing less than a decrease in productivity, price rises, even a perceptible decline in living standards.

The most practical route would be to increase energy efficiency. Western industries achieved huge efficiency gains in the 1970s after the oil crisis. With energy prices still subsidized, the East never made these gains. Eastern European economies consume two to five times as much energy per unit of GDP as Western economies. Economic reforms are designed to make industry more cost-sensitive, and less inclined to waste energy. In Poland, for example, deregulation at the beginning of 1990 meant a jump of up to 500 per cent in coal and gas prices. Poles no longer regulate the heat in their apartments by opening their windows. They turn down the thermostat. The best long-term solution would be economic recovery. New-found prosperity would generate the funds needed for more efficient production processes and for pollution-control devices.

For the foreseeable future, however, expensive desulfurization equipment and air-filters will remain beyond the budgets of most strapped Eastern Bloc governments. Only the wealthy West can help with money, technology and expertise. Although historically Westerners have not cared much about pollution in the Eastern Bloc – anything which drained communist resources was seen as a boon to the West – the global environmental crisis has changed perspectives. Chernobyl's radioactive rays provoked cries of alarm throughout Western Europe and the United States. New worries about the global Greenhouse effect reinforce the idea that pollution in Czechoslovakia causes as much potential harm to faraway Americans as to nearby Czechs and Slovaks.

When I traveled to Scandinavia, officials in both Finland and Sweden told me that about two-thirds of the acid rain threatening their forests came from abroad, much of it from Eastern Europe. "For the Nordic countries, what happens in Poland, East Germany, Czechoslovakia isn't an abstract issue," said Markku Wallin, an environmental specialist at the Central Organization of Finnish Trade Unions. "It directly affects our health – personal and economic."

It would be cheaper and more effective for Finland or Sweden to finance the fight against pollution in Poland and East Germany than at home. "Since we have a lot less pollution than in Poland, we must spend a lot more than them to lower pollution levels," explained Aira Kalela, director of the International Affairs Division of the Finnish Ministry of the Environment. "But politically it's difficult to justify paying for projects abroad." Another problem involved technology transfer. While Western coal power-plant filters guarantee a 40–50 per cent reduction in nitrogen-oxide emissions, Eastern European equipment produces only a 10–15 per cent reduction. Before they signed new anti-pollution agreements, the Eastern Europeans demanded that the West donate its anti-nitrogen-oxide technology, a request the West refused out of security considerations. "At a certain stage in the negotiations, we always found ourselves in front of restrictions on high-technology exports," a Hungarian diplomat complained.

Some progress was made across the ideological divide. Talks on environmental cooperation began in 1979 as a follow-up to the Helsinki Accords. "Leonid Brezhnev asked himself, 'In what area could we all cooperate?' " recalled Finland's Aira Kalela. "Environment was a 'safe issue.' It didn't provoke East –West conflicts like human rights did." Ecology was becoming a topical issue in Western Europe, particularly in pivotal West Germany. "After the rise of the Greens and the problems deploying American missiles, the West German position changed 180 degrees," remembered Lars Björkbom, of the Swedish Ministry of the Environment. "Bonn began pushing the negotiations."

The sulfur negotiations moved to quick completion. The thirty-two European countries who met in Geneva all adopted a protocol on air pollution, and an accompanying protocol was adopted requiring signatories to reduce their sulfur-dioxide emissions by 30 per cent by 1993. Another protocol froze emissions of nitrogen oxides at 1987 levels by 1994. To help pay for these moves, bilateral cooperation agreements are becoming common. Czechoslovakia and West Germany agreed to pay for some sulfur-dioxide "scrubbers" in power stations and jointly to develop equipment to fight water pollution. Under another treaty, Austria and Hungary promised to share information on ecological problems.

Just as in the West, however, powerful interests in the East continued to regard pollution as a lesser evil than a decline in production. Economic interests often overwhelmed environmental joint efforts, and environmental concerns remained mostly a concern of the rich rather than the poor. Before unification, agreements between West German and East German towns on garbage disposal proliferated. Western towns found it cheaper and politically acceptable to dump their waste in the East. The East, strapped for hard currency, accepted the refuse. Western producers also contracted – often illegally – to dump hazardous waste in Polish and Hungarian dump sites.

As they attempt to satisfy growing public demands for more and better consumer goods, many of the new Eastern European regimes could end up neglecting the environment. Somewhat paradoxically, market-oriented economic reform could add to the problem. With salaries tied to productivity, workers could oppose environmental constraints that cut their wages. Each Eastern European country now boasts a Green Party, but no Green movement has won significant political power. For Eastern European politicians, the fight for democracy comes before the fight for the environment, while for most Eastern Europeans, better food and housing for their families come before cleaner air. The new Solidarity Minister of Industry wanted to shut the polluting Nowa Huta steel mill outside Kraków. Once settled in office, however, he found that he could not touch it: almost all the country's industry was dependent on its steel.

After the cancelation of the Danube dam project in Hungary, I went to visit János Vargha. The soft-spoken Vargha was never a man to exhibit exuberance, I was still amazed to find him so pessimistic. "Environmental consciousness remains so low in this country," he said. Already he had decided to close down Danube Circle. "With no concrete issue, it no longer has much popular support," he explained. He himself, Eastern Europe's foremost environmentalist, was joining the Free Democrats and running for Parliament. "Human rights are our first priority," he said. "Environment will just have to wait."

Chapter Thirteen

The Jews: Stirring Ghosts

Revolutions aren't good for Jews. They create a vacuum of power, and when there's a vacuum of power, it's Jews who suffer the most.

Martin Weisman, Bucharest Jew January 1990

When I began traveling to Eastern Europe, the first attraction was not political. It was personal. Fannie Wolf and Saul Gross, my mother's parents, had emigrated from Vienna. The family of my father's grandmother Pearl Commando came from Budapest. My namesake, my father's grandfather, the Echikson, originated in a Jewish village in Latvia just outside Riga. As he told the story, his name was Isaacson but was changed by chance by an immigration officer at Ellis Island.

Wherever I went, I recognized smiling plump *babushka*s who looked like my grandmother. They had the same mannerisms, the same lilt in their voices, the same firm walk. I ate jellied carp, just like my grandmother's home-made *gefilte* fish. The men resembled my grandfather. They wore the same type of wide-brimmed hat, the same faded tweed vest, the same intense, quizzical facial expression. In their faces and in their mannerisms, the "World of my Fathers" lived on.

One of my first stops in Warsaw was the city's only remaining synagogue. I found no rabbi, just a few old, haggard men. Their gray coats were ragged and their faces covered by a few days' stubble. Their mouths revealed toothless gaps. One gave his name as Nathan. He spoke a bit of Hebrew, and led the way to Mila Street in the center of the old Ghetto. In September 1939 about a third of the population of Warsaw was Jewish. Almost all the Jews perished during the war; most of those who did survive fled to Israel or the West, and the ragged few who stayed behind were persecuted in communist-sponsored purges. Now in the Ghetto row after row of gray, mass-produced housing stretched to the horizon. Among the housing units, Nathan pointed out a large granite-and-bronze memorial to the Ghetto fighters who rose up against the Nazis. Unlike other memorials in Poland, this monument was not wreathed with commemorative flowers. Nathan smiled, and asked for a few dollars.

After this experience, I tried putting aside my search for roots – the path looked too strewn with emotional shrapnel – only to discover that forgetting was impossible. Throughout Eastern Europe, Jews and Judaism are a burning issue. If anything, lifting the lid on totalitarianism has reinforced fears of a resurgence of anti-Semitism. When I went to Poland to cover the appointment of Solidarity Prime Minister Tadeusz Mazowiecki, everyone seemed obsessed not by the amazing political breakthrough, but by the controversy over the Carmelite nunnery in Auschwitz. I traveled to Hungary to cover the election, and discovered that anti-Semitism had become a major campaign topic. And in East Germany I found Jews frightened about the revival of a neo-Nazi movement. "You begin to attack the communists," East Berlin Jewish leader Irene Runge said, "and you always end up with the Jews."

On the surface, the fears of renewed anti-Semitism in the 1990s seemed absurd. Almost no Jews live in Eastern Europe. Only Hungary, with 80,000, is home to a large Jewish population. In East Germany there are only a couple of hundred aging pensioners. In Poland a generous count comes up with a figure of 15,000, down from a pre-war Jewish population of 3.5 million. Like the haggard beggar Nathan whom I met, almost all the remaining Eastern European Jews are old and poor.

Something else, I realized, was at issue: ghosts. Eastern Europeans and Jews lived side by side for more than 1,000 years. Jews suffered. They also created a flourishing culture. Before the war, world Jewry was centered there. All the Jewish religious, national and cultural movements – Hasidism, Bundism and Zionism – originated there. In the Old Jewish Cemetery in Prague, dating from 1439, tombstones tumble over each other. Because of a lack of space, the graves have been piled on top of one another, up to twelve layers deep.

No subject which I reported caused me more anguish. There was the personal connection; there was also the sheer emotional energy which it generated. When the subject of Jews and Judaism was raised, normally rational, sane individuals – Jews and non-Jews, Eastern Europeans and non-Eastern Europeans – became hysterical. Each side claimed the status of unique victim, a strange sort of competitive martyrdom. Among my

Jewish American friends, I encountered hot hatred of Eastern Europe and its people. They kept asking, "How can you go there? How can you go back to where our parents fled?" Eastern Europeans responded with their own hatreds. Some fabricated a Jewish conspiracy to ruin their countries, claiming that communism had been a Jewish plot. Others asserted that they were always hospitable to their Jewish neighbors, failing to recognize the region's deep strain of anti-Semitism.

Sorting out the facts from the emotions proved impossible. Along with anti-Semitism, I discovered philo-Semitism. Jewish and non-Jewish youngsters packed courses on Jewish history and culture. When I traveled to the smallest town, my host invariably pointed out an abandoned synagogue and noted, "The Jews lived there." In countries which live through their history, the deep memory of the Jews pricks and torments consciences. Under communism, the troubled Jewish past was buried in silence. Increased freedom means confronting the old memories. Ghosts, I guess, are supposed to give nightmares.

The most powerful, painful nightmares stem from the Holocaust. The killers were the Germans, the death camps were located in Poland and most of the victims came from Eastern Europe. Six million Jews were killed. Three million were from Poland. Three million non-Jewish Poles were also killed. Even with the best of intentions, sorting out these memories is bound to raise heavy emotions. When *Shoah*, a history of the Holocaust, was screened in Warsaw, Poles saw their peasants depicted as callous and detached from the horrors of the Jewish fate. Although the Polish government protested that the film was unfair, it did catch some terrible truths.

On my first visit to Auschwitz, an official guide, Stanisłav, described the prison work in detail: the collecting of eye-glasses, gold fillings from teeth, and other personal belongings from condemned prisoners, and the workings of the crematoriums. The barracks had been transformed into memorials for all nationalities, everyone from Bulgarians to East Germans. Until I asked, he never mentioned the word "Jews." "This was also a Polish tragedy," he explained. "It wasn't just Jews who died here."

For Jews, this omission affronted their catastrophic losses. Of the approximately 4 million people who perished at Auschwitz, at least 2.5 million were Jewish. Some experts contend the percentage of Jews was even as high as 90 per cent. What no one disputes is that the Jews were killed just for being Jews, and that only Jews were brought in from other countries of Europe to be murdered. In America, my friends blamed the Poles. "You know why the Germans built the concentration camps in Poland?" one asked me. "Because the Poles were only too glad to help them."

Such statements in turn infuriate Poles and, to be fair, they falsify history. Poland hosted the greatest number of Jews scheduled to be annihilated. The Nazis put their killing camps close to the targets. Unlike in Western Europe, Poles harboring Jews were punished by summary execution. And unlike other nations, Poles had no leaders who collaborated at an official level with the Nazis. The underground Home Army declared the betrayal of Jews as punishable with death. "Poles feel they are unjustly treated," argued Jacek Wosniakowski, editor at the Roman Catholic publishing house ZNAK. "They didn't murder the Jews; they weren't the mass murderers."

Polish losses were immense. The Nazis leveled most major cities and killed more people in Poland than in any other occupied country. The Polish state emerged from the war emasculated, deprived of its independence. Given this situation, Poles tended to concentrate on their own suffering and ignore Jewish losses. "Poles are ignorant of the Holocaust. They don't grasp the difference between what happened to them and what happened to the Jews," worried Konstanty Gebert, a leader of the Polish Jewish community. "They think of themselves as victims, so it is hard for them to see others as victims."

These conflicting emotions exploded in the dispute over the Carmelite monastery at Auschwitz. In 1985, fourteen Carmelite nuns moved into an old brick building on the outer edge of Auschwitz which had been used by the Nazis as a warehouse to store gold fillings from their victims and some of the Zyklon B poison used in the gas chambers. Part of the ensuing controversy centered on whether the convent was located within the death camp. When I went to investigate, I found that while the building stood outside the barbed-wire perimeter fence, it was shown on a camp map and was visible from the barracks inside.

The nuns received permission from the Polish Minister of Culture for their convent. They hired workers to repair the structure. The adjacent vacant lot was turned into a garden, with a twenty-four-foot wooden cross as its centerpiece. In front, an eternal flame glowed. Off to the side stood an alabaster statue of the Virgin Mary. By all reports, the cloistered nuns inside spent their days in prayer and peaceful contemplation – prayer for those who died and contemplation to prevent such an evil from recurring. I say "by all reports," because they refused all interview requests. One nun was designated to pick up the mail. I waited for her, but she too declined to make any comment.

Theological questions fired the dispute. Through their own sacrifice and suffering, the nuns believed Auschwitz's sin could be overcome. For Poles, nothing could honor the memory more than such prayers. When I asked local residents, they saw the endeavor in terms of Christian duty and charity. "Those nuns just fixed the place up," said Jan, a mason. "It was crumbling before." "What could be more natural than to pray, to have quiet?" asked Marion, a railroad machinist. "It can't offend anyone."

In Judaism, however, there exists no similar concept of redemption through prayer. The Jewish prayer of mourning, the Kaddish, exalts God. It does not even mention the dead. From the Jewish perspective, the presence of the nuns at Auschwitz was offensive. "This began as the type of religious dispute which offended religious sensibilities," Gebert of the small Polish Jewish community said. "People of good faith here in the Catholic Church just weren't aware of the reasons for our hostility to the Carmelites."

After a series of meetings between Catholic and Jewish leaders in 1986 and 1987, an original compromise had been reached. Church officials promised to relocate the convent to a nearby center for Jewish–Christian dialogue by February 1989. The dispute died down until the deadline passed without the relocation. By this time it was clear that something deeper was at issue – the two differing versions of the Holocaust. Church officials said that building a new home for the nuns had proved more difficult than expected, and Jewish groups responded with a series of demonstrations. A rabbi from New York and a group of followers jumped over the fence and construction workers roughed them up and doused them with water. For Jews, the images broadcast around the world showed Polish anti-Semitism in its most violent form. Polish Catholics were outraged that a demonstrator, Jew or non-Jew, would violate the sanctity of a convent. For Maciej Kozlowski of the liberal Roman Catholic newspaper *Tygodnik Powszechny*, the Jewish demonstrations evoked memories of communists closing monasteries in the 1950s. "All we saw was somebody preventing Polish sisters from praying on Polish soil," he said.

Polish Primate Józef, Cardinal Glemp, uttered the worst

words. Speaking before 100,000 people at Czestochowa, a shrine to the Virgin Mary, the Primate departed from his prepared speech to launch a virulent attack against the Jewish demonstrators. He accused them of wanting to kill the nuns, and of using their "control" over the media to spread anti-Polish sentiment. The West exploded in outrage. Fortunately, the Pope and Solidarity Prime Minister Mazowiecki, himself a practicing Catholic, distanced themselves from Glemp and insisted that the convent would be moved. Krzysztof Śliwiński, managing editor of the Solidarity newspaper *Gazeta Wyborcza*, criticized the Cardinal in a front-page editorial. "We have to understand that what the Cardinal said doesn't just upset Jews," he told me. "Swedes find it just as offensive, even though almost no Jews live in Sweden."

Even after the convent was moved, a fundamental misunderstanding between Poles and Jews lingered on. Sliwinski said he received a great many letters and phone calls about his column – most of them negative. Most Poles I talked to backed their Primate. Even intellectuals failed to perceive the real reasons for Jewish anger. ZNAK's Mr. Wosniakowski wrote that the convent should be moved, not out of respect for Jewish understanding of the Holocaust, but because it offended them. "We signed a contract to move the convent, we should keep it," he explained. "But Jews should not monopolize suffering. They should realize that millions of others were killed, among them Poles."

Honest, open discussions about the Holocaust have not taken place in Eastern Europe. When the German Wehrmacht occupied Hungary on March 9, 1944, Hungarian Arrow Cross detachments began fanning through Budapest rounding up Jews from prepared lists and herding them into special ghetto areas. Before the war, Hungary's 600,000 Jews were among the most educated, affluent and assimilated in Europe. In four months, 450,000 were deported to Auschwitz, despite the heroic efforts of Swedish diplomat Raoul Wallenberg, who saved thousands by providing false papers and passports, setting up "Swedish houses" protected by the Swedish government. For many years the Hungarian government refused to honor Wallenberg's memory after his arrest by the liberating Soviet army. The silence was broken only on the Holocaust's fortieth anniversary. A moving Wallenberg monument was erected in Budapest, and the press began to discuss the role of the Iron Cross in the deportations.

Surprisingly, the one Eastern European country which emerged from the war with a reinforced reputation for tolerance was "backward" Bulgaria. Under pressure from the Nazis to deport the country's 48,000 Jews, the Bulgarian government procrastinated. It sent some of the Jews to villages. It acquiesced to the deportation of Jews from Bulgarian-occupied territories of Yugoslav and Greek Macedonia. But even in the darkest period of German intimidation, not a single Jew within the Bulgarian borders was surrendered to the Nazis. Parliament members, government ministers, intellectuals and professionals, and not least of all King Boris I, all protested against Jewish deportations, and by September 1944 all anti-Jewish decrees had been abolished.

At the other extreme, East Germans had the most difficulty coming to terms with what took place. In contrast to the fledgling West German state which admitted moral responsibility for the Holocaust and paid billions in reparations to Jews, East Germany's communist leaders refused any guilt. German communists had resisted the Nazis, they argued, so the East German state had no responsibility for fascism. "We don't have any moral responsibility for Hitler," one East German diplomat insisted. "The German Democratic Republic has done everything to uproot fascism, anti-Semitism and racism – our state is an anti-fascist state."

This explanation left many Holocaust survivors bitter. Israel never recognized the communist half of Germany. East Berlin acted as if it didn't seem to care, taking strong pro-Arab positions in the Middle East conflict with strident attacks against Israel. I'll never forget visiting the Buchenwald concentration camp near Weimar. At least at Auschwitz there was a pavilion devoted to Jewish suffering. Here no mention was made of Jewish victims. The memorials noted only murdered communist martyrs.

A timid effort was made to rectify the most glaring omissions in the waning days of the Honecker era. East Berlin's synagogue on Oranienburgerstrasse, desolate and deserted since the war, was renovated to serve as a place of worship for the remaining 350 Jews and as a museum of Jewish history. Rediscovering German–Jewish ties was part of a larger design to rediscover German history – the same as putting back the statue of Frederick the Great on the Unter den Linden, celebrating Martin Luther's anniversary, and even rehabilitating Bismarck. "We now realize that we can't just break with history; we have to deal with it," admitted Hans Wilke of the Office of Religious

Affairs. "There is Luther, Bach, Handel, the Huguenots, Moses Mendelssohn, and the Kristalnacht."

Restoring contacts with the World Jewish Community was designed to improve East Germany's image internationally, especially in the United States. The East Germans wanted Most Favored Nation trading status from Washington. Similar motives colored the Polish, Hungarian and Romanian governments' treatment of Jews during the 1970s and 1980s. The talks were always difficult. In 1988 East German leader Erich Honecker met with Rabbi Israel Miller, president of the Jewish Claims Conference, and offered to pay $100 million to Jewish victims of the Holocaust. Still the East Germans refused to accept "responsibility" for the genocide, and Jews who were less interested in the money than in seeing the East Germans accept moral responsibility, refused. "It's like trying to square a circle," concluded a Western diplomat following the issue. "Honecker was willing to set up a Jewish cultural center and do almost anything to respect the role of Jews, but he wouldn't stand up and say he or his state was guilty of murdering them."

A change in policy would take place only after the East German revolution. In one of its first acts, the first freely elected East German Parliament accepted moral responsibility for the Holocaust, and offered to begin paying reparations, and to open diplomatic relations with Israel.

Relations between communism and Judaism resembled those of close but warring relatives. Many pre-war Eastern European communists were born Jewish. Shedding the hermetic existence of religious orthodoxy, they searched for a secular substitute to escape persistent persecution. Many turned to Zionism, which envisioned an idealized Jewish socialist state. Others sought salvation in communism, with its pledge to rid the world of all social distinctions and discrimination. A typical example were the parents of Miklós Haraszti. When the war came they fled from Budapest to Jerusalem, where Miklós was born in 1945. His parents, preferring communism to Zionism, returned to Hungary to build socialism. Miklós was raised an atheist, never taught anything about Judaism. But later, as he shed his Marxist beliefs to become one of his country's most fearless fighters for democracy, he began to revaluate his religion. He doesn't practice, but he doesn't deny either, and he finds something strangely comforting in his identity. When we met and he discovered my Jewishness, there was a moment of quiet complicity between us. We shared something important.

In the immediate post-war period, Jewish communists such as the Harasztis became prominent in many Eastern European communist regimes. The Soviet-trained communist leadership in Hungary included a majority of Jews, led by Mátyás Rákosi. Romanian leader Anna Pauker was a former Hebrew teacher. Jews were often put in charge of the secret police. Some scholars say this was a clever move by Stalin, because he knew that the Jews had long memories of the anti-Semitism of their fellow citizens.

When the Stalinist purges started, they soon focused on Jews. In the autumn of 1952 Rudolf Slánský, former Secretary-General of the Czech Communist Party, and thirteen other former officials in the Party and government went on trial in Prague for high treason. The charges were "Zionist conspiracy." An openly anti-Semitic tone pervaded the trial. Of the fourteen defendants, eleven were Jews. Countless other Jews were mentioned as co-conspirators. The defendants were depicted as tools of Jewish leaders in the United States and Israel, determined to overthrow the communist regime through espionage and sabotage. Slánský was even accused of trying, with help from the American Joint Distribution Committee, to poison President Klement Gottwald. All the defendants were declared guilty, and all but three were executed.

Similar anti-Semitic purges and trials took place in the rest of the communist world. In Stalin's mind, Jews appeared as a repository of the "deviationist" Trotskyite and Titoist socialism which the Soviet ruler feared. It didn't matter that Slánský himself was a veteran hardline Stalinist. For local communist rulers, purging Jews was seen as a way of anchoring their legitimacy and proving that they were good native patriots. Anti-Semitism provided a distraction from internal economic failures. Throughout the Bloc, Jews were expelled from their positions in government, Party and industry. In Romania Anna Pauker was deposed; and in Hungary Rákoski tried to save his skin by jettisoning his Jewish colleagues, but in February 1953 the order came down from Moscow that he should leave his post as Premier. Numbers of Jewish communal leaders were jailed and tried on charges of "economic crimes."

Repression eased after Stalin's death in March 1953, only to be revived periodically. In Poland, the 1956 liberalization unleashed an upsurge of popular anti-Semitism. Poison-pen letters appeared in the newspapers, urging Jews to leave the country. Jewish children were taunted, some even assaulted. Polish leader Władysław Gomułka, with a Jewish wife, was not himself an anti-Semite, and gave permission for Jews who wanted to leave for Israel. Thousands rushed to the passport offices to secure exit visas.

Another anti-Semitic campaign erupted in 1968, this time the consequence of a three-way rivalry for leadership within the Communist Party. General Mieczysław Moczar, the Interior Minister, mounted a press campaign accusing "Zionists" of forming a Fifth Column. Day after day, his supporters fabricated articles claiming that the country's institutions were riddled with "non-Poles." Intellectual discontent boiled over when Adam Michnik led a rally of Warsaw University students, protesting the cancellation of Mickiewicz's play *The Forefathers*. Much was made of the fact that Michnik and several of the other student leaders were Jewish. A painful purge followed. Ministries, universities and hospitals were asked to compile lists of staff who were thought to be Jewish or to have Jewish relatives, Jewish ancestors or Jewish spouses. Thousands lost their posts and all but a handful of Poland's remaining Jews emigrated.

State-sponsored anti-Semitism revealed the bankruptcy of the socialist utopia for many of the committed, convinced Jewish communists. Men such as Bronisław Geremek, the grandson of a Kraków rabbi, became committed democrats. Among the Polish students arrested in the Mickiewicz demonstration, Adam Michnik, Jan Lityński and Seweryn Blumsztajn, all of whom had given little thought to their Jewish origins, remained active in opposition politics.

Religious Jews throughout the region took a different approach. They learned to keep their heads down, while community leaders struck bargains with the communist rulers. There was a price to pay, and the price was more or less active support of odious regimes. Romania's Rabbi Rosen, nicknamed the "Red Rabbi" for his willingness to work with the communists, exemplified and perfected this collaboration. "Collaboration" is really too strong a word to describe what was a delicate moral choice. Throughout their history as a minority in exile, the Jews often found themselves at the mercy of hostile societies. For protection, the leader of a Jewish community turned to the country's ruler. Moses Rosen played this role.

When I met the Rabbi in his Bucharest office, he impressed me with his savvy intelligence. In addition to Romanian and Hebrew, he spoke French, German, Russian and English, all fluently. His small, plump figure camouflaged a man of remarkable energy, and his long white orthodox Jewish beard hid a man of considerable secular knowledge. Rosen was born in 1913 in the little Bukovian town of Suceava. Before taking up rabbinical studies, he trained as a lawyer. After experiencing first hand a violent anti-Jewish pogrom in Suceava in 1940, he moved to Bucharest. There he escaped another pogrom by hiding in a synagogue. He became Chief Rabbi in 1947. Under pressure from the regime, he joined the communist front "Peace Committee" and endorsed the Party line in its attacks on "Western Imperialism." But he resisted pressure to condemn the new state of Israel. During the Stalinist anti-Zionist purges, police placed him under virtual house-arrest. His phone was tapped. Unless he relented and criticized Israel, police warned him of "serious personal consequences." He tried to resign. "No one resigns in Romania," the police warned him. "He disappears." "Stalin's death saved me," Rosen told me. "I asked myself, was I foolish to try to work with such people? But there was no choice."

After Stalin's death in 1953 the regime began to permit emigration to Israel. At the time Romania was home to some 300,000 Jews, the largest enclave of Jews in Eastern Europe apart from the Soviet Union. All except 20,000 left. Romanian Jews today make up the largest foreign-born group in Israel after Moroccans. While all other Eastern Bloc countries broke relations with Israel after the 1967 Six Day War, Romania kept its ties with the Jewish state. Dictator Ceausescu even saw himself as something of an "honest broker" between Israel and its Arab enemies.

Jews who stayed behind in Romania were protected. Aid programs sponsored by Western Jews were shut down elsewhere in Eastern Europe, but the American Joint Distribution Committee was allowed to continue its work in Romania. It spends $4 million a year in the country. Among the results are an impressive $2.5 million Jewish nursing home and kosher kitchen operation. Just as in New York, needy elderly Jews receive "meals on wheels." Seven mini-vans deliver 700 meals a day. When I found myself hunting for food in Romania, I counted on Sabbath dinner at the Jewish Community Center for sustenance.

The price for these favors was high. Ceausescu demanded payment for letting the Jews leave; the pay-off reportedly was $3,000 per Jew, paid by an authorized agent of Israel's intelligence service. Rosen even became a sort of personal ambassador for Ceausescu in Washington, traveling to the United States every year to plead with the American Jewish community to support continuation of the precious Most Favoured Nation trading privileges. According to Rosen, Ceausescu believed Jews commanded the world's banks and money supply. "Ceausescu was an anti-Semite who believed all these myths about the Jews controlling the world," he insisted. "I couldn't change his beliefs; I could only use them to my advantage."

As conditions for other Romanians deteriorated, the Jewish community began to resemble a state within a state. Rosen himself acted like a king. He was chauffeured around town in a stately black Mercedes, and articles in the Jewish newspaper referred to him as "His Eminence." In a country where people had long hidden the fact that even part of their ancestry was Jewish, many Romanians now came to Jewish offices to claim fictitious Jews in their family trees. Outside Rosen's office hangs a sign: "We take no conversions to Judaism. It is pointless to ask."

Often I wondered how Rosen could have cut such a bargain. How could he have kept coming to the United States and testifying to Jewish leaders that all was well on the human-rights front in Bucharest? Wasn't it immoral to lie? Although a few voices criticized Rosen's autocratic manner and tactics after Ceausescu's downfall, they were all foreign. Romanian Jews appreciated their venerable leader. "The Rabbi has done so much good for Jews," said Martin Weisman, a community member. "I doubt there will be a revolt against him, and in any case I don't see any possible successors." Rosen himself felt no regrets. He had acted to save lives, pure and simple. "If I had to deal with Hitler to save Jews, I would deal with Hitler," he says in his own defense. "Ceausescu wasn't my friend, but we had to deal with him."

Elsewhere in Eastern Europe, many Jews responded to the coming of *glasnost* by rejecting Rosen-style *Realpolitik*. In both Czechoslovakia and Hungary, a younger generation of Jews revolted against the entrenched collaborationist Jewish leaderships. They rejoiced in their Jewishness and identified with Israel. Instead of coddling up to the government, be it communist or democratic, they affirmed their independence.

The first revolt came in Hungary, where the Jewish community was the fiefdom of Geza and Ilona Seiffert. Geza, a lawyer, served as president of the Central Board of Hungarian Jews for ten years until his death in 1976. Afterwards, his widow took over. In 1985 when I first visited the Central Board offices next to the impressive Dohany Synagogue, I found a silver-

haired, stylish and sophisticated matron. Twenty-six synagogues functioned in Hungary, she explained, as well as three
Jewish old people's homes, a Jewish day school, a Jewish
newspaper, a Jewish hospital and even a Jewish holiday home.
Eastern Europe's only rabbinical seminary was in Budapest.
"All those people who said that this community had no future
after Hitler were wrong," Mrs. Seiffert insisted. "All those
people who said we had no future in this social system were
wrong."

The price for this freedom was high. Because Romania never
broke diplomatic relations with Israel, Romania's Rabbi Rosen
never had to hide his Zionist sympathies. Ilona Seiffert and all
other Eastern European Jewish leaders lived under constant
fear of being branded as "Zionist–Imperialist" agents. She kept
silent about Israel while voicing loud support for Kádár. "When
I was five years old, anti-Semitism was directed by the government," she told me. "Today, the government helps us."

When I paid another call on Mrs. Seiffert three years later,
the crumbling Kádár status quo no longer satisfied younger
Jews, who had begun publishing a samizdat magazine called
Shalom. The young dissidents supported Israel, questioned the
Hungarian role in the Holocaust and demanded recognition of
Raoul Wallenberg. They wanted a more aggressive community
leadership, one willing to speak out against anti-Semitism, one
that wasn't traumatized by the Holocaust. "My grandchild
comes to me and says, 'Grandma, why don't you criticize
this?' " Mrs. Seiffert admitted with a deep trace of sadness.
"We were thankful to be alive, to begin rebuilding our lives."

In the 1980s a religious revival took place. At Sabbath services
I met teenage Jews who rejoiced in their religion. "My parents
tried to hide their religion," sixteen-year-old Anna Donath told
me. "I want to be more Jewish. I like the traditions."

I met Endre Rosza, founder of the Alternative Federation to
Maintain Jewish Culture, at a café on Lenin Boulevard. He wore
a skullcap and a bushy beard, signs of an observant Jew. Rosza
said his parents sent him to church and never told him he was
Jewish. "They wanted to assimilate, to hide," he explained.
"They thought it was dangerous to be Jewish." At the age of
twelve, a schoolfellow became angry with him and yelled, "You
dirty Jew." Young Endre was shocked. "I went and talked to
my father," he recalled. "He responded with all this blah, blah,
blah." Endre didn't know what to do. He dropped the issue.
He was thirty-seven when he rediscovered Judaism. He had
four children. "When my children asked me," he explained, "I

wanted to give them a clear response." He began studying Hebrew. He began lighting the Sabbath candles. And he organized the Alternative Jewish Federation. "I don't want to be like Seiffert, with just a closed religious community," he explained. "I want the community to open up to all those 'hidden' Hungarian Jews. I want it to act as a lobby for Jewish interests."

In neighboring Czechoslovakia, Leo Pavlat's parents, both Holocaust survivors, never told him that he was Jewish. "They were scared, they just wanted to forget," he recalled. "When I asked my mother about the mark on her arm, she just replied, 'It's the war.' I asked, 'Were you sent to the camps because you were a communist? That's what we're taught in school.' 'No,' she said. 'I am Jewish.' " After Israel was menaced with extinction in 1967, Leo began a long search to construct a meaning around his Jewish identity. "In 1967 I was seventeen years old and I felt frightened," he recalls. "Israel's victory was a victory for me."

The next year, a gust of freedom swept through Czechoslovakia. Censorship was eased. A burst of pro-Israeli, pro-Jewish feeling took the country. At a crucial writers' conference, Milan Kundera and other leading artists demanded the re-establishment of diplomatic relations with Israel. But a few months later, Soviet tanks invaded. As a grim process of "normalization" descended on the country, the most prominent Prague Spring participants found themselves cut off from their jobs and futures. The Prague regime turned anti-Israeli. Leo and a few fellow "reborn" Jews continued their studies, working at Hebrew in secret – there was no rabbi or school where he could learn. He began wearing a skullcap and keeping kosher – even though there was no butcher in Prague who respected the Jewish dietary laws.

While Hungarian Rosza was attempting to revive a community of 80,000, which already enjoyed a complete range of Jewish services, only a few thousand Jews remained in Czechoslovakia. In 1985 the community's talented president Desider Galski was forced to resign after organizing an exhibition of Prague Jewish treasures, "The Precious Legacy," which toured the United States to rave critical reviews. Politburo ideology chief Vasil Bílak, angered that Galski had received so much positive publicity in the American press, appointed as leaders of the Jewish community two communist bureaucrats, Bohumil Heller and František Kraus. They proceeded to sponsor an official "peace action" of Jewish communities throughout Europe, supporting a communist plan to create a nuclear-free zone in Central Europe. After large anti-government demon-strations in January 1989, Kraus and Heller wrote to the Party paper *Rudé Pravo* expressing their support for violent police action used to crush the peaceful protest. They issued frequent declarations condemning Israel. When I met Kraus, I found a frightened, uneducated man, who had worked as a cook before being catapulted to the head of the Jewish community. He defended his attendance at the communist-sponsored "peace conferences," saying "without peace, there is no life."

In protest, Leo and other young Jews organized a petition demanding the resignation of Kraus and Heller. It called for a more positive attitude towards Israel, for the re-opening of two Prague synagogues closed for several years for "repairs," for more Hebrew classes for adults, and for the publishing of more books on Jewish themes. Kraus threatened to have the rebels prosecuted. "These young people want to separate Jews and other Czechs," he complained. "We have complete religious freedom." In August 1989, police arrested Leo Pavlat. Kraus had given them the petition and named him as the chief con-spirator. Leo was interrogated for five hours. The police per-secutors accused him of fomenting a "Zionist" conspiracy.

When the revolution came, Leo and the other young Jews convened a meeting of the Jewish community. They drafted a new petition demanding Kraus's resignation. It gained almost complete support from the small community, and Kraus suc-cumbed to the pressure. Desider Galski was brought back as community president. "We had our own revolution," a happy Leo told me.

Throughout liberated Eastern Europe, Jews seemed frightened and uncertain about the future. In Romania they did not cel-ebrate the overthrow of hated despot Nicolae Ceausescu. "I fear a vacuum of power," Rabbi Rosen said. "More often than not, Jews are the victim." Several Jews were prominent in the new Romanian government, among them Prime Minister Petre Roman. Rosen feared attacks against them by the budding opposition parties, particularly the revived National Peasant Party. "I look at the Peasant Party with great fear," he said. "We must remember that democracy is weak in Romania, that the fascists could return."

Jews made good targets. They could be blamed for their past role in the Communist Party and their present role in the democratic opposition. In the Hungarian electoral campaign, charges of anti-Semitism focused on István Csurka, a noted playwright and leader of the nationalist Democratic Forum. When I met him, he denied the accusations, but in a troubling manner. "We can't accept this constant harangue over anti-Semitism," he insisted. "It is true that we fight against the mass media and the television directors were named by [former leaders János] Kádár and [György] Aczél. Anytime we note that Aczél is a Jew, then we are accused." Earlier, while covering the Polish election, I was shocked when a spectator interrupted a campaign meeting for longtime opposition activist Jacek Kuroń, asking, "How should we respond when people tell us everything in Poland is directed by Jews like you?" Kuroń turned red. He handed the microphone to his campaign adviser, who explained that Kuroń was not Jewish. "I was so embarrassed," Kuroń explained afterwards.

But the signs were not all negative. Jews felt confident enough to take advantage of the new democratic freedoms to voice their concerns. One of the first actions by the new Eastern European democracies was to restore diplomatic relations with Israel. In the last part of 1989 and the first few months of 1990, Poland, Czechoslovakia and Hungary all reopened their embassies in Tel Aviv. This represented more than mere diplomacy; it evoked strong emotions. When the Israeli Philharmonic Orchestra visited Warsaw, Poles lined up for hours to try to get tickets. The orchestra began its concert with Israel's National Anthem, followed by Poland's, and many in the audience wept. "It's not just the music," my friend Agata Koszak explained. "Everyone now says they have a Jewish grandparent."

Many Eastern Europeans, fed up with communism, seemed to take a nostalgia trip back to before the war to rediscover Judaism. Studying Hebrew and Jewish culture became chic. In Poland, meetings sponsored by the influential Catholic Intellectuals Club to discuss Polish Jewish topics drew hundreds of people of all ages. University students wrote dissertations on Isaac Bashevis Singer and the role of the Jew in Polish literature. By learning about Jews, Catholic Poles searched for roots, not scapegoats, asserting that the path out of communism's spiritual desert included a rediscovery of their country's Jewish past.

Typical was my friend Krzysztof Śliwiński. As a child, he remembered Jews from his apartment block being deported to the concentration camps. As an adult, he became interested in Jewish tradition, learning Hebrew, Jewish theology and Polish Jewish dialogue. He wanted to read the Old Testament, especially the Book of Job, in its original. For him as a Pole, the story and the Jewish history were relevant. The situation of

Poles, he reminded me, resembled that of the Jews. During much of their history, both peoples had lived without a state. National consciousness was transferred through a religion, a language, a culture. Even today, he said, Poland shares much with Israel. Both are nations trapped in a geographic dilemma, fighting against overwhelming odds, struggling to save their souls. Both see themselves standing up against the entire world. Israel was even conceived in Eastern Europe, and particularly in Poland: the founders of the Jewish state came from there. "My greatest dream is to go to Israel," Śliwiński told me. "It would be a sort of return home."

In the West, the picture of Jews in Eastern Europe was often drawn with daggers, described as a war between good and evil, truth and lies. That was too simple. While communism's collapse has opened the door to long-repressed emotions and raised the specter of renewed anti-Semitism, the promise of democracy has also brought new hope. I find it easier to discuss the Holocaust with a West German than an East German, or even a Pole. The West German usually expresses regret about the Holocaust, often going to remarkable lengths to bow before the awe of the Shoah. The Easterner does not. Raised in ignorance, he can only see his own nation's tragedy. Democracy means a free open debate, and I believe that eventually this freedom will produce a long-needed soul-searching. "I'm confident about the future," said Mr. Gebert, the Polish Jewish leader. "These problems get worked out in democracies."

Chapter Fourteen

The Nations:

Patriotism, Chauvinism and History

The struggle of man against power is the struggle of memory against forgetting.

Milan Kundera, The Book of Laughter and Forgetting

The policemen came at 7 p.m. There were four of them, three armed and in uniform and a plainclothes officer.

"What is your name?" the officer demanded.

"Suleyman," responded Suleyman Mumenov.

The officer became angry. "Your name is not Suleyman," he said. "From now on, you have to choose another name."

The police took his passport. When they returned it a week later, "Suleyman" had become "Boyan," and "Mumenov" "Martinov."

That fateful event, part of a ruthless assimilation campaign, took place in Kardzali, Bulgaria, on January 7, 1985. In addition to changing their names, the estimated one million ethnic Bulgarian Turks were forbidden to speak Turkish in public or to practice certain rituals of their Islamic religion. Anyone who refused to hand over their passports took a great risk. "Two people in my building were left unconscious," Suleyman said. Turks from villages in the neighboring hills say their homes were encircled by armored personnel carriers and armed soldiers. Resisters were shot. "They came early in the morning, around 5 a.m., and surrounded the entire village," recounted Safia in the village of Selovina. "Two people in the next village were killed."

Through the centuries, Eastern Europe's indiscriminate mix of nationalities has caused countless confrontations, uprisings and wars. The question of nationalism is a tangled, complicated one, defying easy definitions. Nationalism can be conservative or revolutionary, reactionary or progressive, sterile or creative. What is benign in moderation is dangerous in excess. There is negative Bulgarian-style nationalism. Call it chauvinism. It places the motherland at the top of the heap, denying and denigrating the rights of other nations. There is also positive nationalism. Call it patriotism. It represents a necessary renewal of national pride.

The revolution of 1989 was a revolution of renewed national pride. After throwing off the communist yoke, people were once again proud to be Czech, Polish, Hungarian or, for that matter, German. They waved the national flag. They sang the National Anthem with renewed vigor. None of this necessarily implied hostility towards other nations. As an American, growing up with the Stars and Stripes and the Dawn's Early Light, it was hard to see what is destructive about this type of patriotism.

The new democratic regimes have already shown themselves less chauvinistic than their communist predecessors. Poland's Tadeusz Mazowiecki took a liberal line on both the Jewish and German questions, drawing criticism from the communists. Czechoslovakia's Václav Havel apologized for the way Czechoslovakia expelled the Sudeten Germans after World War II. He too was criticized by the communists. The Romanian revolution began when ethnic Romanians joined together with ethnic Hungarians to protect Hungarian Pastor László Tökés.

World War II purged the region in horrible fashion of its two greatest minorities – the Jews, of course, and also the Germans. Poland is now inhabited almost entirely by Poles, Hungary by Hungarians, and Czechoslovakia by Czechs and Slovaks. Although conflicts between the different national states could still emerge as they did before World War II, fewer potential tensions are visible compared with the Central Europe of 1939 – at least in the northern half of the region.

The same cannot be said of the south. Romania's map has been redrawn so many times that it now encloses large pockets of Hungarians, Serbs, Germans and Gypsies. Yugoslavia's different nations are near open warfare, and Bulgaria is home to a million-strong Turkish minority. The Balkans were long called Europe's powder keg. Ever since the gradual break-up of the ailing Ottoman Empire in the nineteenth century, the expression "Balkanization" has described unhealthy, undesirable political fragmentation. The weak countries which emerged from the mess were marked by misrule and oppression, corruption and poverty, warfare and violence, heroism and treachery.

Antagonistic nationalism destroyed the multinational Hapsburg Empire. The problem was one of double standards. What Hungary wanted from Vienna it refused to Croatia. What

Croatia demanded from Hungary it, in turn, refused to give to the Serbs living within its borders. This double standard of dealing with the rights of one's own nation and those of alien minorities remained dominant features of the new states which emerged from the ashes of World War I. At Versailles it proved impossible to distribute ethnic groups without leaving large and small minorities stranded from their mother country – Hungarians in Romania, Romanians in the Soviet Union, Albanians in Yugoslavia and Turks in Bulgaria.

The construction of a communist utopia was supposed to sweep away these tensions. Proletarian internationalism demanded that previous antagonistic governments cooperate, sharing the goal of ending the old feudal and capitalist exploitation. Practice was different. In their decline during the 1980s, Eastern Europe's communist regime embraced aggressive chauvisnism as a substitute for their bankrupt ideology. After his military *coup* in 1981, General Jaruzelski abandoned the language of Marxism for the language of a patriotic Pole. Under János Kádár, the Hungarians remained reluctant to express almost any national feeling. His successors embraced the cause of the Hungarians in Transylvania. Even the East German Communist Party, for which the word "nation" was long taboo, attempted to reclaim the Prussian past.

"National communism" proved a most dangerous tactic, like playing with fire. Once lit, it was difficult to bring back under control, and as the Soviet Union relaxed its grip on Eastern Europe, ethnic tensions burst out. The great fault line between East and West changed in character. It no longer divided capitalism and communism but Byzantium and Rome – Orthodox Serbs and Catholic Croats, Orthodox Romanians and Catholic Hungarians, and, above all, Orthodox Bulgarians and Turkish Muslims. Time seems to have moved back to the turn of the century when Turkish power in the Balkans disintegrated, releasing new national emotions. The result then was World War I.

Of all the ethnic disputes I encountered, the most terrifying, in its violence and its hot hatreds, was between Christian Bulgarians and Muslim Turks. Animosity between Turks and Bulgarians goes back some 600 years to the time when the Ottoman Empire absorbed Bulgaria. Turkish rule was not noted for gentleness. It left Bulgarians shouldering a morose and fragile sense of national destiny. One of the most important dates of the Bulgarian calendar is the holiday, celebrated on

February 17, commemorating the execution by the Turks in 1873 of the Bulgarian guerrilla leader Vasil Levski.

After independence, about 10 per cent of the population remained Turkish. They were concentrated in villages in two rural mountainous regions, one in the north of the country around Shuman, the other in the south around Kardzali. The high Turkish birthrate – four times the rate of the Slavic Bulgarians – frightened the communists, who tried to assimilate the Turks. Turkish schools were merged with Bulgarian ones, school lessons in Turkish were eliminated and mosques were closed. Then in 1985 the dramatic name-changing campaign was launched.

Bulgarian leader Todor Zhivkov insisted that the Bulgarization was voluntary. Western human-rights groups claimed that entire villages were sealed off and people were forced at gunpoint to sign documents. Independent confirmation was hard to obtain. The Bulgarian authorities closed off the Turkish regions to foreigners. When I tried to visit Kardzali in 1988, police kept me confined to the city of Plovdiv. "You need authorization to go there," a policeman insisted. When I protested that the region was open to visitors, he didn't care. I telephoned the international press center in Sofia and officials there insisted that I would have no problems making my visit. I tried a second time to leave Plovdiv towards Kardzali. Again, policemen stopped me. What struck me most was the lack of public anger about the Turkish plight. Bulgarians told me, with straight faces, that no more Turks lived in Bulgaria; only a few, insignificant "Islamicized Bulgarians" remained.

The lie could not bury the truth. Turkish resistance stiffened in the spring of 1989 and violent demonstrations took place in the Kardzali region. Zhivkov responded by expelling several thousand of the Turks who had led the protests. The unrest swelled. A passport was issued to any Turk who wanted one. In the space of a few weeks, some 310,000 people fled before Turkey, overwhelmed by the inflow, closed its border. The exodus helped precipitate Zhivkov's fall after thirty-five years in power. Vigorous condemnation came from the budding Bulgarian democratic opposition and from Westerners deploring human-rights abuse. Longtime Foreign Minister Petar Mladenov took over and reversed course on the controversial Turkish policy, issuing a decree allowing Turks to take back their names, speak their language in public and practice their religion.

Frightened Bulgarians responded with their own anti-Turk

demonstrations. I decided to try again to visit Kardzali, site of some of the largest, most vociferous protests. This time I had no problem reaching my destination. It was a grim, underdeveloped Third World town, its one main street lined by unprepossessing gray apartment blocks. Residents told me that about 60 per cent of its 60,000 people were ethnic Turks. The other 40 per cent were Slavic Bulgarians.

Fear and loathing were palpable among the Bulgarian residents. They seemed traumatized by a "Cyprus syndrome," an ingrained fear of an invasion like the one of the Mediterranean island by Turkish troops to protect its Turkish minority. Shopkeeper Kaloyan Koloyanov told me how Turkish troops had killed his grandfather in the 1913 Balkan War. "Give them any rights and they'll be at our throats," he said. "Islam is a religion of violence."

My most frightening experience in Kardzali took place in the Damska Moda department store. Suleyman Mumenov, a twenty-six-year-old watch repairman, began telling me how his name had been changed to Boyan Martinov. As we talked, Bulgarian employees and shoppers began to gather round us. Soon they were shouting at Suleyman.

"Here you must speak the Bulgarian language," one lady said. "Otherwise you make us feel we are in Istanbul."

"In Turkey, you can have Turkish names," another added. "Here you should use Bulgarian ones."

"In America," a third interrupted, talking to me, "you have to take an American name, after all?"

Suleyman and I stood in the center of the angry crowd as the invective mounted, and I began to fear a riot.

"You like your name Boyan, don't you?" one lady told him. "Yes, Boyan, you like it."

The two of us fled the scene. Suleyman continued his story in a nearby unheated café, which served no coffee or tea. He explained how, after his name change, a ban was imposed against speaking Turkish in public. Anyone caught had to pay a fine. "I have been fined thirteen times," Suleyman said. "The first time I was speaking with my brother about buying a bus ticket when a plainclothes policeman came over to me and said, 'You cannot do that.' I had to pay 5 leva." He spoke of the pain of living with two names, the schizophrenia of being called Boyan at work and Suleyman at home, and said that unless his real name was restored he would emigrate to Turkey. "I have been so humiliated," he said. "All I want is my own name."

*

261

Humiliation and fear, I soon learned, colored all Eastern Europe's ethnic disputes. Hungarians and Romanians have been fighting over Transylvania for thousands of years. Most records of the area's early inhabitants were destroyed during a Mongol invasion in 1241. For centuries Transylvania was part of, or associated with, the Kingdom of Hungary – later within the Hapsburg Empire. It was integrated into Romania after World War I, lost in 1940 and then regained after World War II. Romanian nationalism has always focused on Transylvania, gaining it, keeping it and integrating it.

After the war, the Hungarian Autonomous Region was dismantled and Hungarian rights whittled down. The separate Hungarian university in Cluj was closed. Hungarian-language secondary schools were shut down. Then, under a scheme of rural reorganization, Hungarian villages which had existed for centuries were scheduled to be demolished, replaced by almost uninhabitable apartment blocks, many with communal kitchens and outdoor latrines. Combined with Romania's deteriorating economy the situation became intolerable for many of the 2 million Hungarians in Romania, and many began fleeing to neighboring Hungary.

I visited the Rakosszentmihaly Presbyterian Church on the outskirts of Budapest, where refugees met every Friday evening to receive food, money and clothes. Told in anguished voices, I heard story after story striking the same tragic theme. Andras recounted how he could not "study in his mother tongue, Hungarian." Dora disclosed how police jailed her "for singing the Hungarian National Anthem." Anika described how her Romanian boss "discriminated against Hungarians, giving them the worst wages, confiscating their ration cards." All the refugees insisted on anonymity in order not to endanger family members left behind. Some crossed the border illegally without passports. Others had passports valid for thirty days. "The flow gets greater each week," recounted Pastor Attila Komlos. "They all just say, 'I feel like a second-class citizen in Romania. I didn't want to come, but I can't take it any longer there.' "

The plight of these Hungarian refugees represented more than just another gripping human tragedy. It was the first time that one communist country had accepted refugees from another, and signaled an unprecedented public row between two neighboring Warsaw Pact allies. "We're just carrying out glasnost," said one Hungarian diplomat. "These tensions existed before Gorbachev, but we just didn't talk about them."

Within Hungary, the plight of the Hungarian minority in

Transylvania became more important than the fight for democracy or human rights. Maps of "Imperial" Hungary, encompassing large territories of Slovakia, Romania and Yugoslavia, began to appear on Budapest streets. The Democratic Forum, the largest opposition group, mounted a vigorous campaign on the Transylvania problem, while the communist authorities used the issue to deflect dissatisfaction over falling living standards. "When we held a meeting about Transylvanian Hungarians, the hall was packed," said Zoltán Bíro, a member of the Democratic Forum and former Party official. "Both the radical opposition and the Party can agree on this matter."

The ethnic issue shifted Hungarian foreign policy westwards. It became impossible for the Budapest regime to consider the Romanians as allies and the Austrians as enemies. While controls on the Hungarian–Austrian border eased, the Hungarian–Romanian frontier turned into the real Iron Curtain, one of Europe's meanest borders. In 1988 the Hungarians cosponsored a United Nations resolution to investigate alleged human-rights abuses in Romania. It was the first time such a step had ever been taken by one Soviet Bloc country against another.

The Romanian revolution brought long-repressed minority issues out into the open. On the day of Ceausescu's fall, pamphlets began appearing in Transylvania in both Hungarian and Romanian. Banned radio stations resumed multilingual broadcasting. I met the leaders of the new Democratic Union of Hungarians. They demanded freedom of travel, freedom of religion, the re-opening of Hungarian-language schools and an end to job discrimination. But they worried about radicals who were calling for the establishment of an autonomous region, and even reunification with Hungary. "We must concentrate on minority rights, not political rights," the Union's president, Géza Dokos, said. "If people start talking about independence, there could be a bloodbath."

His dire prediction was soon confirmed. Romanian nationalists opposed the re-opening of Hungarian-language schools and universities. In March 1990 bloody clashes between Hungarians and Romanians broke out in the Transylvanian town of Tirgu Mures. Men wielding axes and pitchforks attacked each other. Three people – two Hungarians and one Romanian – were killed and 269 people – 200 Romanians, 68 Hungarians and a British tourist – were wounded before tanks, troops and armed police succeeded in separating the two communities. On his visit to the United States I met with Father László Tökés, the Hungarian pastor whose arrest had sparked the revolution. His initial euphoria had vanished. "Many Romanians say they want a democracy, but they don't want to give us our rights," he said. "There can be no democracy in Romania if this minority of 2.5 million people is not free."

Other ethnic groups in Romania also worried about the future. The German minority, estimated at 200,000, came to the country centuries ago, first with Saxon crusaders and later as colonists of the Austro-Hungarian Empire. In the Ceausescu era many emigrated, and now most of the rest prepared to leave. The million or so Romanian Gypsies found themselves in an even more precarious situation. They had no place to flee. I discovered outright racism directed against them for their alleged black-marketeering and bohemian ways. In Hungary a literate Gypsy leadership emerged, voicing demands for Gypsy rights. But in Romania the Gypsies remained leaderless and defenseless – an easy scapegoat for a souring revolution.

Similar ethnic divisions threatened to tear up Yugoslavia. Before World War II, Yugoslavia had been dominated by the Serbian royal house. In 1934 an assassin linked to the Ustaša, a Croatian terrorist group, killed King Alexander, aggravating a climate of communal hate between the Orthodox Serbs and the Catholic Croats. Hitler proved quick to take advantage. During the war the Ustaša was given control of Croatia and undertook to massacre whole villages of Serbs. Post-war Yugoslavia under Tito, half-Croat and half-Slovene, repressed Serb nationalism. Once Tito disappeared in 1980, a gradual process of liberalization took place, resulting in a resurgence of those national feelings. Yugoslavia's 8.6 million Orthodox Serbs once again found themselves in open political conflict with the 4.6 million Catholic Croats.

While the Serb-Croat conflict was contained with words, the Serb conflict with the 1.7 million Muslim Albanians in the southern province of Kosovo sharpened to the point of outright violence. Serious Serb–Croat enmity stems from World War I; serious Serb–Albanian tensions date all the way back to the epic battle of Kosovo Polje in 1389, when the Serbian hero Lazar lost his kingdom to the Ottoman Turks. Kosovo was the heartland of the medieval Serb nation. During the long centuries of Turkish rule, Albanians moved in, and by 1981 Kosovo's population was already 87 per cent Albanian and 13 per cent Serbian.

Under Tito's constitution, Kosovo's Albanian majority gained significant control over its own affairs. Frightened Serbs continued to emigrate from the province, claiming that the Albanians were terrorizing them out of their homes. The Albanians kill our pigs, they said. They smash our windows with stones. They vandalize our graves. They rape our women. When I visited Kosovo Polje, evidence of such crimes was hard to find. Asked whether they could point to a specific incident, Serbs invariably fell silent. At the Gracanica convent, Sister Tatiana told me in a tone of mounting hysteria how an Albanian policeman squeezed her hand and tried to pull her into an embrace. She called it attempted rape.

Serb leaders demanded that Kosovo be incorporated into Serbia to rectify these perceived injustices. In March 1989 they achieved this goal. As Serbs sang and danced in Belgrade, thousands of Albanians took to the streets around Kosovo. They were met by helmeted riot police, armored personnel carriers, even tanks. MIG fighter jets screamed low overhead. When the Albanians attacked, most hurling rocks, some firing rifles, the police replied with water cannon, tear gas – and then rifles and automatic weapons. Defiant Albanian youths, faces covered by bandanas, raced through alleys hazy with tear gas. Police pursued them in helicopters. Automatic weapons clattered. When it was over, the official count came to twenty-four dead, including two policemen. Outside observers put the toll at more than 100.

Less than a week later, I returned to Priština, Kosovo's capital. Cafés had started selling grilled Turkish sausages called *cevapcici*. Children had begun returning to school. Families were once again taking the ritual after-school Balkan stroll, the *korzo*, down Marsala Tita Avenue. But beneath this "normal" surface, tensions simmered. A 10.30 p.m. curfew remained in effect. Helmeted riot police armed with machine guns stopped people on the *korzo* to check their identity papers and to tell large groups to disperse – it was illegal for more than three people to gather. More than 1,000 Albanians had been detained, facing up to fifteen years in prison on charges of "counterrevolution." In schools, factories and offices, a classic Stalinist-style purge had begun, weeding out "unreliables" who refused to denounce their compatriots. At the end of the twentieth century, Yugoslavia had plunged back into the tribal hatreds of the Middle Ages.

Ethnic tensions emerged in even the most civilized, tolerant country of Eastern Europe – Czechoslovakia. The Czechs and Slovaks speak closely related languages, intelligible to each other, but in many ways they are different in temperament and tradition. The Czechs, 10 million strong, are sober and serious; the Slovaks, only 3.6 million, lighter and merrier. Beer is the Czech drink, wine the Slovak favorite. The Czech countryside is well manicured, with old industrial towns; the Slovak lands are mountainous and rural. There are large numbers of Protestants in the Czech provinces; the Roman Catholic Church dominates in Slovakia.

Historically, the two nations never united into a single state. For 1,000 years the Slovaks lived under Hungarian influence and the Czechs under Germanic control. At independence in 1919, the two had reached different levels of development. The Czechs had played an important political and economic role in Austria; the Slovaks had possessed almost no political rights in Hungary. In the First Republic, the Czechs predominated. Presidents Masaryk and Beneš were Czechs, and their concept of a "Czechoslovak" nation denied that a separate Slovak nation existed. Many Slovaks accepted the notion of Czechoslovak national unity. Others stressed the separate Slovak identity and urged autonomy for Slovakia. Although the Slovaks attained great cultural and political development under the First Republic, resentment of Czech domination simmered. After the capitulation at Munich the Slovaks achieved autonomy, and during the war the Nazis sponsored a puppet "Slovak" state under conservative, clerical–fascist leadership.

Czech predominance resumed after the war. In the early 1950s a campaign against Slovak nationalism resulted in the execution of Slovak Party leader Vladimír Clementis and the imprisonment of his deputy Gustáv Husák. If anything, the new communist Czechoslovakia became a state ruled by Czechs with an even greater indifference to Slovak rights than the First Republic had shown. A new constitution proclaimed in 1960 eliminated all forms of Slovak self-government. Then during the Prague Spring, Alexander Dubček became the first Slovak to lead the Communist Party, and proposals for a new federal state were approved. The Slovak authorities were given extensive powers over education, culture, health, trade and construction. Polls revealed that an overwhelming majority of Slovaks approved of the plan. The Czechs, showing little interest in the matter, assented.

Federalism was just about the only achievement of the Prague Spring to survive the Soviet invasion. Husák the Slovak replaced Dubček as Party leader and in the ensuing years of normalization large amounts of investment were devoted to industrializing Slovakia. Slovaks were moved into positions of responsibility in the administration. Before 1968 only 14 per cent in the foreign service were Slovaks, and in other ministries there were even smaller percentages. Now, for every Czech appointed a Slovak accompanied him. If the President were a Slovak, the Prime Minister would have to be Czech; so during the twenty-year rule of President Husák, he was always balanced by a Czech Prime Minister. The affirmative action satisfied Slovaks while annoying Czechs. Numerous jokes appeared about "dumb Slovaks" receiving important posts in Prague.

Two men meet in a Prague pub.

"What do you do?" one asks the other.

"I work in the Ministry," comes the answer.

"Oh, yes, and what's your job?"

"I'm the Slovak."

Despite such grumbling, Czechs accepted the need for a federal state and Slovak autonomy. Although most Charter 77 signatories came from the Czech lands, and its successor Civic Forum would be a Czech-dominated organization, Václav Havel and all its other Czech leaders showed great sensitivity towards Slovak feelings. A Slovak counterpart to Civic Forum, "Public Against Violence", was formed. Its leader, the Catholic activist Jan Čarnogurský, became Vice Premier. Slovak Alexander Dubček was brought back to become president of the National Assembly and Slovak Marian Čalfa was named Prime Minister.

Tensions soon emerged none the less. They focused on the country's name. Obviously the Czechoslovak Socialist Republic was no longer appropriate. Czechs proposed the simple Czechoslovak Republic. Slovaks felt their distinct identity should be better recognized and proposed the Federation of Czecho-Slovakia. As farcical as the issue may have sounded, it reflected deep-rooted tensions. The Slovaks feared renewed Czech domination. The Czechs, in turn, resented what they perceived as Slovak uppitiness. Both nations argue over who had profited from communist rule. The Czechs insisted that the Slovak economy had been subsidized. The Slovaks retorted that Czechs were still exploiting their lands.

Another, darker side of Czechoslovak nationalism concerned relations with Hungary and Germany. The Hungarian minority, numbering about 600,000 and living in southern Slovakia, complained of discrimination in education and jobs. Industrialization had brought a large influx of Slovak workers into formerly Hungarian-dominated regions and in the city of Bratislava Hungarians worried about losing their Magyar identity. "When my children go to university, they must speak Slovak, so I'm forced to send them to Slovak grammar schools," one mother said. "We aren't oppressed. But I speak Slovak at work. My kids are taught in Slovak. Bratislava has become Slovak."

The problem with Germany is more explosive. Conflict with the Germans has always been a central issue in Czech history. The clash of the two nations within the Austro-Hungarian monarchy was reversed in the First Republic when the Czechs became the rulers and the Germans the ruled. Although the 3.5 million Germans in the country enjoyed full democratic freedoms, even substantial cultural rights, simmering resentment made them easy prey for the Nazis. By 1937 the majority supported the secessionist demands of the Nazis. After the war the Czech government expelled the Germans. Democratic President Edvard Beneš took the decision.

The Communist Party, before the war a strong supporter of minority rights, approved of the move. It even took an active role in resettling the vacated territories with Czechs and Slovaks from other parts of the country. Given the tremendous sufferings inflicted in the previous six years by the Nazis, the consensus was not surprising. Historian Gordon Skilling noted:

> The move gave the Czechs, like the Poles, a powerful national interest in an alliance with the Soviet Union as a guarantor of their territorial integrity against the threat of German revisionism, Cooperation with East Germany was only in partial contradiction to this, as the existence of such a state, which recognized Czechoslovakia's western frontiers and weakened the position of the German nation by keeping it divided, served both the ends of Communist policy and Czech national interests.

It was only after Charter 77 was formed that a few independent Czech thinkers did some soul-searching. To the philosopher Jan Patočka, mentor of Václav Havel, the expulsion of the Sudeten Germans represented "the first act of totalitarianism in the country." By endorsing collective guilt, it broke with the humanist principles on which the First Republic was founded. It had "morally disarmed" the country. When Havel became President, one of his first public statements on television was that Czechoslovakia owed the Sudeten Germans an apology. The initial public response was negative, but the country's great moral figures eventually rallied to Havel's side. Cardinal

František Tomášek issued a statement saying that "these illegal, inhumane acts have left a stain on our national honor."

Havel moved ahead to support German unification. His first trip abroad as President was a one-day jaunt to both East and West Germany. The new Europe, he said, "need have no fear of a democratic Germany. Democratic awareness and a democratic system in Germany are more important than the possibility that it might become one nation of 60 or 80 million people."

Even more than in Czechoslovakia, post-war nationalism in Poland focused on relations with foreign powers, specifically Russia and Germany. After 1945, Poland became an ethnically unified state with only small national minorities. When the Polish underground press began to discuss the question of the German minority in Poland, the main focus of the question was: "Does a German minority exist?" In the former German regions of Silesia and Pomerania, almost all the Germans fled after World War II. The Bonn government, however, insists that a million-strong German community continues to exist, and awards automatic citizenship to its members. Ironically, many Poles desperate to leave their impoverished country for prosperous West Germany search for papers showing that a relative had served in the Wehrmacht. They then receive automatic West German citizenship.

For years the fear of German revanchism was one issue which united Cardinal Glemp with General Jaruzelski. On the fortieth anniversary of the annexation to Poland of Szczecin (formerly Stettin), both men traveled to the Baltic port, where they issued a joint declaration of the inviolability of its Polishness. Shortly afterwards, I visited Szczecin with a television crew. When we tried to take a picture of a queue in front of a butcher's shop, a bystander spotted our West German license plates and began screaming, "Get the Krauts out of here! It's their fault that we're in this mess."

My guide in Szczecin described the ancient Slavs who settled in the region a millennium before. Her claim masked the capture of the city by knights of the Teutonic Order in 1226. "No amount of sophistry can dismiss the fact that the German element was dominant in those parts for the last six or seven hundred years," commented historian Norman Davies. Polish insecurities concerning the border remained palpable. Although Willy Brandt acknowledged the Oder–Neisse line in 1970, the West German constitution continued to call for Germany's unification within

269

the Reich's 1937 borders. Helmut Kohl's ambiguous statements in the early months of 1990 provoked near panic among officials in Warsaw. "When we talk to the Germans about setting up a consulate in Wrocław, they say 'Yes,' but it must be called Breslau," complained Mieczysław Tomala, secretary of the Polish–German Friendship Forum. "The West Germans must understand that we're sensitive about this issue."

Many Poles began to work for a new positive relationship with Germany. Those born after World War II admired prosperous, democratic West Germany. The youthful Freedom and Peace group took the lead, nurturing contacts with West German Greens and constructing a monument to a German soldier who was executed in World War II for befriending Poles. "Our government must not be permitted to encourage stupid attitudes," insisted Jacek Czaputowicz, Freedom and Peace's leader. Solidarity accepted the idea of German unity, for both practical and moral reasons. Bronisław Geremek said that the division of Germany had helped the communists consolidate their power. If Poland refused unification, he feared that the issue could once again be exploited by anti-democratic forces. "We decided it would be better to accept the process and try to influence it than to refuse it and see it accomplished against Poland," Geremek said. Morality provided a clinching reason. "We could not aspire to self-determination for Poles," he added, "and refuse the same self-determination for others."

Solidarity hoped German unity would be accomplished within "a European framework." During their long years of opposition, activists defied strict police surveillance to work together. Czech and Polish dissidents met on the border and announced the creation of the "Circle of Friends of Polish and Czechoslovak Solidarity." Later, they included members of the Hungarian and East German democratic opposition in statements demanding the right to conscientious objection and respect for minority rights in Romania. In power, these same men speak of a pan-European federation, or, more immediately, a confederation of Poland, Czechoslovakia and Hungary. "Our great hope for the future is to work together," said Geremek. "It is our only hope."

The confederation strategy must overcome centuries of cold, contentious history. As insecure, small nations, the Eastern Europeans developed a tendency to lash out against each another. The people of these nations have long memories. Wherever I went, I met men and women who remembered distant events as though they had taken place yesterday. To them, history did not mean studying abstract, long-forgotten events. Young Poles learned about the bloody 1863 revolt against the Russians, young Czechs recalled their defeat by the Austrians at the White Mountain back in 1620, while young Hungarians grew up remembering the 1848 and 1956 uprisings.

The brilliant Czech novelist Milan Kundera has described how communist regimes tried to make citizens forget their history, their traditions and their national identity. They manipulated the past, teaching a "correct" and "incorrect" version of an event. Polish communists refused to accept that Russian troops were guilty of massacring Polish officers at Katyn, while for years Hungarian and Czech communists insisted that the events of 1956 and 1968 represented "counterrevolutions."

The struggle against communism concentrated on persuading people not to forget. Anniversaries of sensitive events were not academic affairs. They became front-page news, coded commentary on the present when anger exploded and deep feelings were revealed. Every year Poles would demonstrate against their government on the day of the Katyn anniversary, Czechs on the anniversary of the founding of their democratic First Republic and the 1968 Soviet invasion, and Hungarians on the anniversary of the 1848 and 1956 uprisings. "In this part of the world, history is not a simple search for the truth," explained Polish historian Krystyna Kerston. "It is a weapon in the fight for national identity."

I was struck by the powerful memories of young Eastern Europeans. In June 1989, when Hungarians reburied the martyrs of 1956, twenty-year-old Éva Huszbik arrived at sunrise at Budapest's Heroes Square. She hung a Hungarian flag without the communist hammer and sickle on a street-lamp, and laid flowers on the coffins. She stood in silence for an entire minute. With tears in her eyes, she sang the Hungarian National Hymn with its moving refrain: "We will never be slaves again." Would a twenty-year-old American become tearful at a ceremony marking such a historic tragedy, even one evoking as many emotions as John Kennedy's assassination? "It's the difference between East and West," Eva told me. "If you live in a state of oppression, the history of the nation lies much heavier on the heart."

As much as this emotion was necessary in maintaining national identity, it could be misused and abused to raise old fears and insecurities. In Bulgaria the long memory of Turkish occupation prevented the acceptance of Turks' receiving their basic human rights. In Yugoslavia, the Serbian defeat at Kosovo 600 years ago justified present-day oppression of Albanians. The task, I concluded, is to learn history's lessons, or to risk making the same mistakes as the past. Recapturing national identity means beginning to open discussion on its merits. This is the only path towards defusing ethnic tensions and forging a new cooperative relationship between the region's different nations.

Some countries are better endowed than others in this search. East Germany, devoid of a legitimate history, found itself naked when confronted with its past. Czechoslovakia, by contrast, looked back with pride to Tomáš Masaryk and the First Republic. In Poland the nationalism of two early twentieth-century politicians, Roman Dmowski and Józef Piłsudski, battled once again for supremacy.

Dmowski viewed the nation as a natural phenomenon, the result of God-given divisions of mankind into distinct entities, each possessing its own exclusive language, territory and history. He blamed many of the evils of modern Europe on the indiscriminate mixing of peoples. Poland's future, in his view, was as a unitary, Polish Catholic nation.

Piłsudski, by contrast, saw the nation as a product of history, a community sharing the same values and loyalties, though not necessarily the same ethnicity. As Norman Davies writes: "Within such a nation, there was room for many nationalities as long as each of the parts stayed loyal to the whole." Piłsudski's model for the "multinational nation" was undoubtedly drawn from the old Republic of Poland–Lithuania, although it had much in common with British and American ideas on the subject. In this view, ethnic and cultural variety within the nation was a source of strength and vitality.

Throughout Eastern Europe, the battle today over nationalism hinges on this division between the followers of Piłsudski and those of Dmowski. World War II, the Holocaust and four decades of communist oppression gave the intolerant nationalists a strong base of support. But the idea of Solidarity also enjoyed a powerful appeal. In Solidarity, Poland as a nation found amazing strength. In Civic Forum's solidarity, Czechoslovakia found strength. In Hungarian–Romanian brotherhood, Romania found strength. In their muddles, East Germany, Hungary, Bulgaria and Yugoslavia looked weak and vulnerable. To paraphrase Tom Paine, divided the Eastern Europeans fell. United they may win.

Epilogue

Finlandization or

Latin Americanization

Only uncivilized tribes fight to the last man.

Finnish statesman J. W. Snellman

It is a small country living in the shadow of the Soviet Union, tied to its giant neighbor by a compromising security treaty. It is also a strong parliamentary democracy, earning top ratings in the human-rights record book. A generation ago, it was a rural backwater dependent on a few old paper mills. Today, it is rich and prosperous, with income per capita greater than that of Britain or France. Unemployment and inflation are low. Militant communism has dwindled to a fringe group. Relations with Russia have become stable and predictable. The good fortune is summed up in a new, confident national motto: "Being born here is like receiving a winning ticket in life's lottery."

The blissful country is none other than secure, stable, successful Finland – the model for a future Eastern Europe. As it once was for the Finns, the great task ahead for the freed small countries of the Soviet Empire is to achieve a balance between Western freedoms and prosperity and good relations with its overweening neighbor. A happy "Finlandized" future is far from assured. If the transition from totalitarianism to democracy comes unstuck, Eastern Europe could revert to its pre-war status as a protectorate and dependency of the West. Parts of the region – certainly East Germany in unification, probably Czechoslovakia and maybe Poland and Hungary in freedom – look ready to succeed in achieving a Finnish-like integration into Western Europe. Other parts – the Balkan backwaters Romania and Bulgaria – face the danger of "Latin Americanization" – by which I mean they will be dominated by authoritarian governments with generals at the helm or lurking in the background. Destructive nationalism rather than destructive Marxism would become the reigning ideology, covering up a congenital identity crisis and a lack of self-confidence.

For centuries Eastern Europe has oscillated between East and West, sharing characteristics of both worlds. Well into the twentieth century, most of the region retained a feudal Eastern "Russian" social structure, dominated by autocratic land-owning gentry, the Esterhazys in Hungary, the Radziwills in Poland, to give just two examples. Except in the Czech lands, no numerous middle class emerged. In Hungary and Poland, the bourgeoisie was dominated by Germans or Jews, and concentrated in the professions rather than in business. The state continued to play a larger economic role in Austria-Hungary and Germany than in Britain or The Netherlands.

Democracy never put down strong roots. Although many argue that Austria–Hungary was a constitutional state with a respect for the law, the Hapsburg Empire was not a parliamentary democracy of the French or British type. It was an empire marked by a powerful, often overweening, bureaucracy. The most chilling descriptions of totalitarianism came out of this peculiar Central European milieu in the writings of such authors as Robert Musil, Joseph Roth and, of course, Franz Kafka. Both tolerance and racism battled it out for centuries in Central Europe and, more often than not, racism triumphed.

The new nation-states after 1918 tried to create Western-style democracies. They wrote constitutions resembling France's Third Republic. All except Czechoslovakia failed. While some freedom of association, of the press, of travel, were maintained, right-wing authoritarian regimes dominated the region by the early 1930s. These regimes fed off bleeding national disputes. Poland claimed part of Czechoslovakia, Hungary claimed Transylvania, parts of Slovakia and Ruthenia, Yugoslavia coveted Slovene-populated parts of Austria. Internal weakness and external vulnerability left the inter-war Eastern European states exposed, first to Nazi and then to Soviet conquest.

As defined by Milan Kundera, the "small nation is one whose very existence can be put into question at any moment: a small nation can disappear and it knows it." At the end of World War II, the time appeared to have passed for independent small nations. The Eastern Europeans emerged from five long years of partial or complete Nazi occupation to find an alien Soviet communism imposed upon them. Moscow even obliterated the Baltic States from the map. The others became "satellites," with

Soviet power leaving them in suspended sovereignty. The death of small nations wasn't confined to countries living in the Soviet shadow. In the West, too, it was believed that the future lay in the destruction of old outdated national boundaries, through the appearance of multinational companies and in the construction of some sort of a United States of Europe.

Today the map looks quite different. If a yearning remains for constructing what Mikhail Gorbachev calls a "Common European House," this house must respect individual identities. More small nations exist than ever before: membership in the United Nations is three times greater now than in 1945. Neither the Nazis nor the Soviets managed to obliterate the individual existence of the small Eastern European states. We called them "satellites," in the sense that Moscow's power seemed decisive, but the people living in these "satellites" continued to think of themselves as distinct, national entities. Once Moscow hesitated, Eastern Europe's small nations raised their voices and broke free. It is not only the Soviet Union which has lost control of its subjects: Western Europe, following a remarkable economic recovery, has reasserted its independence of the United States. In the West the process has been peaceful and gradual. In the East, coming amidst economic crisis and political vacuum, it has been revolutionary.

This book has documented the forms of resistance which enabled the small Eastern European nations to survive Soviet subjugation. Survival in and of itself must be considered a success, but it only assures that these small nations, which look so fragile, will not be wiped off the map. A new strategy is needed to chart the path ahead. Here the Finnish example fascinated me, because it showed how, though a small nation might be too weak to impose its will on others, it might none the less have the power to preserve its unique identity and protect its fundamental interests.

We in the West tend to dismiss Finland as a lucky survivor, granted pardon by an otherwise evil Soviet Union. But was it all luck? Might not the Finns themselves have had something to do with their success, just as the Eastern Europeans had something to do with their own liberation? When I went to Helsinki in 1987 and 1989, I came away with the firm conviction that Finns indeed had to be given credit for maintaining democracy and creating prosperity under the ominous Soviet shadow. They were autonomous actors, not mere pawns. If they had taken different decisions, they could have ended up an impoverished captive nation. Sometimes the Finns showed it was necessary to fight. At other times they demonstrated that it was necessary to accommodate.

After World War II the 5 million Finns were forced to cede 11 per cent of their territory to Moscow, accept heavy war reparations and sign the compromising Treaty of Friendship, Cooperation and Mutual Assistance. The epithet "Finlandization," held up as a nightmare for Western Europe, described a country facing inevitable demise through blackmail and subtle subversion by the Soviet Union. Only in recent years did we realize that the term had become a positive achievement worthy of admiration. In Warsaw, Prague and Budapest I found a deep interest and admiration for the Finnish model. "I went to Finland and found something unique," said Sándor Csoóri, a leader of the Hungarian Democratic Forum. "Just like them, we are thinking of a Third Way – some way of ensuring the survival of a little nation caught in the unfortunate situation of being between the Russians and the Germans."

The vagueness of the Finlandization metaphor – an Eastern European dream but a Western European nightmare – made me cautious about any facile comparison. Finnish observers in Helsinki stressed some differences between their country and Eastern Europe. A geographic position on the northern perimeter, they insisted, made their country less vulnerable than Poland or Czechoslovakia or Hungary in the heart of Europe. The political structure of post-war Finland was not hammered together in a deal between the victorious powers, imposed from the outside. Alone among small countries involved in World War II, Finland was never occupied. Mobile ski troops slaughtered hundreds of thousands of Russians in the 1939–40 Winter War. The Finns' martial valor made a profound impression on Stalin. During a discussion on Finland at the Tehran Conference in December 1943, he told Roosevelt and Churchill that "any country that fought with such courage for its independence deserves consideration."

"Finlandization" for Eastern Europeans cannot mean that they too must give the Russians a bloody nose in a winter war, but the Finnish example shows some rationale for resisting the overweening demands of Great Powers. The Hungarians fought the Russians in 1956 against impossible odds and were crushed. Over the next few decades they enjoyed a greater degree of independence than Czechoslovakia, which submitted to superior Nazi force in 1939 and then to superior Soviet force in 1968. A key lesson Eastern Europeans can learn from Finland is how to manage defeat. Finland was beaten in World War II, losing many of the nation's brightest youth and much of its best land. But Finland was not conquered, spiritually or physically. Its democratic system never stopped functioning and its social fabric remained intact. The nation united in a national effort to resettle some 400,000 Finns who lost their homes and land under the peace treaty signed with Moscow.

The comparison with Poland and the rest of Eastern Europe is sharp. Nazi occupation ripped apart the social fabrics of those countries and Soviet troops occupied the devastated countries. "Free and unfettered" elections promised at Yalta were doomed to failure because the Soviets did not allow them – and because most Eastern Europeans themselves had little experience before the war with "free and unfettered" elections. Only Czechoslovakia enjoyed a democratic tradition similar to Finland's. After the war, the two countries held free elections in which the local Communist Parties scored well and entered governing coalitions. Stalin forced both countries to sign compromising treaties of "mutual cooperation," and at the beginning of 1948 fears of a communist *coup d'état* swept both Prague and Helsinki.

The communists took over in Czechoslovakia. They failed in Finland. Why? Max Jakobson, the former Finnish Ambassador to the United Nations, offered some compelling reasons in his English-language profile of his homeland. "Communism was stronger in Czechoslovakia than in Finland," he observed. "The Czech Party had the support of 40 per cent of the voters, the Finnish Party 23 per cent. In Czechoslovakia, communists held important positions in the civil service and armed forces; in Finland they had hardly any influence at all in the central organs of the government. Attitudes to Russia also differed: the Czechs and Slovaks on the whole looked upon the Soviet Union as a friend and ally, the only power that in 1938 had declared its readiness to come to the aid of Czechoslovakia, while most Finns still considered the Soviet Union their arch-enemy."

When Czechoslovak President Edvard Beneš gave in to communist demands without resistance in 1948, Finnish President Juho Paasikivi took strong action against the communist threat. The Finnish leader ordered troops to mobilize, alerted police and deployed a gunboat in Helsinki harbor opposite the presidential residence. In July 1948, the Finnish Communist Party suffered heavy losses in parliamentary elections and was left out of the new government. "In Czechoslovakia the communists were strong enough to seize power by their own efforts," commented diplomat Jakobson. "In Finland only a massive

Soviet intervention by military force could have overthrown the elected government."

Stalin chose not to intervene. After the *coup* in Czechoslovakia, the shocked Western powers began conceiving a system of common defense, NATO. The Soviet leader's quarrel with Tito was moving towards a climax. He must have asked himself why take on more troubles with Finland, which in 1939 had shown its willingness to fight for its independence. President Paasikivi meanwhile moved to mollify Soviet fears, arguing that Russian interest in Finland was strategic – to guard the defenses of Leningrad from attack, and that this defensive "interest" could be satisfied without danger to Finland's freedom. In order to show Stalin that he could trust the Finns, Passikivi took a number of goodwill steps: he refused American aid from the Marshall Plan and gave priority to paying back Russian war reparations. He even held trials convicting eight of Finland's leading politicians of making war on the Soviet Union.

Eastern European security treaties with Moscow imposed unlimited obligations to political consultations in time of peace. Paasikivi held out for a pact which noted Finland's neutrality, its "desire to stay outside the conflicts between the Great Powers," and narrowed the obligation of the two countries to hold consultations only when there was a direct threat of military aggression. The lesson, I believe, is that in certain circumstances a small nation can profit from accommodation. In the Finnish context, this meant keeping quiet when Western nations lambasted the Soviets. When Moscow invaded Afghanistan in 1979, the Finns abstained in the United Nations vote. Finns found Western criticism of this attitude beside the point, even hypocritical. What good would Finland's vote have done for freedom in Afghanistan? None, they answered, but it would have compromised freedom in Finland. Why, Finns asked, did Westerners long salute Romania with its Stalinist system and criticize Finland with its democracy? Finnish President Mauno Koivisto's retort to those asking more of Finland was simple. "If you want drama," he said, "go to the theater."

History taught the Finns the value of keeping quiet. At the time of the 1830 and 1863 Polish uprisings, the Finns were part of the Soviet Empire and avoided siding openly with the Poles against the Russians. Finnish statesman J. W. Snellman warned his country that such a foolish gesture would only hurt Finland without helping Poland. "Only uncivilized tribes fight to the last man," he cautioned. For the Eastern Europeans, the Finnish lesson is that the greatest courage a nation can show is to avoid emotional egotism. Nations must act out of interests. This *Realpolitik* does not mean giving up national sovereignty. On the contrary as Max Jakobson argues, if sovereignty is considered in terms of the will to pursue national interests, the Finns have shown supreme respect of their own sovereignty, basing their security on an unsentimental calculation of strategic realities.

The Finnish–Soviet relationship does not mean that the Eastern Europeans have to love the Russians. They must only learn to live with them and respect their security interests. Both culturally and economically, Finns look to the West, not the East. In commercial terms the Soviet Union accounts for less than one-fifth of all trade; the vast majority goes to Western Europe or the United States. In Helsinki, only a few miles from the Soviet border, McDonald's does a booming business; clothing stores are packed with Levi's; the cinemas show the most recent American films, including the latest James Bond; and the radio features American entertainers and the Top 40. Some 86 per cent of all Finnish students choose English as their first foreign language; only 0.4 per cent choose Russian. Finnish friends said they received Moscow television but didn't tune in. Instead they preferred to watch the American shows and American sports broadcasts on satellite. When I was in Helsinki, a new craze for American football was sweeping the country. "We're not Finlandized," my Finnish friends joked. "We're Americanized."

Why do the Russians leave alone this attractive island of Western consumer culture? The arrangement serves their interests. Moscow enjoys cast-iron guarantees of its vital security interests and trades for first-rate Finnish goods, not substandard Eastern Bloc manufactures. When Soviet leaders speak of Finland as a "good neighbor," they mean it. Unlike in any of the former satellites, Gorbachev does not have to worry about an anti-Russian revolt in Finland. A national consensus in Finland supports cooperation with the Soviet Union; the infamous security treaty, contested in Finland when it was first signed in 1948, has been renewed several times without any opposition. All the political parties in the free parliament support close ties with Moscow. "When a couple of academics started discussing breaking off the treaty, no one took them seriously," recalled Martti Valkonen, an editorial writer at the daily *Helsingin Sanomat*. "There's an almost unbelievable consensus about our policy towards the Soviet Union."

By treating Eastern Europe like Finland, the Soviets hope to discover that they are better off this way. Instead of subsidizing their allies, they will profit from them. Instead of worrying about unrest, they will enjoy stability on their frontiers. Gorbachev has reversed Russia's traditional method of seeking security and power by territorial expansion and subjugation of neighboring nations. In the nuclear world, he realized that territory no longer buys defensive advantage; and in the computer world, he recognized that keeping nations under control in the old Imperial fashion is not worth the cost.

The Eastern Europeans must similarly adapt to the new world. They must look hard at their own past, beyond communism's failure and the nostalgia for the misty years before World War I, expressed in the fascination for the vague term "Central Europe." They must count on themselves, not on foreigners. None of these impoverished nations, except for vanishing East Germany, should expect much more than nice words from the West. At worst, German unification will revive the danger of an expansionist, powerful neighbor on their western border, just as Soviet power recedes in the east. At best, it threatens to divert resources to the eastern half of the new Germany. "We were on the verge of signing an agreement for $100 million in aid," recalled Leszlaw Kuzaj of the Kraków Entrepreneurial Association. "The day the Berlin Wall came down, the Germans said they would have to reconsider. I haven't heard from them since."

This adversity could turn out to be a disguised blessing, mobilizing national energies and overcoming a deep-seated sense of fatalism. The Finns never took foreign aid. They even paid large war reparations to the Soviets. As the first bold step in a dramatic struggle to achieve manhood, Eastern Europe's successful revolutions resembled Finland's Winter War. The next steps require Finnish-like caution and accommodation. This means holding no grudges against Soviet misbehavior in the past, and constructing a new positive relationship with Gorbachev's Moscow.

Looking ahead, the Eastern Europeans must not lose sight of their priority: the creation of prosperous, democratic societies. Lost lands are secondary issues. When I heard leaders of the Romanian Peasant Party insisting on the return of Moldavia, or Hungarians dreaming of getting back Transylvania, I cringed. I remembered how, during World War II, the Poles helped compromise their own future by haggling with Moscow over their future borders. The Finns have not been obsessed by the loss of Karelia to the Soviet Union. To them, Karelia was the necessary price to pay to preserve Finland's freedom.

A democratic consensus offers the best insurance policy for freedom. The Soviets invaded Finland in 1939, hoping to play on its internal ideological divisions – to resurrect the old lines of the Finnish Civil War. The Finns instead united behind their freely elected government. A strong President continues to ensure continuity and consistency in Finnish foreign policy, while the Finnish parliamentary system depends on broad majorities. The system prevents any sudden shift between right and left. Change comes as part of a wide agreement in society. Intrigued by this formula, the Hungarians have sent a delegation to Finland to study its governing institutions. In Poland and Czechoslovakia, Solidarity and Civic Forum have shown a remarkable ability to overcome ideological differences. Even where scores of new parties have sprouted, as in Hungary, the first free elections produced clear, decisive results and potentially strong governments.

I came away optimistic for the future. The communist era was over. The system which had proclaimed itself the future of the world was buried. Any police or military backlash would prove only a temporary set back. People like Jiří Dienstbier and Miklós Haraszti, Lech Wałęsa and Václav Havel killed communism. Meeting them and seeing their fight for freedom was an unforgettable experience. Personally, I felt honored to find friendship and intellectual comradeship with such courageous individuals. Professionally, I was thrilled to thrash out ideas in smoke-filled private kitchens and grimy public cafés, to feel the abstract notion of fundamental human rights and self-determination come alive. If these words hold the danger of sentimental idealization from a privileged Westerner who has never faced such difficult choices, so be it. The courage and dignity of Eastern Europe's new leaders cannot be denied.

Compared with those in a Latin American country such as Argentina, the Poles, Czechs and Hungarians are united in their goal: the creation of prosperous democracies. Compared with the drift I felt in my own country when I returned to the United States, the energy of these reborn societies was impressive. The leaders who had brought about the momentous changes were of great integrity and dedication. They had survived the age of darkness. When points of moral reference failed, they had retained a measure of moral credibility, an ability to inspire their nations. If, as Václav Havel put it, the liberation of Eastern Europe was a victory of right over wrong, truth over lies, self-confidence over pride, then the people who led the revolution were not just politicians: they were people acting with a real mission and purpose, with a sense of morality. In his moving inaugural address in January 1990, Havel best expressed these sentiments, not just for his own Czechoslovakia but for all the neighboring nations struggling to be free.

"Our nations have raised their heads high of their own initiative without relying on the help of stronger nations or powers; it seems to me that this constitutes the great moral asset of the present moment," he said. "Let us teach ourselves and others that politics should be an expression of a desire to contribute to the happiness of the community rather than of a need to cheat or rape the community. Let us teach ourselves and others that politics can be not only the art of the possible – especially if this means the art of speculation, calculation, intrigue, secret deals and pragmatic maneuvering – but that it can even be the art of the impossible."

Bibliography

Almost all of this book is based on my own reporting. But as I explored Eastern Europe I read as much as possible about the region. What follows is a selective list of some of the most interesting and enjoyable books. They make up a mixed bunch – history, essays, fiction, academic and journalistic – and I have chosen to list them below by such groupings, each with a brief description.

Original Texts

Milovan Djilas, *The New Class: An Analysis of the Communist System*, Thames & Hudson, London, 1957; Praeger, New York, 1957. A clear, concise analysis of the Nomenklatura and its corrosive effects.

Wolfgang Leonhard, *Child of the Revolution*, Collins, London, 1957; H. Regenery & Co., Chicago, 1958; new edition Ink Links, London, 1979. A first-hand account of how communism came to East Germany – and how bright, idealistic people after World War II were drawn to the socialist faith.

Miklós Haraszti, *Worker in a Workers' State: Piece-Rates in Hungary*, Universe Books, New York, 1977. A penetrating first-hand description of factory life under communism. The best book illustrating how the workers' state abused the worker.

Miklós Haraszti, *The Velvet Prison: Artists under State Socialism*, Basic Books, New York, 1987; I. B. Tauris, London, 1988. How Hungary's Kádárist compromise, which seemed to promote a modicum of freedom, actually corroded intellectual life. A dense and difficult, but revealing, document.

Václav Havel, *Living In Truth* (ed. Jan Vladislav), Faber & Faber, New York and London, 1987. Remarkable essays which outline the Czechoslovak playwright's transformation into political philosopher. Essential reading for understanding the thinking behind Eastern Europe's opposition – and its new democratic governments.

Václav Havel, *Letters to Olga*, Alfred A. Knopf, New York, 1988; Faber & Faber, London, 1989. Havel's moving prison letters addressed to his wife Olga. His philosophical musings are a bit dry. The concrete description of prison life is much more gripping.

Jan Jósef Lipski, *KOR: A History of the Workers' Defense Committee in Poland, 1976–1981*, University of California Press, Berkeley, 1985. Although often dry and sometimes tedious, this history of the Polish opposition provides invaluable insights into the birth of Solidarity in 1980.

Adam Michnik, *Letters From Prison and Other Essays*, University of California Press, Berkeley, 1986. Michnik at his best – commentaries on Polish history and the present which are tough, touching and thoughtful.

Czeslaw Milosz, *The Captive Mind*, Alfred A. Knopf, New York, 1953; Secker & Warburg, London, 1953. The Nobel Prize-winning poet describes how communism captured his fellow intellectuals. His predictions look all wrong today, but an invaluable document.

History

Neil Ascherson, *The Struggles For Poland*, Michael Joseph, London, 1987; Random House, New York, 1988. A clear, concise journey through Polish history. Based on a television series, it doesn't delve too deep.

Norman Davies, *God's Playground: A History of Poland*, 2 vols., Columbia University Press, New York, 1979–82; Clarendon Press, Oxford, 1981. A grand, epic history, which turns Poland's past into a thrilling narrative. Opinionated but judicious.

Norman Davies, *Heart of Europe: A Short History of Poland*, Oxford University Press, New York and London, 1986. A one-volume summing up of *God's Playground*. Also fascinating and insightful.

Hugh Seton-Watson, *Eastern Europe Between the Wars, 1918–1941*, Westview Press, Boulder, Colorado, 1986. Somewhat outdated, but well written and insightful.

Max Jakobson, *Finland: Myth and Reality*, Otawa Publishing Co., Helsinki, 1987. A short book, ostensibly about Finland, really about the struggle of all small countries for independence and dignity. Written in a clear, stylish English by the Finnish diplomat.

Max Jakobson, *Finland Survived: An Account of the Finnish–Soviet Winter War*, Otawa Publishing Co., Helsinki, 1984. A masterpiece of diplomatic writing about one of the twentieth century's most moving David-vs.-Goliath stories.

György Konrád, *Antipolitics*, Harcourt Brace Jovanovich, New York, 1984; Quartet, London, 1984. The Hungarian novelist takes on politics or, as he puts it, the antipolitics of dissident thinking in Eastern Europe. Seems somewhat outdated now, but still a magnificent piece of writing.

Ernst Pawel, *The Nightmare of Reason: A Life of Franz Kafka*, Farrar, Straus & Giroux, New York, 1984. The best biography available on Kafka – and the best portrait of turn-of-the-century Prague.

Joseph Rothschild, *East Central Europe Between the Two World Wars*, University of Washington Press, Seattle, 1974. A dry read, but Rothschild is thorough and precise in his analysis of this crucial period of Eastern Europe's history.

Joseph Rothschild, *Return to Diversity: A Political History of East Central Europe since World War II*, Oxford University Press, New York, 1988. Still hindered by stilted prose, but the best short general history of the region under communist rule. Takes the story up to the 1989 revolution.

Journalism

Neil Ascherson, *The Polish August*, Penguin, Harmondsworth, 1981. A well-done report from the revolutionary Poland of 1980–81.

Timothy Garton Ash, *The Polish Revolution: Solidarity*, Jonathan Cape, London, 1983. The best book on the incredible events of 1980–81. Infused with both immediacy and a sense of perspective, Garton Ash is a unique mixture of reporter and historian.

Timothy Garton Ash, *The Uses of Adversity: Essays on the Fate of Central Europe*, Random House, New York, 1989. The historian–journalist's pieces from the *Spectator* and the *New York Review of Books* from 1981 until the beginning of the 1989 revolution. Sometimes overreaching but always provocative.

Michael Kaufman, *Mad Dreams, Saving Graces: Poland, a Nation in Conspiracy*. Random House, New York, 1989. Picks up Poland's story in the aftermath of the 1981 martial law and carries it up to the 1989 revolution. A fine piece of reportage by a talented *New York Times* correspondent portraying the underground society which kept alive the struggle for freedom.

Lawrence Weschler, *The Passion of Poland, from Solidarity through the State of War*, Pantheon Books, New York, 1984. Another insightful reportage by a *New Yorker* writer from the 1981 Solidarity revolution.

Academics

Abraham Brumberg (ed.), *Poland: Genesis of a Revolution*, Random House, New York, 1983. A helpful collection of essays. Particularly good is Alexander Smolar's on the Nomenklatura.

Stephen Clissold, *Djilas, the Progress of a Revolutionary*, Maurice Temple Smith, Hounslow, Middlesex, 1983. A clear biography of an extraordinary man – which doubles as perhaps the best history of post-war Yugoslavia.

Charles Gati, *Hungary and the Soviet Bloc*, Duke University Press, Durham, North Carolina, 1986. Gati is that rare breed of academic who infuses his learning with clear prose. The best available description of the Kádár era.

William E. Griffith (ed.), *Central and Eastern Europe: The Opening Curtain*, Westview Press, Illinois, 1989. The best academic book on the forces leading up to 1989. The essay by Mark Palmer, former American Ambassador to Budapest, was influential in shaping Western policy towards the changing Eastern Europe.

Vladimir Kusin, *The Intellectual Origins of the Prague Spring: The Development of Reformist Ideas in Czechoslovakia, 1956–1967*, Cambridge University Press, Cambridge, 1971. A helpful book by a Czechoslovak émigré and the head of Radio Free Europe's research department explaining the 1968 events.

H. Gordon Skilling, *Czechoslovakia's Interrupted Revolution*, Princeton University Press, Princeton, 1976. A mammoth study of the 1968 events. Examines all the issues in great detail and with great skill.

BIBLIOGRAPHY

H. Gordon Skilling, *Charter 77 and Human Rights in Czechoslovakia*, Allen & Unwin, London and Boston, 1981. Good background on the key Czechoslovak dissident movement.

Sarah Terry (ed.), *Soviet Policy in Eastern Europe*, Yale University Press, New Haven and London, 1984. Outdated but still worth a look for background reading.

Jiří Valenta, *Soviet Intervention in Czechoslovakia: Anatomy of a Decision*, Johns Hopkins University Press, Baltimore, 1979. For those readers who want a detailed account of the fateful invasion of Czechoslovakia in 1968.

Novels

Kazimierz Brandys, *Rondo*, translated by Jaroslaw Anders, Farrar, Straus & Giroux, New York, 1989. The Polish wartime experience as seen through the eyes of this eminent émigré novelist.

Witold Gombrowicz, *Diary: Ferdyduke*, Grove Press, New York, 1961. A scintillating portrait of pre-war Poland.

Jaroslav Hašek, *The Good Soldier Schweik*, Penguin, Harmondsworth, 1951. These turn-of-the-century tales of the conniving, boozing, draftee defined the Czech spirit as submissive and weak-willed; a closer reading shows that Schweik really is an example of provocative anti-conformism.

György Konrád, *The Case Worker*, Harcourt Brace Jovanovich, New York, 1974. *The City Builder*, Harcourt Brace Jovanovich, New York, 1977. *The Loser*, Harcourt Brace Jovanovich, San Diego, 1982. Fiction from the Hungarian author of *Antipolitics*. Unsparing descriptions of life under 'goulash' communism.

Ivan Klima, *My First Loves*, Harper & Row, New York, 1988. Short stories from a Czech Jewish writer who chose to stay in Prague after 1968.

Tadeusz Konwicki, *A Minor Apocalypse*, Farrar, Straus & Giroux, New York, 1983; Faber & Faber, London, 1983. My favorite from Konwicki. A satiric nightmare focusing on a dissident's effort to immolate himself "for the cause."

Tadeusz Konwicki, *A Minor Apocalypse*, Farrar, Straus & Giroux, New York, 1983; Faber & Faber, London, 1983. My favorite from Konwicki. A satiric nightmare focusing on a dissident's effort to immolate himself "for the cause."

Milan Kundera, *The Joke*, Harper & Row, New York, 1982; Faber & Faber, London, 1983. Czechoslovakia's best-known writer's best-known book, written before his exile in France. One of the artistic monuments from the 1968 Prague Spring.

Milan Kundera, *The Unbearable Lightness of Being*, Harcourt Brace Jovanovich, New York, 1984; Faber & Faber, London, 1982. *The Book of Laughter and Forgetting*, Alfred A. Knopf, New York, 1980; Faber & Faber, London, 1982. Kundera's two classics, full of raw sex and bitter politics. Through the looking-glass of Czechoslovakia's tragic history, asks whether we can control our destiny, and answers with a resounding no.

Stanisław Lem, *The Cosmic Carnival of Stanisław Lem: An Anthology of Entertaining Stories by the Modern Master of Science Fiction*, edited and translated by Michael Kandel, Continium, New York, 1981. Science fiction from a Polish master, who mixes fun and thrills with provocative insights.

Olivia Manning, *The Balkan Trilogy*, 3 vols., Heinemann, London, 1960–65; Doubleday, New York, 1961–66. A classic describing life from a British teacher's point of view in pre-war Bucharest. Unforgiving and unforgettable of Balkan crass and corruption.

Joseph Skvorecky, *The Bass Saxophone*, translated by Kaca Polackoba Henley, Alfred A. Knopf, New York, 1977; Chatto & Windus, London, 1977; Anson Cartwright Editions, Toronto, 1977. *The Engineer of Human Souls*, translated by Paul Wilson, Alfred A. Knopf, New York, distributed by Random House, 1984. *The Swell Season*, translated by Paul Wilson, Ecco Press, New York, 1982; Hogarth Press, London, 1982. *Dvořák in Love*, translated by Paul Wilson, Lester and Orpen Dennys, Toronto, 1986; Alfred A. Knopf, New York, distributed by Random House, 1986.

Index

INDEX